Microsoft SharePoint 2010 End User Guide: Business Performance Enhancement

Taking the basics to the business with no-coding solutions for SharePoint 2010

A from-the-trenches tutorial filled with hints, tips, and real world best practices for applying SharePoint 2010 to your business

Michael McCabe

Peter Ward

BIRMINGHAM - MUMBAI

Microsoft SharePoint 2010 End User Guide: Business Performance Enhancement

Taking the basics to the business with no-coding solutions for SharePoint 2010

First published: February 2011

Production Reference: 1090211

Published by Packt Publishing Ltd.
32 Lincoln Road
Olton
Birmingham, B27 6PA, UK.

ISBN 978-1-849680-66-0

www.packtpub.com

Cover Image by Mark Holland (MJH767@bham.ac.uk)

Credits

Authors

Michael McCabe

Peter Ward

Reviewers

Robert Crane

Richard Paterson

Manish Patil

Michal Pisarek

Acquisition Editor

James Lumsden

Development Editor

Stephanie Moss

Technical Editor

Erika Fernandes

Copy Editor

Janki Mathuria

Indexer

Rekha Nair

Editorial Team Leader

Vinodhan Nair

Project Team Leader

Ashwin Shetty

Project Coordinator

Joel Goveya

Proofreader

Jonathan Todd

Graphics

Geetanjali Sawant

Production Coordinator

Shantanu Zagade

Cover Work

Shantanu Zagade

Foreword

I have travelled the world as a SharePoint evangelist talking to all levels of End Users, and Information Workers, Site Managers, SharePoint Power Users, and Site Collection Administrators who come to me with the same question, no matter where I'm speaking, "Are there any resources for our End Users?" Getting users up to speed on the day-to-day use of SharePoint is a universal problem in all companies from the largest Enterprise, to the smallest business utilizing SharePoint.

The problem has compounded since the release of SharePoint 2010 and the UI Ribbon. Talk about a tough situation. Not only do we have to get buy-in from the people moving into a new system, but End Users are pretty much on their own when it comes to using it in the context of their jobs.

The book you are holding in your hands is part of the solution to that problem. When I was first sent the drafts, I thought to myself, "This is good... really good." I was drawn in by the simplicity of the language used and the concentration on real world uses for solving problems, combined with the lack of technical jargon. What kept me interested, was the authors' insistence on thinking of SharePoint as a problem solving solution, not a technological solution.

The question is not just "How should I use SharePoint?", but "Why should I use SharePoint?" Describe to me why something is done as you show me how something is done, and I will understand it at a much deeper level.

Dux Raymond Sy, Richard Harbridge, Sue Hanley, Andrew Woodward, and Paul Culmsee are at the forefront of a revolution in SharePoint. They are the ones who are evangelizing the message that **the statement of the problem and a description of the desired outcome, without consideration of the technology**, is what is essential to get through the next maturity phase in SharePoint.

This book is a good starting point not only for understanding why something should be done in SharePoint 2010, but also how to do it. It's not an easy thing to do. This is information you will want within arm's reach as you continue to mature and evolve your understanding of SharePoint.

I wish that every one of these chapters was an article on `EndUserSharePoint.com`. If you know me and my work, you'll understand that's the highest recommendation, I can give.

Mark Miller
Founder and Editor, EndUserSharePoint.com
Chief Community Officer and SharePoint Evangelist, Global 360
Founding Member, NothingButSharePoint.com

About the Authors

Michael McCabe currently works for Microsoft and focuses on the SharePoint product. He has 18 years' of experience in technology and has taught the first classes of Chase employees to use personal computers. Pre-Windows technology; those were the days. He has worked on collaboration technologies for Lotus, IBM and currently is a Technology Advisor with Microsoft. He has broad experience in financial services having worked at JP Morgan, Financial Guarantee Insurance Company, and as a consultant for the State of Connecticut. Michael has worked abroad and is fluent in German. He has studied at the Universities of Bonn (Germany) and Innsbruck (Austria). He earned a Masters from Cornell University and an undergraduate degree from the University of Notre Dame.

I would like to thank my husband Eric for all his support and encouragement during this project and always.

Peter Ward is a Business Collaboration Manager for a New York-based Microsoft partner. In this position, Ward is responsible for the continued success of implementing Microsoft's Information Worker product suite, which includes SharePoint, InfoPath, SharePoint Designer, and Office.

His experience enables him to find creative, yet pragmatic solutions to collaboration challenges in a broad cross section of industries, including consumer goods, online gambling, government, financial services, and transportation. Although originally from Britain (and proud of this), he currently lives in Long Island City, the fashionable part of Queens, and views Manhattan as a small island, 3000 miles off the coast of Europe.

Other factoids about him:

- Always a software guy. Not much of a gadget guy. In fact, more of a late adopter.
- Teaches yoga in NYC.
- Tries to cook up the perfect vegetarian dish.

I would like to thank my wife Peggy for being the executive first draft editor of each chapter, and the following people who provided input, direction, and technical clarification: Paul Andrushkiw, Hannah Beren, Scot Bobo, Kathy Mathews, and Narsan Lingala.

This made a tremendous difference to the format and contents of the book.

I would like to thank everyone at Packt Publishing who made this book idea a reality.

About the Reviewers

Robert Crane has a degree in Electrical Engineering as well as a Masters of Business Administration. He is also a Small Business Specialist and Microsoft Certified SharePoint Professional. Robert has over 15 years of IT experience in a variety of fields and positions, including working on Wall St in New York. He continues his involvement with information technology as the Principal of the Computer Information Agency.

Apart from resolving client technical issues, Robert continues to present at seminars locally and internationally, as well as write on a number of topics for the Computer Information Agency, including being involved in the SMBit Pro community in Sydney. He also develops and presents technology courses on a regular basis through local community colleges. Robert is committed to a process of ongoing business and technical education to continue developing the skills required to assist clients with their business challenges. He can be contacted directly via `director@ciaops.com`.

Richard Paterson is a co-founder and director of the international SharePoint consultancy BrightStarr. He provides technical and architectural leadership to a team of consultants, architects, and software developers. Richard has been involved in web development since its inception, and is passionate about its application in the business environment.

He has worked as a developer and architect in a broad range of industries, including weapons modeling and psychometric profiling. In 2009, he was selected as one of the United Kingdom's top 30 young entrepreneurs in recognition of the rapid growth of BrightStarr.

Richard has an honors degree in Physics and is a Microsoft Accredited Software Developer. Outside of work, Richard is a committed family man and an enthusiastic runner and cyclist.

Manish Patil is a graduate in Electronics Engineering and has been working as a software professional in the IT industry since the last five years.

He serves various business verticals with several brands of IT industry through his technical expertise on Microsoft Technologies ranging from SharePoint, MS.NET, SQL Server to Office Development, along with some exposure to Siebel On Demand.

While working, if you don't find him doing coding then he will be seated on a team member's machine or else doing paperwork. In his free time, he blogs, plays with his niece, or else thinks about something unusual. Also, a few times he has provided coaching to aspiring freshers and college students.

I would like to give my sincere thanks to Joel and Ashwin for their sound coordination, Stephanie for her direct/indirect guidance, and Dhwani for introducing me to Packt Publishing and giving me an opportunity. Also, I would like to thank my parents and friends for not caring about my absence at social events and providing much-needed support. And special thanks to my wife for keeping cool.

Michal Pisarek is a SharePoint specialist who assists clients in defining, planning, and executing projects for maximum business value and end user engagement. He brings a unique blend of technical acumen and business skills to help clients through the murky waters of SharePoint.

A Microsoft Certified Trainer and Microsoft Virtual Technical Specialist, Michal holds several SharePoint certifications in addition to sharing his thoughts on his blog: SharePoint Analyst HQ. He was recently an organizer of the prestigious SharePoint Saturday event in Vancouver and is an active member of the Vancouver SharePoint Users Group.

Michal's other interests include cooking (he used to be a chef) and travelling, and he is highly addicted to CrossFit.

I wish to thank my employer Habanero Consulting Group and my amazing partner Robyn for giving me the opportunity to review this book instead of working.

www.PacktPub.com

Support files, eBooks, discount offers and more

You might want to visit www.PacktPub.com for support files and downloads related to your book.

Did you know that Packt offers eBook versions of every book published, with PDF and ePub files available? You can upgrade to the eBook version at www.PacktPub.com and as a print book customer, you are entitled to a discount on the eBook copy. Get in touch with us at service@packtpub.com for more details.

At www.PacktPub.com, you can also read a collection of free technical articles, sign up for a range of free newsletters and receive exclusive discounts and offers on Packt books and eBooks.

http://PacktLib.PacktPub.com

Do you need instant solutions to your IT questions? PacktLib is Packt's online digital book library. Here, you can access, read and search across Packt's entire library of books.

Why Subscribe?

- Fully searchable across every book published by Packt
- Copy and paste, print and bookmark content
- On demand and accessible via web browser

Free Access for Packt account holders

If you have an account with Packt at www.PacktPub.com, you can use this to access PacktLib today and view nine entirely free books. Simply use your login credentials for immediate access.

Instant Updates on New Packt Books

Get notified! Find out when new books are published by following @PacktEnterprise on Twitter, or the Packt Enterprise Facebook page.

Table of Contents

Preface

This book seeks to bridge the gap between SharePoint's functionality and end users' desire to use SharePoint to assist with their business processes. While other books will tell you what SharePoint can do from a technical standpoint and may leave you wondering if the product is appropriate for your day-to-day needs, this book will provide you with the information and hands-on direction so you can immediately apply solutions to your work environment.

Like its predecessor SharePoint 2007, SharePoint 2010 is the *Swiss Army Knife* of web platforms. Its extreme versatility means that SharePoint does not fit neatly into one single software category in terms of its definition, functionality, or user-approach. It also means that a company's investment in SharePoint can deliver more than just a *document management system* to the organization, but rather can replace website technology, intranets, and bespoke applications, as well as file servers.

Because of the flexibility in SharePoint functionality, end users are often challenged to understand where to begin applying SharePoint's capabilities to their daily activities or job functions, and to understand which functionality is appropriate to their needs. The objective of this book is to demystify the SharePoint product for end users by providing non-coding business solutions and applying out of the box functionality of the SharePoint product.

Information challenges for an end user

With the information overload through intranets, e-mails, calendars, tasks, SMS, and instant messages, like it or not we have become **Information Workers**. Though they have no physical impact, the amount of information can provide knockout punches if vital pieces of information are missing, forgotten, or even misread. However, it is not just the actual information that can bring the end user down, but also the endless calls for attention about the request, its status, who has acted on it or where it is in the process, who is taking action on it, and so on.

As the new decade is upon us, things will only continue to get worse for the following reasons:

- Companies have been doing more with fewer people.

- The world has gotten smaller with the globalization of economies.

- Companies have a real need for transparency, measurable results via metrics, and instant gratification. Organizations want greater visibility into what their workers are doing; not just seeing the end result of a document or project, but where they are in the process.

- **Limitation of existing technology**: E-mail was and still is a great tool, but it was designed as an electronic memo system for one-on-one communication and not as a project management tracking system, or for company-wide global communication, or a purchase order tracking tool. The limits of e-mail usage and functionality have not only pushed the envelope to the limit, but busted it.

The preceding list may seem like a depressing read, but like it or not it is the reality in many organizations.

The aforementioned problems can be solved by introducing SharePoint to an organization as a strategic platform with a phased rollout, with user buy-in. The key to its success is its presentation. If end users see this tool as an aid to their productivity for managing information and not an initiative dictated by the IT department, they will be more likely to embrace it. Those who invest time to change their work habits with the use of this technology will have the ability to gain control of their work days, increase their productivity and efficiency, and maybe even garner a promotion along the way.

Most end users do not realize that they need to learn new skills beyond e-mail functionality and Microsoft Office. These skills may have been adequate in the early Internet days when AOL and AltaVista were the tools of choice, but these desktop applications on their own do not work well if people continuously need to access the information that resides on a user's desktop as there are security and accessibility issues. Learning new techniques with the SharePoint technology is not a major undertaking, but will require some time investment that will pay off multiple times over.

Most end users have been taught only to save information in these applications and e-mail it when necessary, which of course means there is more clutter in your Inbox. Considering the time constraints of the average worker, there has to be a better way.

The days when work ends at the sound of the whistle on the factory floor at five o'clock are long gone. Today, our work and personal lives have become intertwined. Often at times, we work at home and shop at work. The result of this work style is that information and updates about it need to be available at all times for people to be productive, but this is unlikely if information is stored on one individual's desktop.

There exists an *always on* mentality, in which an employee seems to have his Blackberry glued to their hand. Endlessly checking e-mails and responding to requests have become the norm. No one ever assumes they were employed to read and write e-mails as part of their job description, but this activity can be a considerable amount of time in the work day. To improve enterprise productivity and collaboration exponentially, end users must be extremely organized in how they utilize and store information. This is a challenge as end users often use the information that is unstructured, out of sync with lines of business applications, and stored in a format that is not accessible to other team members. At best, the information may be e-mailed to other team members where it may be unread or misfiled.

Where does SharePoint 2010 fit in?

Just as Microsoft's products have become the de facto standard with daily desktop tools such as Word, Excel, PowerPoint, and Outlook, SharePoint is becoming the de facto standard web platform for team and company collaboration. There are other products that provide collaboration, but few integrate as seamlessly with a company's existing IT investments just as Office, Active Directory, Windows 7/Vista/XP, or SQL Server has, thus making the deployment process rather palatable to the IT department and workers within a company.

Another huge benefit of SharePoint is that it seamlessly integrates with the desktop technology of Outlook, Word, Excel, Access, and Visio, so an end user's acceptance is much easier and quicker as they feel that this is an extension to their tool set, and not a replacement.

[Even non-Microsoft browsers are supported in SharePoint.   ]

FAQs

- **Q**: Do I need to be technical to do this?
- **A**: No. If you have an MP3 player then you are more than qualified.

- **Q**: Is this book appropriate if we use SharePoint 2007?
- **A**: The functionality discussed is for SharePoint 2010. However, much of the content is relevant for SharePoint 2007.

- **Q**: If we use SharePoint 2010 and an earlier version of Office, will the book be of value?
- **A**: Yes, but not all the Office integration points exist in versions of Office prior to 2010.

- **Q**: Do you reference third-party products that work with SharePoint?
- **A**: No. However, you may contact the authors for further information and references.

- **Q**: Do I need SharePoint Designer installed on my desktop?
- **A**: No, not for this book. SharePoint Designer functionality is not referenced.

- **Q**: Will the stated functionality work if our SharePoint server is hosted externally?
- **A**: Yes. One of SharePoint's greatest traits is that it delivers content and functionality from anywhere to anyone.

- **Q**: Is mobile device integration discussed in the book?
- **A**: No. Mobile integration with SharePoint is a broad subject and could even have a separate book dedicated to it.

- **Q**: How large does my company need to be to gain value from SharePoint?
- **A**: This is a difficult question to answer, because SharePoint can be used in many ways. The right question to ask is: *How much information does my company use on a day-to-day basis and do I or my team have problems finding important information and keeping it up-to-date?*

  Our rule of thumb is that if you are receiving more than 100 e-mails a day, you probably need a better tool than Outlook to be more organized.

- **Q**: Does SharePoint work with Internet Explorer 6 or previous versions?
- **A**: It may work, but these versions are not supported by Microsoft. SharePoint 2010 does work with other browsers.

- **Q**: What is *webinizing* information?
- **A**: *Chapter 1, Where Should End Users Start with SharePoint?* explains about webinizing information.
- **Q**: How do I start *webinizing* my information?
- **A**: Start by writing down what you did today or over the past couple of days. Ask yourself questions such as: *How much follow-up with co-workers was required? Was finding information a challenge? How do I control the document version? Was finding the status of a certain task an issue?*
- **Q**: Does this book address the different editions of SharePoint 2010?
- **A**: Yes.

What this book covers

Chapter 1, Where Should End Users Start with SharePoint? identifies the typical end user and discusses information and technology considerations with the SharePoint technology.

Chapter 2, SharePoint Essentials covers fundamental essentials that the end users should know about SharePoint technology and how it is relevant to them.

Chapter 3, SharePoint Team Sites begins to further introduce the key SharePoint components to help you understand what SharePoint Team Sites (Sites) are and what purposes content and information in a Site provide. This will ultimately allow you to architect an entire portal.

Chapter 4, List Management helps you to gain knowledge of List Management and understand how to track information and learn efficient ways to store this information for business activities.

Chapter 5, Library Management explains Library Management, how files can be stored and managed, and how to collaborate on documents with team members. The integration with Office and SharePoint is introduced.

Chapter 6, Workflows Fundamentals explains workflows and how these benefit the business world, both in terms of streamlining office functions as well as cutting costs. The chapter explains the workflows options available with different SharePoint versions and how to integrate workflows modeling using Visio 2010 SharePoint Designer.

Chapter 7, Office Integration with SharePoint builds on the functionality explained in previous chapters and explains the integration between this functionality and the Microsoft Office 2010 client applications. It covers Ribbon Interface, Office Web Apps, Co-Authoring, Social Computing, Backstage, Slide Show Broadcasting, Visio Web Services, and SharePoint Workspaces. The chapter also identifies time saving techniques of integrating Office and SharePoint technology for tasks and activities.

Chapter 8, Managing Metadata explains both the basic terminology and concepts of metadata, and where and how to apply it to both hierarchical taxonomies and to unstructured folksonomies. Administrative tools for managing hierarchical taxonomies are reviewed.

Chapter 9, Getting Better Search Results with SharePoint 2010 introduces SharePoint search functionality such as wildcard and phonetic searches, and how to customize search results.

Chapter 10, Alerts and Notifications explains SharePoint's alert capabilities and why this important functionality is often overlooked by end users. Alert management in Outlook is also discussed.

Chapter 11, Enterprise Content Management discusses SharePoint's functionality in managing content with procedures to ensure accurate, up-to-date, and compliant content. The chapter's main functionality discussion points are record management, content types, and information management policies. Other discussion points include how to organize and promote true enterprise-wide content management and the challenges to do this in an organization.

Chapter 12, Blogs, Wikis, and Other Web 2.0 Features further explains the new SharePoint 2010 Web 2.0 features to create and share information collaboratively on the web. The Web 2.0 functionality discussed includes blogs, tagging, comments, wikis, and ratings.

Chapter 13, Pages and Web Parts will extend previously introduced functionality by explaining how page customization can be done by the user, without code. This introduces personalization to the user experience.

Chapter 14, My Sites explains My Sites and how they assist users to keep track of their personal content and information, along with discovering information about other users. This chapter's objective is to make you aware of the importance of My Sites and to ensure you learn how to effectively use them in your organization.

Chapter 15, Applying Functionality for Business Initiatives discusses where SharePoint's functionality can be applied to business areas in an organization, such as Sales Department, IT Department, Project Management Office, and Human Resources. The chapter also introduces functionality that is most appropriate to users' main collaboration activity.

Chapter 16, Creating Exceptional End User Experience for You and Your Team looks at where SharePoint's functionality can be applied to give exceptional user experience to lists, libraries, notifications, search, pages, team sites, and My Sites. *What is exceptional end user experience* is discussed and how this can be applied to a SharePoint deployment. Other topics covered include tips and techniques on how to apply SharePoint functionality, as explained in the previous chapters.

Chapter 17, Golden Rules for End User Deployment outlines what SharePoint is not, what is special about SharePoint, why there is considerable value in using this technology, and the User Requirement Challenges that a deployment will cause.

Appendix A, Glossary, provides definitions to many terms and acronyms related to SharePoint end user functionality, corporate intranets and web user interface.

Appendix B, SharePoint Functionality Comparison gives a functionality comparison of SharePoint's Foundation and Server versions, along with the functionality differences to SharePoint Standard and Enterprise editions.

Appendix C, List Templates gives a functionality comparison of SharePoint's available out of the box list and library functionality as well as business scenarios of when to use each type of list and library.

What you need for this book

The following software needs to be installed on your PC:

- SharePoint 2010 deployed in an environment, or accessible via your browser, along with at least Designer access to a SharePoint site.
- Microsoft Office (Word, Excel, PowerPoint, Outlook), ideally 2010 as there is better integration and interface consistency with the SharePoint 2010 product, although Office 2010/2007 does have integration with SharePoint 2010.
- Internet Explorer 8 for full browsing compatibility; although Internet Explorer 7 is supported by Microsoft, there are some limitations.
- You do need some time to step back from your immediate activities and learn and understand what the SharePoint technology can do and where it is appropriate to your job and role within an organization. We are not talking about days, rather a few hours to identify SharePoint 2010's functionality and where it is appropriate to your job role, department, or organization.

By using the most up-to-date software, instructions in this book will be easier to follow as they reference the Office 2010 product.

Who this book is for

This book is ideal for the end user who wants to take back control of their work day and inbox. It will also be of value to the Information User, Developer, Content Manager/Content Writer, and SharePoint Administrator.

By using SharePoint to complement their Office desktop tools, this book will be a tremendous aid to the employees who are willing to invest a few hours of reading to become even more productive and efficient with how they work with the SharePoint technology.

For this book to be of value, the reader should also know the basic functionality of Outlook, other Office applications, and basic web page functions that are popular today such as the personalization ability on Yahoo and Google's home page.

Conventions

In this book, you will find a number of styles of text that distinguish between different kinds of information. Here are some examples of these styles, and an explanation of their meaning.

Code words in text are shown as follows: "He goes to his intranet and enters `market research`."

New terms and **important words** are shown in bold. Words that you see on the screen, in menus or dialog boxes for example, appear in the text like this: "Right-click on the **Arrange By** header above your list of e-mails."

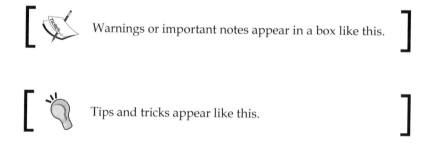

Warnings or important notes appear in a box like this.

Tips and tricks appear like this.

Reader feedback

Feedback from our readers is always welcome. Let us know what you think about this book—what you liked or may have disliked. Reader feedback is important for us to develop titles that you really get the most out of.

To send us general feedback, simply send an e-mail to feedback@packtpub.com, and mention the book title via the subject of your message.

If there is a book that you need and would like to see us publish, please send us a note in the **SUGGEST A TITLE** form on www.packtpub.com or e-mail suggest@packtpub.com.

If there is a topic that you have expertise in and you are interested in either writing or contributing to a book, see our author guide on www.packtpub.com/authors.

Customer support

Now that you are the proud owner of a Packt book, we have a number of things to help you to get the most from your purchase.

Errata

Although we have taken every care to ensure the accuracy of our content, mistakes do happen. If you find a mistake in one of our books—maybe a mistake in the text or the code—we would be grateful if you would report this to us. By doing so, you can save other readers from frustration and help us improve subsequent versions of this book. If you find any errata, please report them by visiting http://www.packtpub.com/support, selecting your book, clicking on the errata submission form link, and entering the details of your errata. Once your errata are verified, your submission will be accepted and the errata will be uploaded on our website, or added to any list of existing errata, under the Errata section of that title. Any existing errata can be viewed by selecting your title from http://www.packtpub.com/support.

Piracy

Piracy of copyright material on the Internet is an ongoing problem across all media. At Packt Publishing, we take the protection of our copyright and licenses very seriously. If you come across any illegal copies of our works, in any form, on the Internet, please provide us with the location address or website name immediately so that we can pursue a remedy.

Please contact us at copyright@packtpub.com with a link to the suspected pirated material.

We appreciate your help in protecting our authors, and our ability to bring you valuable content.

Questions

You can contact us at questions@packtpub.com if you are having a problem with any aspect of the book, and we will do our best to address it.

1
Where Should End Users Start with SharePoint?

We feel that the business community's most logical entry point for the for the SharePoint technology is not a deep dive into the technology, but to identify the typical end users and discuss the information and technology considerations to identify what is possible with this deployed technology with your organization. Most end users will always try to get more work done with their existing tools such as e-mail, Word, and Excel; in reality, these tools have their limitations in terms of personal and team productivity. With the release of the SharePoint technologies in 2001, 2003, and 2010, there has been a tighter integration of the Office applications and corporate web server technologies that have resulted in additional functionality and team processes to the Office applications, such as **version control**, **workflow**, and **issue tracking**.

This chapter will cover the typical end user in an organization and how they currently use information and apply this to their work processes with the SharePoint technology, all without the direction of the IT department. It will also address some frequently asked questions about SharePoint that *should* be asked by end users. This chapter will cover the following topics:

- The typical end user
- Webinizing information
- Key takeaways
- Technical considerations for an end user
- Integration with other technologies
- External access
- Governance

The typical end user

End users are people who **use** the SharePoint product, as opposed to those who **develop** or **support** it, so it is important that the SharePoint technology adds value to an end user's work day by making tasks more structured within a team, and information easier to find. The end user may or may not know what to do if something goes wrong, or indeed will not usually have administrative responsibilities or privileges. However, it is more their behavior and attitude toward a product such as SharePoint that will make a difference in their day-to-day activities. End users typically fall into the categories described in the following sections:

"I'm fine, leave me alone"

This is the person who is content with their existing toolset of Word, Excel, and Outlook. Their inbox may be full of unorganized e-mails, and their desktop is overflowing with saved documents. However, the idea of investing time and changing behavior is either completely alien or unwelcome. Using desktop technology to increase productivity will be a challenge if the person is unwilling to learn. Their excuses will range from *I'm too busy*, *It's too difficult to use*, or *I don't have time*. Their effectiveness as a team player in using information is limited and self-imposed as they are unwilling to learn and change their behavior. This kind of a person is a late adopter to a SharePoint deployment. These people are also categorized as *Low Touch, Low Adopter*. The good news with this kind of end user is that they are honest and will be vocal that they are not using the technology.

"That's great, it'll help me"

This person is supportive in the deployment and understanding of the technology, but that is as far as it goes. What they are really saying is that this technology is great, but for everyone else to use. Their effectiveness as a team player with information is also limited and self-imposed as they also are unwilling to learn and change their behavior. Unfortunately, collaboration requires **everyone** to be on board for it to work effectively.

"This is amazing"

This wide-eyed user is eager to learn, willing to change his behavior patterns, and ready to use the quick productivity wins that SharePoint provides. This kind of end user is willing to learn SharePoint functionality, but the steps have to be easy and should not require too much work.

"Show me and tell me more"

This is your **Power User** who will typically know how to perform the advanced formulae in Excel and will have a very efficient inbox, by having rules set up, and an organized folder structure. This kind of end user will invest time to advance his knowledge with SharePoint. If anything, they will find that administrative restrictions hold back their use of all of the functionalities.

It is important that an end user (or a trainer) knows what categories they belong to so, they know how to get the most mileage and use from this book. If the reader is honest and recognizes that he is not in the last two categories then this book will only provide an entertaining read. If you are in the last two categories, we urge you to change your daily habits as you learn SharePoint's functionality.

Webinizing information

Producing, storing, and responding to information in SharePoint is viewed as **webinizing** the information so it is accessible to a group of people or a team. Information is stored in a user-friendly format (text), and it can be task driven. There is much more to SharePoint than uploading documents to a site. Quick wins to this process include version control, workflow approvals, and check in/out processes, which provide team activity tracking.

We recognize that there is an information overload in the workplace. Everyone knows this and end users have found ways to work with information in the following ways:

- Read it
- Glance at it
- File it
- Ignore it (filter)

Despite the different approaches to reading, managing, and storing this information, we format and produce it in the same way — with a one-size-fits-all-approach, usually in Word and then e-mail, or we upload it into a SharePoint list. *So why doesn't this approach work? Aren't Word documents and e-mail information 'communicating tools', just like the phone?*

Given the four stated approaches to information, let us try to understand why these approaches (with existing desktop tools) do not provide the most efficient productivity gains.

Reading information

Despite popular belief, most people do not fully read most information that is sent to them, particularly if it is more than five pages or sent as an attachment. Yet we spend a lot of time writing and formatting documents only for them to sit in other people's inboxes and remain unread.

This is because in order for people to actually read the information, they have to take time out of their already busy day to detach it, digest the information, and then be ready to act on it, all of which requires time and attention. This is an unspoken activity in the workplace today. How many times have you been on the phone with co-workers and they have said, *"Just remind me what was in that document that you sent over to me?"* What the person is really saying is, *"I know you spent a lot of time writing up the document, I haven't read it, so just tell me what I need to know."*

Typically, the recipient of the document has to perform the following tasks: download it, open it up (in hopefully the correct version of Word), mark up, save it, store it, and when necessary, reply to the e-mail by attaching the corrected document. And back and forth this goes. So, time is wasted in producing the document with additional formatting and re-editing of the original document. The additional steps can add up to hours or even days for the end user, especially if there are multiple users all editing.

Glancing at information

Unlike at school, where you can hide away in the library and be isolated from interruptions from instant messengers, e-mail, and the phone, today it is very difficult for workers to dedicate large amounts of time to read information. People generally skim through text and look for activities attached to their names, which may require steps to be taken. So, having information as a text in a straight e-mail, which can be read and replied to with few mouse clicks (and which can be read on a mobile-friendly device) is a very effective way of writing, reading, and replying to the information. This is how the majority of people use information, so we need to ensure that our information is formatted to take advantage of its real world use.

 Text is king! Why? There are no file downloads, and no need to fire up an application to read and then resave the information. Above all, people usually just want the information, the message, and understand what needs to be done. They generally do not care about the formatting.

File information

Storage behavior is where people don't even bother to read the information. They know that there is value with it so they will save it to their desktop or drag it into a folder in Outlook for future reference.

This activity does have some benefit if the information saved has value, but given the storage location, it is only of value to the individual who stores the information, not to the group or a team. There is no one source of the truth that you can achieve by storing information in a central, controlled location and eliminating the need for users to perform the same actions. When information is reliant on multiple people filing information in their e-mail inbox and the folder system has become your filing cabinet, any documentation related to projects or teamwork will cause a problem as there is a strong chance that team members will be viewing and acting on wrong versions of information, with unproductive consequences. E-mail is certainly still useful, but when it comes to teamwork, SharePoint's collaborative features such as wikis and document repositories provide a superior set of tools for working together and being able to keep track of the latest version of that work.

A question such as, *Who's got the most current version of this document we're working on?* is an all too common question in offices, as well as *I never got that e-mail*, can lead to a black hole of communication.

By contrast, SharePoint allows you to cut the time needed to reach consensus on a document against a deadline by providing a single, easy-to-manage environment, and may just be your best hope for escaping the e-mail hell that people live in. And, as you know, faster decision-making means faster action and a quicker ROI that ultimately can translate directly to the bottom line

Ignore it (filter)

This is done either intentionally or unintentionally. What is clear, however, is that information is ineffective when someone writes it up, sends it to an end user, and then it is ignored. It is not uncommon for developers to ignore e-mails knowing that if it is important, someone may phone them to discuss it. So, why spend time and effort responding to an e-mail when you know the phone will ring anyway?

The four stated responses to information are limited in terms of individual productivity and organizational effectiveness, and this is an inevitable outcome of e-mail being used as the main communication tool, or when documents are stored in Outlook. The result of a lack of transparency and sharing of information that Word and e-mail promotes does limit organizational and individual effectiveness.

E-mail was invented as an electronic replacement to a memo pad, which was normally addressed to an individual rather than a group of people (someone did not read the instruction manual with their Outlook). We are using e-mail in a way that it was not designed for—bulk communications, storage, virtual management meeting, contact sheets, you name it. Yet we carry on using this tool, even though we know it is not the best option in the toolbox.

Remember, no one was ever employed to read and respond to information, yet we are filling up our work day with these activities. This is why SharePoint is not a solution *looking for a problem*, it is a solution to a problem.

The aim of this book is to educate the end user on how to manage information in a collaborative, structured, and task-driven way with SharePoint.

Key takeaways

Let's take a moment to consider the main points we have covered so far:

- **Remember, you have a day job**: End user designing and thinking as well as setting up activities should not involve a lot of work. To reduce scope creep, create only the activities that you need to be more effective. Read the Glossary when you have finished a chapter as this will reinforce terms and SharePoint features.

- **Take your time**: Read a few chapters of the book first before you start delving into the SharePoint technology.

- **What you learn in this book is a journey**: It is a constant process of adding SharePoint functionality to your day-to-day activities.

- If you have requirements that are not immediately obvious from the functionality that has been described in the book then try to find a compromise, or maybe your requirements are not appropriate for the SharePoint technology.

- If a SharePoint process does not add value to the activity, it probably should not be in SharePoint.

- Share what you have learned with your co-workers as they will provide feedback and ask questions. Remember, *collaboration cannot be done on your own*.

- If e-mail is used, the best tip is—Get to the Point.

Technical considerations for an end user

From SharePoint 2007 to SharePoint 2010, there have been significant improvements with functionality and the end user's experience. The shortcomings of Office, Outlook, and SharePoint 2007's integration and social aspects have been rectified to provide a Web 2.0 social user experience, and in true Microsoft style, the look and feel of the Office Ribbon is now part of SharePoint's user interface.

With Office 2010, there is tighter integration with the SharePoint product with both user interface and functionality. This functionality includes:

- Outlook Social Connector, which shows SharePoint My Site activity in the Outlook client

- **PowerPoint Broadcast service**: This feature allows you to broadcast your presentation over the Internet to up to 50 users simultaneously

- Simultaneous editing of Word documents with multiple people

- Opening Office documents in the browser

End users have heard a lot of buzz about SharePoint and it is often difficult to understand what it does out of the box, what is required of the IT department, and what it requires of the development team. Let's look at the technical considerations for an end user in a non-technical manner and demystify the product.

This book is written with the assumption that the end user has Office 2010 with Outlook 2010 deployed on their computer. Earlier versions of Office with Outlook may still perform the same functionally, but the look and feel will be different.

SharePoint 2010

With each new release of SharePoint, there are small changes to the names of the SharePoint technology.

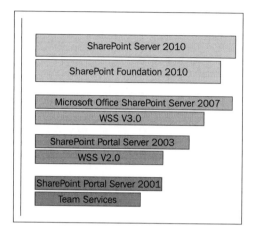

The full name for SharePoint 2007 was *Microsoft Office SharePoint Server* — **MOSS** for short. The **MOSS** part has now been removed in the 2010 release.

SharePoint Foundation 2010

SharePoint Foundation, formerly known as **WSS**, is ideal for smaller organizations or team-oriented web-based collaboration, as well as entry-level document management. The following figure illustrates SharePoint's functionality and what is available with SharePoint Foundation:

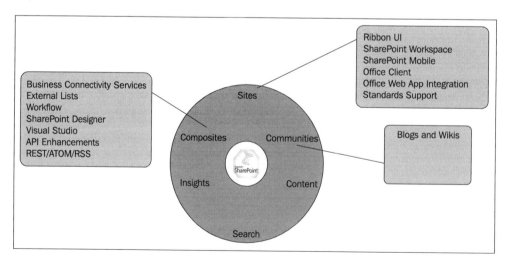

This is a free version and is an ideal entry point for an organization that is new to SharePoint and is trying to figure out its functional requirements such as team approvals or issues tracking, rather than a tool that works across the entire organization.

SharePoint Foundation can be used as an extranet.

Some noticeable limitations with Foundation are described in the following sections:

Workflow

There is a single out-of-the-box predefined workflow available. Additional workflows need to be developed with third-party tools such as SharePoint Designer. SharePoint Designer is free and can be downloaded from the Microsoft website.

The Three state workflow tracks the status of an issue or item through three different states. For example, when a Three-state workflow is initiated on an issue in an Issues list, SharePoint Foundation 2010 creates a task for the assigned user. When the user completes the task, the workflow changes from its initial state (Active) to its middle state (Resolved), and creates a task for the assigned user. When the user completes the task, the workflow changes from its middle state (Resolved) to its final state (Closed), and creates another task for the user that the workflow is assigned to at that time. When you associate the Three-state workflow with a list, you can choose to specify different state names other than Active, Resolved, and Closed.

 Note that the Three-state workflow is not supported for use with libraries.

Search

The search functionality is limited to individual team sites rather than a Google-style search engine, which can make suggestions with your search, find similar results, or sort by relevance. Search functionality could be enhanced with the free Search Server Express.

Personalization

Although users can add web parts to pages, there are no **My Site** features that allow greater personalization of user behavior job function. This functionality is explained later in this book.

This edition is ideal for:

- Integrating Office documents within SharePoint
- Evaluating a technology without committing to software license purchases
- Simple business processes such as workflows and forms
- Basic collaboration

 SharePoint Foundation could be viewed this way: If you are hungry, you may go to a restaurant where the appetizers are free, but if you really want a good feast with all the fixings, you will need to buy the main meal aka SharePoint Server.

SharePoint Server 2010 Standard Edition

SharePoint Server is an extension of SharePoint Foundations functionalities, which are illustrated in the following diagram:

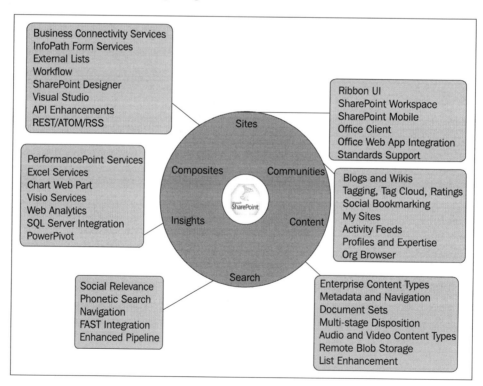

For larger organizations with more demanding collaboration requirements, SharePoint Server is more ideal as out-of-the-box functionality. SharePoint Server has two editions, which are described in the following section.

Standard

This has the core SharePoint capabilities to manage content and business processes and personalization and search functionality.

This edition is ideal when there is a need for:

- Content Management—Document Sets
- Governance policies
- Workflows
- Web 2.0 features—Rating and social bookmarking
- Enterprise Management: tagging and taxonomy
- Enterprise search capabilities

Enterprise

This edition has the functionality of the Standard Edition and also provides integration with Microsoft Office client for rich data visualization, dashboards, and analytics through Excel and Access services as well as InfoPath forms.

This edition is ideal for:

- Integrating information from different systems to the end user in a web-based environment
- Displaying business intelligence information
- Extending data from the web into Excel
- Using web-based InfoPath forms that need to be filled out in the browser

 Both the Standard and Enterprise editions have the same workflow ability, enterprise search and personalization, and content targeting features.

In this section, you can see that the out-of-the-box functionality increases from Foundation to Enterprise. If an organization has more than 50 employees and wishes to standardize business process with the SharePoint technology, we would recommend the Enterprise edition. This recommendation may increase software license and hardware costs, but the additional out-of-the-box functionality provided will bring a beneficial ROI to the business.

A SharePoint Editions Comparison is detailed in *Appendix A, Glossary*.

Integration with other technologies

Despite Microsoft's track record on non-Microsoft technology, the out-of-the-box product is fully platform agnostic with both Firefox and Safari's browsers and an Apple computer. We recommend using Vista/Windows 7 as your client operating system, Internet Explorer 7/8 as your browser, Outlook 2010 as your e-mail, and Office 2010 as your word processer, spreadsheet, and presentation application with the SharePoint 2010 technology.

 Remember the mantra of this book is: *simplify processes to give you immediate traction with the SharePoint product.*

External access

This is important to understand as it will affect how you work with your information, and who has access to it.

To understand the functionality that is available, you should ask the following questions to your IT department so that you understand the limitations of the deployed technology, and if possible make requests to IT for any changes that support your requirements:

- Can I work remotely, and what does it involve?

  In general, the more security that is applied, the more difficult collaboration becomes as it is not convenient to log in and get on with your work or integrate to Office applications. As an end user, there is not much that you can do about this, but it is important to be aware of these limitations.

  If remote access requires VPN or fob security keys then the ease of collaboration is reduced and user experience is reduced because there are additional authentication steps.

- What SharePoint edition does the company have: Foundation, Standard, or Enterprise?

This will affect the web functionality that can be applied to your business processes.

- What version of Office has been deployed to my computer?

  Some of the SharePoint 2010 functionality will work with Office 2003/2007.

- Has SharePoint been deployed throughout the organization? If not, which departments have access to it?

  Office 2010 now has a co-authoring ability so multiple people can edit a document at once. This will influence who can work with your information.

- Can non-employees have access to the SharePoint environment?

  This will influence how you collaborate with non-company employees.

- Has the My Sites feature been enabled?

  The My Site feature is a personal site, similar to a MySpace page, that can be customized and custom content created. With SharePoint 2007, often companies turn this feature off as they feel this will be a distraction to a user's work day or an IT maintenance overhead. With this release, companies want a greater focus on the social elements of the technology.

Governance

When you talk about governance, an end user might think of IT governance, but here it is about a *user's governance* to his information.

What does this mean? Part of the problem with network drives and e-mails is that they become a dumping ground for information that no one is responsible for. In turn, this information is unsearchable and no one has ownership over it.

This information experience should be avoided at all costs. Consider the following six questions:

- **Can the information be metatagged?** If SharePoint's taxonomies feature can be used, locating information will be quicker and easier for you.
- **Who is the owner of this information?** Department or individual.
- **Should I have an archiving policy on the information, to a location that I can easily access, but which is not on my immediate home page?** SharePoint has Information Policies that can be assigned to documents.
- **Does the information require approval by anyone?**
- **Notification of new/changed information. How should I set this up for my team and myself?**
- **Who needs access to this information?** Co-workers/external parties.

When the preceding questions can be answered or addressed, the value of documents and information is dramatically increased because it is more relevant to an organization, it is more likely to be correct, and there is an owner assigned to it who can be accountable for any action.

With SharePoint, there is an element of front loading the information, which will be based on technical considerations such as how often the information is being reviewed or requested.

 Important note: The next five chapters are very important for the reader in order to understand the fundamentals of the SharePoint 2010 product. We would suggest reading this book with your laptop open to visualize and better grasp the functionality that is being discussed.

Summary

The intention of this chapter is for the readers to identify themselves as a particular type of end user in the workplace and recognize this type of end users' behavior, what version of SharePoint their company has deployed, and how it has been deployed with regard to access. Depending on the edition, this will affect the deployment approach as obviously functionalities are different in Foundation, Standard, and Enterprise.

If the Foundation version has been deployed, it is worth asking the IT department if there is a department time frame for Standard or the Enterprise edition to be deployed within the company.

This question should be asked if the user base is still using Office 2003 rather than Office 2010.

Even though you may not fully know all of SharePoint 2010's features, we recommend that you think about what daily team-based tasks can be moved into SharePoint such as action items from meetings, project issue tracking, and team communications

The next chapter details SharePoint's actual components at a high level so you will have an understanding of how SharePoint sites and its content are architected and used by end users.

2
SharePoint Essentials

This chapter will cover fundamental essentials that the end user should know about SharePoint technology and how it is relevant to them. This knowledge is not rocket science, but it is important to know and understand the basics as this is a foundation of the other chapters in the book.

This chapter will cover the following topics:

- SharePoint's core components
- Site hierarchy
- User interface
- Site navigation
- Search

SharePoint's core components

From the user's standpoint, the core component is the **Team Site** (or commonly termed simply **Site**). Within a **Site**, there are **lists** and **libraries**, and these store content such as documents, images, announcements, team discussions, items, and pages:

- **Lists**: These are template-defined areas on a site that store web-based content such as team discussions, links, announcements, contacts, events, tasks, issues lists, or even custom-defined lists.
- **Items**: Items are records in a list. This is where metadata such as author, date, and keywords are stored. Users have the ability to enter and edit an item in their browser. Events such as workflows and alerts can be initiated from an item in a list.

- **Libraries**: These are collections of files that include documents and graphics that you can store or share. Files that normally reside on a local or network drive would be stored here.

- **Documents**: Any form of document, both Microsoft Office or non-Office files, are stored in Libraries. Events such as workflows and alerts can be initiated from an item in a library.

- **Content Types**: This is reusable functionality such as columns, workflow, lists, or libraries and allows you to manage the settings in a centralized and reusable way.

Let us provide an example in layman's terms:

Imagine a building with several rooms containing furniture. Each of the rooms has a defined purpose such as a bedroom for sleeping, a kitchen to cook in, and a living room to entertain guests in. Each room has different furniture items in it, which may only make sense in that particular room; for example, an oven does not work well in the bedroom. It can reside there, but it is not what you expect to find in the bedroom.

If a team site is a building, its rooms are the lists and libraries, which have predefined functionality within it, and the furniture that people use is the content.

On a company's SharePoint portal (a road), there could be many sites (buildings), each with a different purpose such as Project Management, HR, Finance, and IT. This is illustrated in the following figure:

Within the Project Management site (a building), there are several defined lists and libraries (rooms) such as project documentation, issue tracking, and so on. Within lists and libraries, content (furniture) is stored, used, and worked on. This can be illustrated as follows:

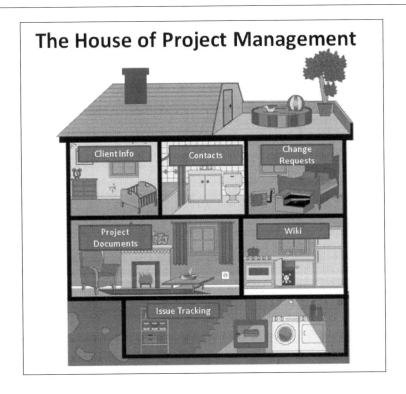

By using content types, this project management functionality can be replicated to different departments. For example, imagine a project management situation in which you have three different types of PMO documents: status reports, purchase orders, and change requests. All three types of documents have some characteristics in common; for one thing, they are all project documents and contain project code data. Yet each type of document has its own data requirements, its own document template, and its own workflow. One solution to this business problem is to create four content types. The first content type, Project Document, could encapsulate data requirements common to all project documents. The remaining three: Status Report, Purchase Order, and Change Requests could inherit common elements from Project Document and also define unique characteristics, such as fields. Each of the content types could be used with any document library in the site hierarchy or even together in the same document library. When project management requirements change, the content types can be modified and updates will be pushed down to any document library where the content type is used.

The use of content types can be fundamental to a SharePoint deployment process as they can replace the number of lists and libraries required. To the novice, they can be complex to understand, and they are covered in more detail in *Chapter 11, Enterprise Content Management*.

Site hierarchy

There are several sites (buildings) that exist within a SharePoint portal, which serve different purposes. This is called a **site hierarchy**, which is illustrated in the following figure:

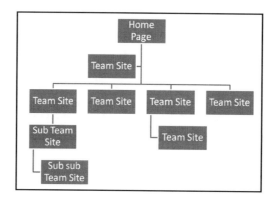

Over time, the site hierarchy can have hundreds of Sub Team Sites.

A Team Site can have a site within a site. This is known as a **Sub Team Site** and has the same functionality of a top-level site.

The preceding figure represents a **site collection**. These consist of a top-level site and one or more sites below it. Each top-level site and any sites below it in the site structure are based on a site template and can have other unique settings and unique content such as security, branding, and workflow setting.

 People often refer to a SharePoint portal, such as `http://SharePointportalhome.com`, as a SharePoint site when in fact this is a series of team sites in what is known as a **site collection**.

The preceding description is slightly misleading in its explanation of sites as it states that houses are immediately next to the road site. This analogy is not the case in the SharePoint world as you can have what is known as **Sub Team Sites**. This is not so much as a house within a house, but rather a *house off a house*.

The analogy may be relevant if a site is called **Project Management Office** and its sub sites were projects.

User interface

SharePoint 2010 has some very noticeable differences compared to SharePoint 2007's **user interface (UI)**. Microsoft has added more to the end user experience, where the most noticeable change is the use of the **Ribbon**, which was first introduced to the Office 2007 products. The following screenshot is the typical 2007 *toolbar menu style*:

Notice with this interface there are a lot of different icon-based tool bars. The Ribbon contains tabs to expose different sets of control elements eliminating the dropdowns.

Some end users had problems accepting the 2007 interface in the Office products because they did not spend any time understanding it, and tried to use it as if it was the 2003 version. This does not increase personal productivity, so we strongly suggest that you embrace the new SharePoint 2010 UI and understand the features that are available. In time, you will find that the UI will grow on you and help you actually find functions more easily.

The Ribbon is becoming the universal UI across all of Microsoft Office's product offerings, so it really has to be embraced.

This chapter's focus is on UI outline and we will expand on functionality in later chapters. For now, take a look at this website that explains and demonstrates the UI in detail:

```
http://channel9.msdn.com/learn/courses/SharePoint2010Developer/
UiEnhancements/TheSharePointFluentUserInterface
```

The Ribbon

The Ribbon is a key user interface feature that extends toolbar functionality. The intention behind the Ribbon UI is to make editing and content search simpler, allowing the user to drill into the Ribbon, and create and edit content more easily.

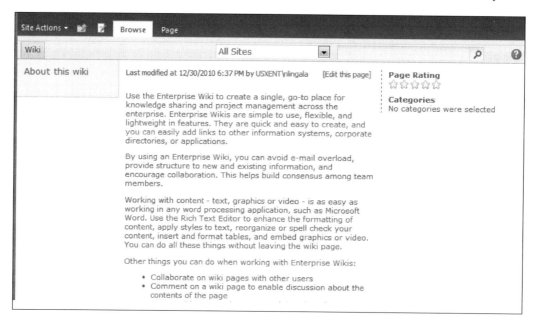

The preceding screenshot shows the Ribbon UI (highlighted) on a typical SharePoint page. By clicking on the **Page** tab, further Ribbon functionality that is purposely hidden is displayed.

 The user has editor permissions on this page.

In the preceding example, functionality has been categorized into sections that include **Edit**, **Manage**, **Share & Track**, **Page Actions**, and **Page Library**. These represent categorized functionality that is available, and so if you wish to edit a document, the button will be in the **Edit** section of the Ribbon.

When clicking on the **Edit** button on the left-hand side, the Ribbon will change again and display text-editing functionality.

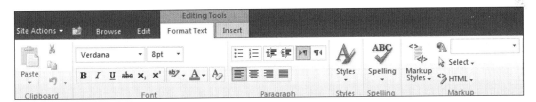

In the preceding example, notice an **Editing Tools** section has appeared on the Ribbon. This is because the user is currently editing text. If there was a requirement to insert a file or image, the **Insert** tab would be clicked and the Ribbon would change further, displaying functionality to add/insert content to the page as in the following screenshot:

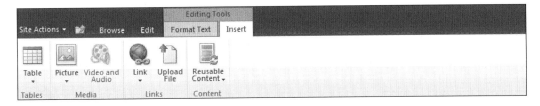

The dynamically changing UI theme is consistent with SharePoint 2010. The advantage of this navigational method is that the user is always on the same screen for editing and creating content and is not redirected to another screen, only to be taken back to the screen they are editing afterwards.

> To add and create content, it is just a matter of the user reaching up to the **Ribbon** to select what they want to do. The user's editing actions are deliberately directed to a single area of the screen to simplify the editing process.

Clearly, the **Ribbon** UI in SharePoint is replicating the Office 2007/2010 interface so there is a single interface experience with Microsoft's suite of applications.

Site navigation

Site navigation is typical of any intranet site, with top and left-side navigational panes, and content in the middle.

The top and side navigational menus can be edited with a site's **Site Settings** page where you can make changes in the **Navigation Editing and Sorting** section.

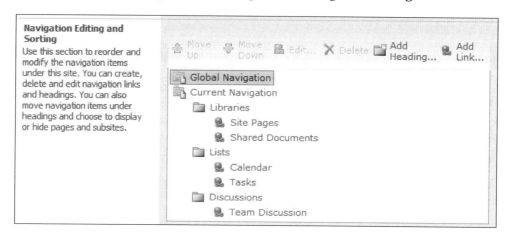

Breadcrumb menus

Breadcrumbs, or what is sometimes known as a **Breadcrumb Trail,** is a navigation aid used in user interfaces, including SharePoint 2007. It gives users a way to keep track of their location within a site. Typically, these appear horizontally across the top part of a web page and represent a site, library, or a folder name. This is illustrated as follows:

A greater-than sign (>) often serves as a hierarchy separator. In the preceding screenshot, **Home** and **Sales** are different sites and **Sales Orders** is the library. **Software and Renewals** is a folder within this library.

In the preceding screenshot, if the user clicked on **Sales Orders**, the Sales Order page would load. The breadcrumb concept has been replaced with a **folder icon** button, which will display the page on the site with an indented hierarchical view of your current location.

When you click on the **Navigational Up** button, the breadcrumb menu is displayed.

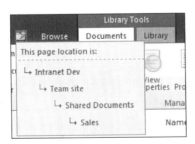

The approach of combining the functionality of a Site Map and Breadcrumb menu is new to website design. This is an innovative approach for Microsoft as this is not done with most websites and is particularly good when sites are large with many sections, which would otherwise result in the breadcrumb menu approach taking up too much of the page. This new method of navigation changes the whole user navigation experience and also, by clicking on the **Navigation Up** button, optimizes page usage by hiding the site hierarchy until it is required.

Creating content

Creating content is one of the primary tasks any user is likely to do. To begin to create content within a site, components such as libraries, lists, or pages need to be created first. To do this, click on the **Site Actions** button on the Ribbon and choose **View All Site Content** or **New Page**, or **New Site**.

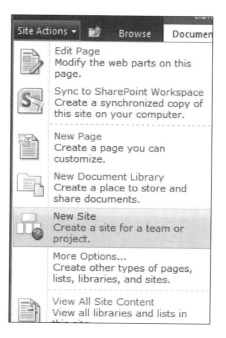

 This is a top site of a Site Collection and the user has full administration rights, so you may not see all of the menu options.

When the next screen appears, click on **Create** to create content.

Further options are offered to create a **List**, **Library**, **Page**, and **Site** within the site. These will be discussed in later chapters.

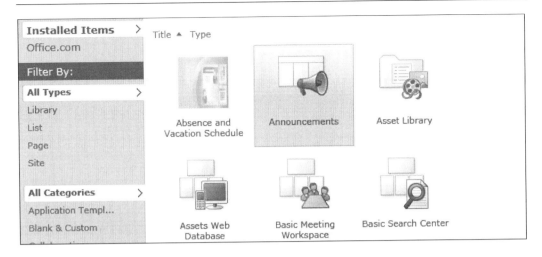

In the preceding screenshot, the **Announcements** template is selected to be created. The announcements list template is where announcement items are created and stored.

Typically, a site has multiple lists and libraries where content is created and stored.

Your profile

With the SharePoint Server edition, there is the ability to change personal information with **My Sites**. By clicking on your **username** on the top right-hand side of the top navigation, you can access the personal information that makes up your profile.

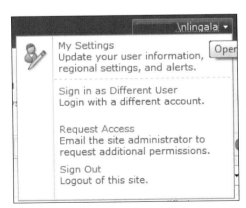

We will go through profiles in greater depth in *Chapter 3, SharePoint Team Sites*.

 There is no My Sites feature with SharePoint Foundation.

Search Functionality

Search functionality is probably one of the most undervalued functionality elements of SharePoint, yet finding information is a fundamental end user activity. This is partly because users are usually more focused on uploading and creating content rather than finding and viewing it. Some users who use SharePoint still drill down a navigation tree to find information even though there is a powerful search feature to find information within two clicks.

 Just as you use Google to find external information to your organization, SharePoint's search function can find information internal to your company even if it is not stored in SharePoint.

Generally, there are two types of behavior types: Navigators (Clicking) and Explorers (Searchers), and given that both behavior types are a user's natural habits and are unlikely to change, the search functionality and navigation caters to both behaviors.

One of the advantages of the search method of finding information is that the contents of documents can be indexed and searched on, thus saving discovery time for the user.

On the right-hand side of the top navigation part of the page, there is a search box.

The **Search** feature can help the user not only find content but also people who can collaborate with them. They can also view other content that collaborators have.

This is important to realize, as it is not only important to find the information quickly, but also to find the author of the information, their skill sets, and what other information that person is adding into SharePoint. This is sometimes referred to as **binding information**.

Key search features

SharePoint's search functionality goes beyond finding the relevant information and can now provide a co-worker's experience to aid the user search process.

Thesaurus support to queries

It is not uncommon that a search query does not always produce an exact match on the search results page. There is now the ability for the search results page to offer other similar search words that you may have originally wanted to find.

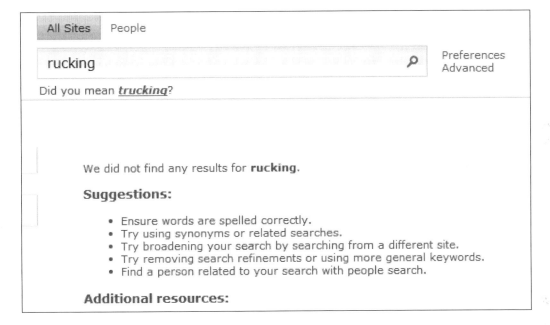

This feature can be extended with **Best Bets** functionality, which is where an administrator can add words to the SharePoint search database; so, if a word is searched, other words can also be included in the search.

Best Bets can link to recommended websites, datastores, and documents that help to explain a keyword and expand upon its meaning. This is useful if someone changes their name and the user wants to see all authored documents with the person's former and current name and is not aware of the person's former name.

The Best Bets functionality can only be administrated by IT, so the user will need to request words to be added to the SharePoint search database.

People and expertise search

The information on a SharePoint site is not just restricted to documents but a company's employee directory and the employees' skill sets. This allows the user to locate skills and co-workers very quickly with a single search.

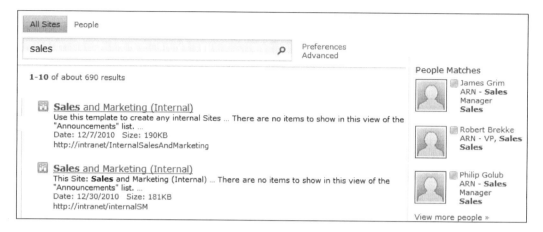

With the preceding figure, employees that have the word **sales** in their profile are also displayed on the **Search** results page.

By clicking on the **People** text on the search page, the user is shown all of the SharePoint users that have the word **sales** on their profile:

There is also the ability to view content by author; hover your mouse over additional search options on the **people search results** page:

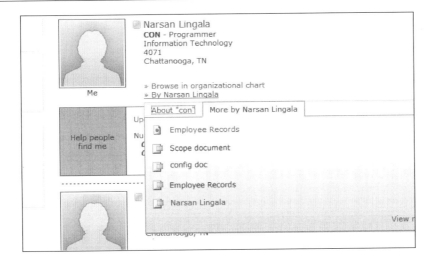

Refinement and Exact Count Sorting

Often with search result pages, the results become too much for the user to make a decision on what to click. With SharePoint, there is the ability to refine the search to metadata items of content with the **Advanced Search** page.

You can find the **Advanced Search** page by clicking on **Advanced** next to the search bar.

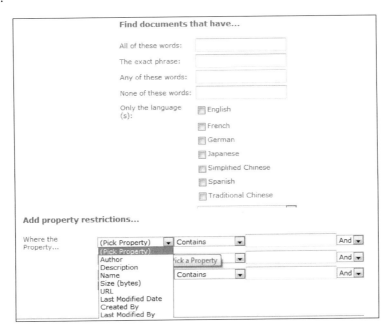

The search criteria can be constructed to provide greater refinement with **AND** or **OR** conditional searching ability.

Phonetics and Nickname expansion

With the global workforce, some employee names can be difficult to pronounce and spell. SharePoint's search engine can intelligently identify misspelled names in search queries.

Recently authored content

It is a very common user behavior to read a document and want to know what other information the author has written. SharePoint now has the ability to easily provide this information on the left-hand side of the **Search** results page.

The user's experience of SharePoint 2010 search has been greatly enhanced from SharePoint 2007 with the Web 2.0 trend of integrating into the search results page both document and list information to the author's role in an organization, and **Active Directory** information such as user location and contact information. As a result, the functionality provides an internal search engine for a document repository as well as finding expertise geographically within the company.

The different editions of SharePoint 2010 provide different functionality and it is important for you to understand the differences. These are outlined in *Appendix A*.

Summary

In this chapter, we have learned about SharePoint Essentials such as **search**, **lists**, **libraries**, **content types**, **Ribbon**, **site hierarchy**, **user interface**, and **site navigation**, at a higher level and what is different from SharePoint 2007 in terms of user experience. In the next chapter, we will discuss team sites and how a hierarchy of a portal can be deployed and managed. The topics include site overview, site creation, site security, navigation, and UI-Themes. We recommend that you open the browser and experience each of the discussed topics in this chapter as this will combine practical hands-on experience with the described functionality in the other chapters of the book.

We also recommend that readers who are familiar with the SharePoint 2007 version understand the difference between these versions and how this affects the way they work as some of your tasks can be simply enhanced rather than changed.

3
SharePoint Team Sites

This chapter is designed to help you understand what SharePoint Team Sites (Sites) are and what content and information a Site can provide for your own specific purposes. This will ultimately allow you to architect an entire portal.

This chapter will cover:

- Site overview
- Libraries and lists
- Creating sites
- Site security for your team
- Managing users and groups
- Creating and managing navigation
- Changing the UI-themes

Site overview

Understanding the site overview can be confusing because there are many terms that people often misuse. The word **Site** can refer to the entire portal when in fact a portal can be a **collection of Sites**, referred to by Microsoft as a **Team Site**. Another term you should also be aware of is **Site Collection**.

Sites

A site usually represents a functional department or activity in an organization, such as sales or marketing in a project. Because there may be multiple collaboration activities, a site would normally be created to accommodate these activities.

Sometimes functionality activity needs to be split into separate sites within a site, perhaps because there is so much content, different branding, or because security is required. When this is a requirement, a **sub site** is created, which is a site within a site.

 Refer back to the previous chapter to learn about sub sites in more detail.

Site collection

A site collection normally has a top-level site with multiple sites below it. Each site in the collection can have a unique template, settings, and content. These features can also be shared among sites to provide a consistent authoring environment with shared site columns, content types, web parts, and workflows.

By deploying sites within a site collection, the benefit to the user experience is unified navigation, branding, and search.

In fact, a SharePoint installation within a company can have multiple Site Collections that can contain multiple Sites. The Site Collections will normally have different business purposes such as an extranet, company intranet, and marketing **business-to-business (B2B)** portal; these are defined by a **SharePoint Administrator**.

The SharePoint components mentioned are illustrated in the following figure:

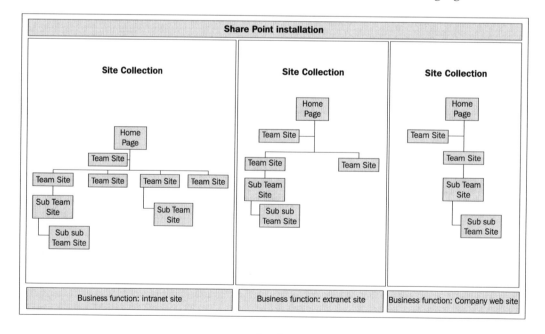

The Sites within the different Site Collections, as illustrated in the preceding figure, store information in **libraries** or **lists**.

Libraries and lists

Libraries have very similar functionality to lists, with the main difference being that they contain documents, not list items. The documents are not limited to MS Office; any document, including PDFs, CAD, and MP4 files (among others) can be found in libraries.

 MS Office 2010 files have greater integration with the SharePoint technology with the ability to apply **metadata** to a file (discussed later in the chapter), start a **workflow**, and experience shortcuts to SharePoint libraries through the **Office Ribbon** interface. Other Office integration features include SharePoint WorkSpace, which allows SharePoint content to be taken offline, and PowerPoint broadcasts, which allows PowerPoint presentations to be broadcast to the Internet.

Links to libraries are listed on the side navigation or **Quick Launch** of a Site, and are categorized. In the following screenshot, the categories are **Libraries**, **Lists**, and **Discussions**.

 The **Quick Launch** side navigation can be manually changed so it is not always the case that a list or library will be displayed on the side navigation. Links on the Quick Launch could link to forums, dashboards, web pages, SharePoint pages, or a non-SharePoint site(s).

To view the **Shared Documents** library, the user can click on the **Shared Documents** link.

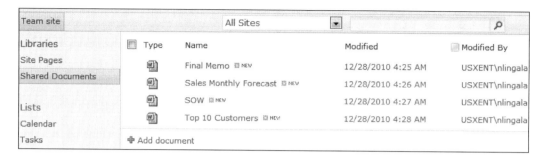

The preceding screenshot shows a typical document library with documents stored in it and document associated data: **Name** (which is the name of the file), last **Modified**, and **Modified By**. These are field information (or metadata) that are associated with the document or information. SharePoint terminology refers to this information as **Columns**. Additional columns can also be added to a document library to provide greater metadata options to the content. **Metadata is data on the data**.

By clicking on the top of a **column header**, the document library is sorted similarly to a column in Excel. Obviously, the more columns that are displayed, the greater the ability to sort and filter displayed information.

> There can only be so many columns on the page until horizontal browser scroll bars are displayed at the foot of the browser, which presents a cluttered user experience. If it is really necessary to have large amounts of field information displayed, create different views in the library. This will keep the user more focused on relevant information.

Information in a Document Library can be viewed in different ways. Select the downward arrow next to the view name on the ribbon as shown in the following screenshot:

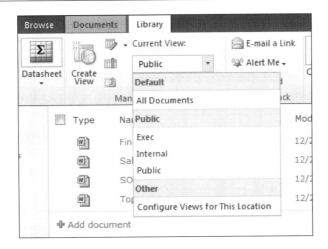

In the preceding screenshot, there is a single view of **All Documents**, and by clicking on it this view will be displayed.

When users first start working with SharePoint's document library, they tend to copy the existing folder structure network drive, with files stored in the same folder location. This is a good practice as it gains user buy-in because they are familiar with the content structure.

Over time, when users become more familiar with their requirements and SharePoint's functionality, they begin to create views within libraries to filter content.

Views are discussed in detail in the following chapter.

Library Ribbons

When a document is selected, the Ribbon dynamically changes to show additional user actions for the selected item, hence the interface is more intuitive and therefore similar to Office 2010.

Before selecting the document, you would see something like this:

Afterwards, the ribbon dynamically changes to this:

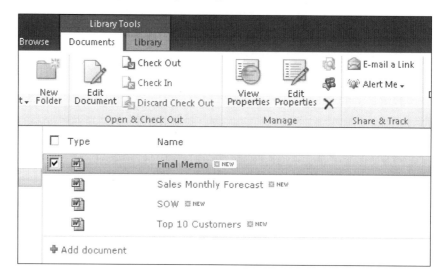

SharePoint has several Ribbons (the preceding screenshot is for libraries). There are two tabs on the Ribbon that are important: **Documents** and **Library**.

- **Documents**: This represents all actions related to the document, such as **Check Out**, **Edit** the document, and so on.

- **Library**: This represents all actions related to a library, such as create versioning, set up an alert notification, or create a view on the library. Some of these actions will require appropriate permissions.

Lists

A SharePoint list is a collection of similar items that contain columns or fields that define the item data or metadata schema. Each item stored in a list shares the same schema.

The built-in lists on a Site are **announcements**, **contacts**, **events**, **tasks**, **discussion** and **issues lists**. When you create your own lists, you can either base them on the designs used for the built-in lists, or you can create a **Custom List**.

A list will contain items such as a **Calendar** entry. The following screenshot illustrates a calendar list in a calendar view, with each calendar entry representing an item.

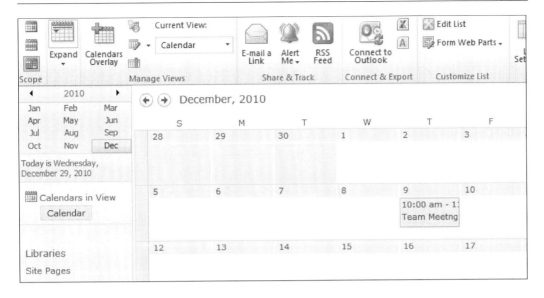

By clicking on the **item**, the whole entry can be seen.

List Ribbons

When an item is in a list, the Ribbon dynamically changes to show additional user actions to the selected item. The following screenshot shows the Ribbon for the Calendar list. Note that there are some subtle differences to the Library Ribbon, including syncing up the calendar on SharePoint with the user's Outlook calendar, exporting the items into Excel, or querying the items in MS Access.

Generally, information that would normally reside in a row on a spreadsheet can be an entry in a list. The advantage of having this information now stored in a list is that it is accessible to members of your team and actions can then be associated with it, such as **workflow**, **alerts**, and **version control**, all of which is discussed in the next chapter.

Workflows, alerts, and control functionality are available in document libraries.

[This chapter is only a brief introduction to the functionality of lists and libraries. This functionality will be discussed in much more detail in the following chapters.]

Creating Sites

To create a Site or a Sub Site, click on **Site Actions | New Site**.

You will be presented with a series of **Site templates**, each of which has a slightly different purpose, but they all have the common **Team Site** functionality of lists and libraries:

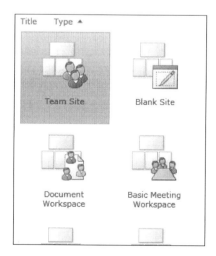

The following table is a description of each site template:

Template Name	Description
Assets Web Database	An assets database to keep track of assets, including asset details and owners.
Basic Meeting Workspace	A site on which you can plan, organize, and capture the results of a meeting. It provides lists for managing the agenda, meeting attendees, and documents.
Basic Search Center	A site that provides the search functionality. The site includes pages for search results and advanced searches.
Blank Meeting Workspace	A blank meeting site that you can customize based on your requirements.
Blank Site	A blank site that you can customize based on your requirements.
Blog	A site on which a person or team can post ideas, observations, and expertise that site visitors can comment on.
Business Intelligence Center	A site for presenting business intelligence data. It provides document libraries for storing documents, images, data connections, and dashboard Web Parts. It also provides lists for linking content from PerformancePoint Services in Microsoft SharePoint Server 2010.
Charitable Contributions Web Database	A database to track information about fundraising campaigns, including donations made by contributors, campaign-related events, and pending tasks.
Contacts Web Database	A contacts database to manage information about people that your team works with, such as customers and partners.
Decision Meeting Workspace	A site on which you can track status or make decisions at meetings. It provides lists to create tasks, store documents, and record decisions.
Document Center	A site on which you can centrally manage documents in your enterprise.
Document Workspace	A site on which colleagues can work together on a document. It provides a document library for storing the primary document and supporting files, a tasks list for assigning to-do items, and a link list to point to resources that are related to the document.
Enterprise Search Center	A site that provides the search functionality. The welcome page includes a search box that has two tabs: one for general searches and another for searches for information about people. You can add and customize tabs to focus on other search scopes or result types.
Enterprise Wiki	A site on which you can publish knowledge that you capture and want to share across the enterprise. It provides an easy content editing experience in a single location for co-authoring content, for discussions, and for managing projects.

Template Name	Description
FAST Search Center	A site for delivering the FAST search experience. The welcome page includes a search box with two tabs: one for general searches and another for searches for information about people. You can add and customize tabs to focus on other search scopes or result types.
Group Work Site	This template provides a groupware solution that teams can use to create, organize, and share information. It includes the Group Calendar, Circulation, Phone-Call Memo, the document library, and the other basic lists.
Issues Web Database	An issues database to manage a set of issues or problems. You can assign, prioritize, and follow the progress of issues from start to finish.
Microsoft Project Site	A site that supports team collaboration on projects. This site includes Project Documents, Project Issues, Project Risks, and Project Deliverables lists that might be linked to tasks in Microsoft Project Server 2010.
Multipage Meeting Workspace	A site on which you can plan a meeting and capture the meeting's decisions and other results. It provides lists for managing the agenda and meeting attendees. It also provides two blank pages that you can customize based on your requirements.
My Site Host	A site that hosts personal sites (My Sites) and the public People Profile page. This template has to be provisioned only once per User Profile Service Application. This template is available only at the site collection level.
Personalization Site	A site for delivering personalized views, data, and navigation from this site collection to My Site. It includes Web Parts that are specific to personalization and navigation that is optimized for My Site sites. This template is available only at the site level.
PowerPoint Broadcast Center	A site for hosting Microsoft PowerPoint 2010 broadcasts. Presenters can connect to the site and create a link for remote viewers to watch a slideshow in a web browser.
Projects Web Database	A project-tracking database to track multiple projects, and assign tasks to different people.
Publishing Portal	A starter site hierarchy that you can use for an Internet site or a large intranet portal. You can use distinctive branding to customize this site. It includes a home page, a sample press releases site, a Search Center, and a logon page. Typically, this site has many more readers than contributors, and it is used to publish the web pages by using approval workflows. This site enables content approval workflows, by default, for a more formal and controlled publishing process. It also restricts the rights of anonymous users so that they can see only content pages, and they cannot see SharePoint Server 2010 application pages. This template is available only at the site collection level.

Template Name	Description
Publishing Site	A blank site for expanding your website and quickly publishing web pages. Contributors can work on draft versions of pages and publish them to make them visible to readers. This site includes document and image libraries for storing web publishing assets.
Publishing Site with Workflow	A site for publishing web pages on a schedule by using approval workflows. It includes document and image libraries for storing web publishing assets. By default, only sites that have this template can be created under this site. This template is available only at the site level when the Publishing Portal template is used to create the top-level site.
Records Center	A site that is designed for records management. Records managers can configure the routing table to direct incoming files to specific locations. The site also enables you to manage whether records can be deleted or modified after they are added to the repository.
Social Meeting Workspace	A site on which you can plan social occasions. It provides lists for tracking attendees, providing directions, and storing pictures of the event.
Team Site	A site on which a team can organize, author, and share information. It provides a document library, and lists for managing announcements, calendar items, tasks, and discussions.
Visio Process Repository	A site on which teams can view, share, and store Visio process diagrams. It provides a versioned document library for storing process diagrams, and lists for managing announcements, tasks, and review discussions.

For further information on team sites, visit the following site:
`http://www.shareesblog.com/?p=601`.

 Because a Site collection can have so many Sites, the Site templates are categorized and can be filtered.

In the following screenshot, the **Collaboration** category on the left-hand side navigation panel has been selected:

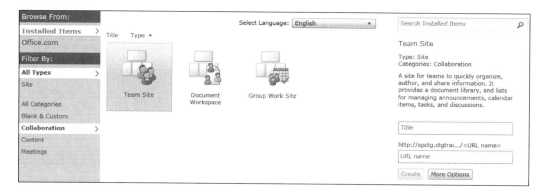

 Unless there is a specific piece of functionality that is required, such as Visio importing, we recommend the Team Site for a selected template as this Site template has the basic list and library elements already configured, such as Shared Documents, Tasks, and Calendar list.

Once a **Site** is selected, type in the Site name and URL, and the **Site** will be created.

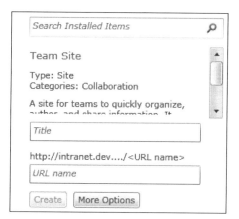

 Try to use relevant names to the title of a site. Although name and description can be changed at a later date, the URL remains the same, and this can be confusing to a user.

As seen in the preceding screenshot, you can select **More Options** to use the same permissions for the new site as the parent site. By default, this feature is set to inherit the permissions.

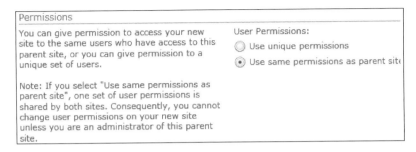

There is also the option for whether the Site will display the top navigational links from the parent site on this newly created Site. By default, this is selected as **No**.

Once a Site is created, the user will be automatically directed to the newly created Site. The following screenshot shows a standard, newly created Site using the Team Site template:

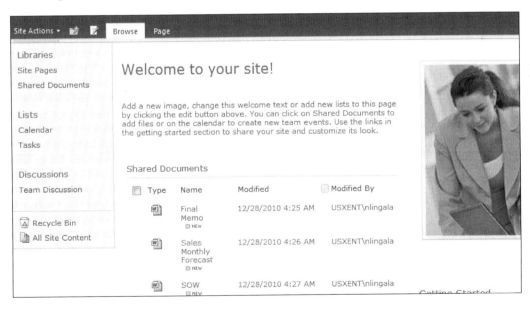

Notice the **Getting Started** box in the lower right-hand corner. This is a list of a few tasks that should be completed to quickly customize the Site for your business needs. It is best to start these tasks from the bottom up as the last action task is to **Share this Site**.

Site Security for your team

Once you have created a Site, it may require that permission be set to the Site, lists, libraries, folders, and documents. SharePoint methodology of site security is known as Site inheritance.

If you do not have manager access to a Site, you will not be able to break inheritance, add groups, and grant permissions.

Hierarchy and Inheritance

Site inheritance is when a defined security automatically inherits permissions from its parent site or even parent element such as a list, library, or folder. By default, a newly created SharePoint Site, list, library, or folder will automatically inherit the permission. The obvious advantage of this is that you do not have to individually security trim every newly defined element.

Security trimming is a term used to define specific access to content or functionality to a small group of people. When security is defined, the security trimming part is that which is normally the last to be implemented. In SharePoint, permissions on any securable object such as Site collection, lists, libraries, folders, and documents are inherited from their parent object. However, you can break this inheritance for any securable object at a lower level in the hierarchy by creating a unique permission on that securable object. For example, you can create a sub site, and break the permission inheritance from the parent if you want to limit (or expand) the group of users who are allowed access, or have permission to access, the Site for security reasons. When inheritance is broken from the parent, the SharePoint element that is now broken has a final inheritance from the parent's permissions. You can then edit these permissions to be unique.

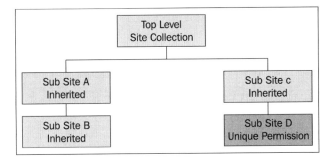

In the preceding figure, **sub Sites A**, **B**, and **C** inherit permissions from the top-level Site. If changes are made to **SharePoint groups** and permission levels on the top-level Site, the permissions will be inherited to sub sites. If a change is made to the **sub Sites A**, **B**, or **C** occur, the parent site is being changed as well, if inheritance is not broken on that site.

 SharePoint does not allow you to manage permission on a sub Site that is already inheriting permissions from its parent Site.

Sub Site D has unique permissions; therefore it is not inheriting any permission from its parent site. If any changes are made to the permission levels and SharePoint groups on **Sub Site D**, they remain in this site.

To view the Site permissions, click on **Site Actions.**

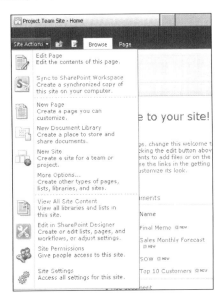

Select **Site Permissions** to view which users and groups have access to the site, and the type of access this is.

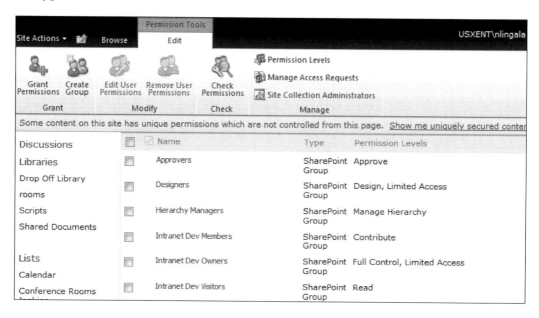

From the preceding example, we can see that:

- The Site is inheriting permissions from the parent site
- All of the groups displayed are SharePoint groups (groups defined in the SharePoint environment)
- The groups have different levels of access to the Site

This inheritance concept can be broken by clicking on the **Stop Inheriting Permissions** button on the Ribbon.

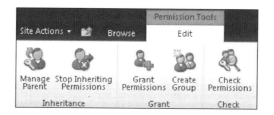

The impact of doing this is that any new groups that are created in the **parent site** will not propagate to this Site and its contents. New users that are created and are within an existing group will still have access to the Site.

We recommend that you think very carefully before breaking inheritance because this increases the administration of user access to Sites. If you are new to the SharePoint technology, breaking permission inheritance can cause access issues with users, because you do not realize sub sites are not inheriting new user permissions until users start complaining.

Often, if a user clicks on a link and they cannot immediately access the information, they normally assume that the information is not available and will fail to report the access issue. Unfortunately, this does not help user acceptance of a new Site.

A Site, list, library, item, and document can re-inherit permissions from the same menu as **Stop Inheriting Permissions**.

To change permissions on a document, select it and click on **Manage Permissions** from the drop-down menu.

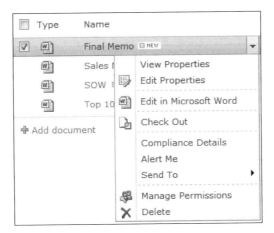

You can also secure a document from the Office client.

If users do not have access to content, they will also not have access to it through SharePoint's **search** functionality.

Managing users and groups

Permissions are granted to users or SharePoint groups so that they can perform specific actions on securable objects, such as a Site, library, list, folder, item, or document on your Site. **Permission levels** allow you to group permissions, and apply them to users and SharePoint groups on various Sites in your SharePoint installation.

When you create a new SharePoint Site, there are five permission levels provided by default:

1. **Full Control**: Allows users or groups full control over a Site. Full Control is the least restrictive permission level. You cannot modify or remove this permission level.

2. **Design**: Allows users or groups to view, add, update, delete, approve, and customize lists, libraries, and pages on your Site, including themes and style sheets.

3. **Contribute**: Allows users or groups to view, add, update, and delete previously created list items and document libraries.

4. **Read**: Allows users or groups to read pages on the Site, including the resource libraries. Read is the most restrictive permission level.

5. **Limited Access**: A permission level that is automatically assigned to a user or group, and therefore cannot be directly assigned by the administrator. This permission level enables users to view specific lists, document libraries, list items, folders, or documents without giving access to all the elements of a site, such as file versions of an alert subscription.

You can add a user who has a valid account, created by a **network administrator**, to SharePoint. When a user is added to the system, you can assign permissions directly to a securable object (web, list, library, and so on) or indirectly through a SharePoint Group.

 Out of the box SharePoint does not provide functionality to create users.

Using SharePoint Groups is the recommended practice when managing security as it is easier to manage changes for a group than for individual users and apply the same change to different objects across your Sites. Also, give the name of the group a relevant name, for example *HR Management*, for executives in the HR department. This makes administration easy for understanding the purpose of the group as the group name is stating the function of the group and its members.

All SharePoint groups are created at the Site collection level (highest level Site), and are available to all sub Sites in the Site collection. You can also create groups that only have permissions to a particular sub Site if inheritance is broken.

For further information visit this site:
```
http://community.bamboosolutions.com/blogs/sharepoint-2010/
archive/2010/11/15/sharepoint-2010-user-management.aspx.
```

Creating and managing navigation

If customization of the **top navigation** needs to be changed, it must change on the parent site as other Sites are inheriting from this site.

On the parent site, select **Site Settings** from the **Site Actions** menu.

Then, select **Navigation** in the **Look and Feel** category.

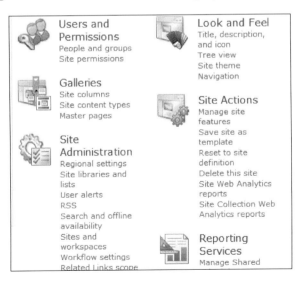

At the bottom of the page, there is a **Global Navigational** link that represents the top bar links. When these are edited, all of the sub Sites' top bar navigation will be affected.

The **Current Navigation** header is the site's **Quick Launch** (Left Side Navigation). The Current Navigation does not inherit from parent sites so this will need to be changed on every Site if required.

To add a category, click **Add Heading**, and to add a link, click **Add Link**.

 As a rule of thumb, Quick Launch items should only relate to the actual Site that they reside on, and not to other Sites. One of the reasons for this is if a link changes then the Quick Launch link will need to be changed on every Site.

Quick Launch items do not have the ability to be hidden by SharePoint's Audience functionality.

To change the **Title**, **Description**, and **icon** of a Site, click on **Site Actions**, then **Site Settings**, and make changes in the **Look and Feel** category.

Themes

In SharePoint 2010, it is possible to brand a site without the knowledge of CSS or HTML, with the use of PowerPoint 2010 and themes. **Site Themes** provide a quick and easy way to apply colors, fonts, background images, text, title fonts, and hyperlinks to a site.

To apply a theme, follow these steps:

1. Open PowerPoint and select a **theme**.

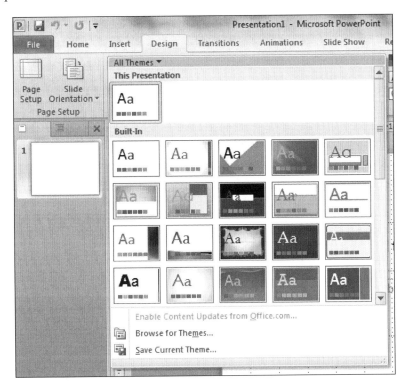

2. Apply the theme color.

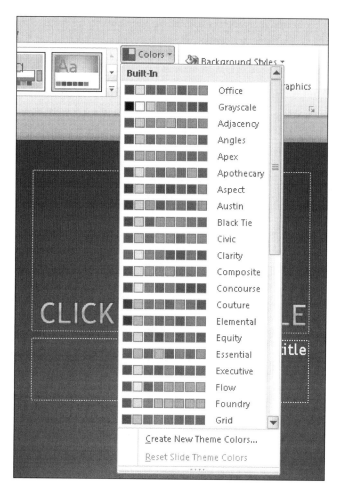

3. Save the presentation as an **Office theme (.thmx)**.

4. In SharePoint, select **Site Settings** under the **Site Actions** menu of the top-level Site (Homepage Site).

5. From the **Site Settings** page, select **Themes** under the **Galleries** section.

6. Select the **Documents** option under the **Library Tools** menu and upload the Office Theme file to the **Themes library**. The saved PowerPoint theme is now stored in SharePoint.

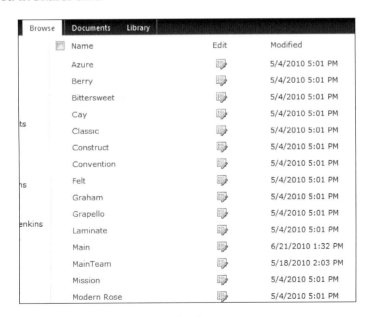

7. Navigate to the **Site Settings** page of the Site that you wish to change the theme.

8. Select **Themes** under **Look and Feel**.

9. From the theme list, select the uploaded theme and click on **Apply**.

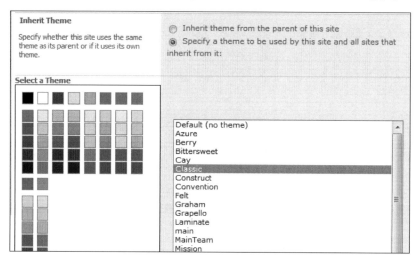

 SharePoint uses the filename as the theme name.

The theme is now applied to the Site.

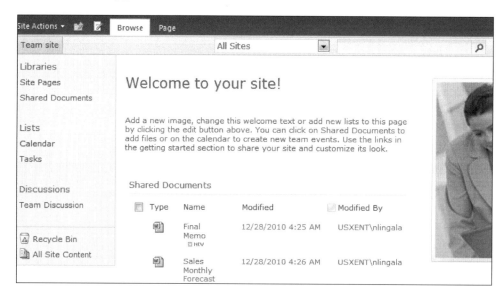

Do not get bogged down in choosing and creating themes for your Site. Content is king, not the color of the Quick Launch.

To create more elaborate custom themes, you will need to have **SharePoint Designer 2010** installed, but creating custom themes or more in-depth site branding is beyond the scope of this book.

Navigation

Navigation to a SharePoint site, is an essential element of user ability. The Ribbon interface can be confusing to users, as there are so many options to choose from. To make the interface more intuitive, there are **Super Tool Tips**.

Super Tool Tips

For every item in the Ribbon, there is what is known as a **Super Tool Tip**. This is a help label that is activated when the curser is hovered over the icon or label. These tips also state if the control on the Ribbon is disabled, and why.

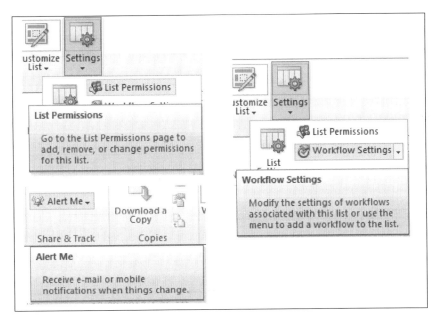

Summary

From this chapter, we can see that SharePoint is a self-service model for creating sites and applying security with usernames and groups, navigation with ribbons, and UI themes with PowerPoint to the sites, all without the need for IT administrators or graphic designers. You were introduced to site collections, site hierarchy with sub Sites, lists and libraries where content is stored, and security site inheritance.

This is a major shift in corporate intranet deployments because the responsibility for the content to be updated, and a site to be architected correctly with the correct corporate brand, now lies with the end user.

The next two chapters could be considered the most important in the book as we will go into a more in-depth examination of the functionality of lists and libraries, which is where user content actually resides.

4
List Management

In the previous chapter, you were introduced to the **SharePoint site** and its purpose in a SharePoint portal. With this release of SharePoint 2010, one of Microsoft's goals is to bring **Enterprise Content Management (ECM)** to all users, rather than to a specific user group. The result is that there is a lot of functionality that was never available to users who were more familiar with network drives or e-mail exchange for collaboration. With the knowledge from this book and without the need for heavy dependence on an IT department, there is now a platform for content to be stored and managed *by* business users *for* business users when SharePoint's ECM functionality is combined with collaboration, Office integration, and social networking.

This chapter explains **Lists** and how to manage them to provide an efficient way to store information and thus provide ECM. We view lists as a key SharePoint functionality for providing basic and complex architecting of corporate and workgroups' information.

In this chapter you will gain knowledge of **List Management** and understand how to track information and collaborate with team members:

- List Management basics
- Creating lists
- Managing lists
- How to add content to a list
- Advanced list features

The basics

A SharePoint list is a collection of similar items that are defined by a set of structure columns or fields, resembling a database table. **Lists** support various field or data types, and can have workflow and alert triggers that react to events such as creating, updating, or deleting items. In addition, lists can be configured to filter, sort, or group items based on item data or properties, which is ideal for visualization of information to both display and edit item data.

An ideal business use for a list is to store information that is normally managed in an Excel file, such as new orders, issue tracking of bugs on a project, or maintenance contracts. The advantages of storing information in a list rather than in Excel are:

- Multiple people can edit different line items of the information
- Read, write, and view permissions can be applied to the line items
- SharePoint business process functionality such as **alerts** and **workflow** can be applied to an item when it has been created or edited
- Information can be targeted to users with the use of views
- There is one version of the truth of the information

There is nothing wrong with using Excel for database-storing activity, but a SharePoint list provides a richer user experience in terms of entering, managing, and taking actions from the data.

Lists in SharePoint are based on **list templates**, such as **calendars**, **contact lists**, **picture libraries**, and others that define the scheme for new lists. You can create multiple lists, based on a single list template.

The following advanced list features are beyond the scope of this book and are provided simply to enhance your knowledge and awareness of SharePoint's functionalities. These include Editing Lists, Customizing List Forms using InfoPath 2010, Customization of List Views in SharePoint Designer, and creating custom Forms.

Creating lists

To create a list, click on **Site Actions** | **More Options...**:

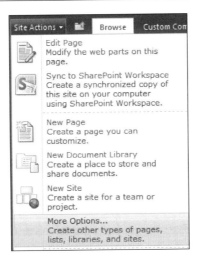

You will be presented with a series of out of the box **List templates**, each of which has a slightly different column names and views, but they all have the common List functionality.

There is the ability to filter the displayed **List templates** with the navigational menu on the left-hand side.

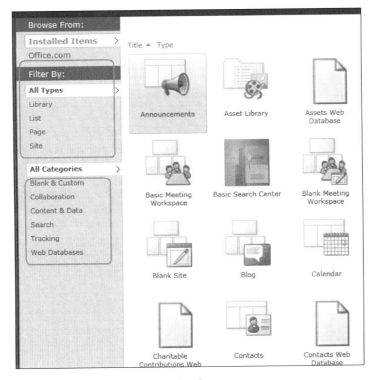

Once you have chosen your **List**, type in the List name and URL, and the **List** will be created.

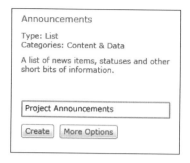

 As best practice, avoid putting spaces in the name as shown in the preceding screenshot. Otherwise, this puts the %20 character in the actual URL of the list. For example, in the preceding screenshot, the generated SharePoint list URL would be `/Lists/Project%20Annoucements/AllItems.aspx`. SharePoint converts non-alphanumeric characters to URL-friendly characters. This **whitespace** can cause problems when the URL is being used with workflows or being pasted by a user into an e-mail as the URL may be truncated when the e-mail has been sent.

Once a list or library has been created, the URL cannot be changed. You can always change the name and put in spaces in the name from the List settings.

In the preceding screenshot, you can select **More Options...** to add a description to the list, or add the list to the Quick Launch navigation of the Site.

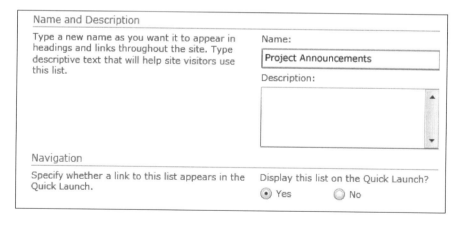

Once a List is created, you will be automatically directed to the newly created list.

List templates

The SharePoint installation has provided many out of the box List Templates that are predefined, and will generally meet your needs with perhaps some minor enhancements by adding a few extra fields.

It is beyond the scope of this book to cover each list template in detail as we believe that it is more productive for you to experiment and create lists yourself and learn the functionality they provide.

For team collaboration, the out of the box list templates such as the Calendar and Discussion List Templates are available in most Site Templates and should be sufficient for your requirements.

 The Team Site template will probably meet most of your collaboration requirements as this site template has Shared Documents, Issue Tracking, Discussions and Announcements Lists, and Libraries.

Out of the Box list templates

As you architect a SharePoint deployment, it is important to know which List templates are available on which sites as this can affect deployment timelines. Take a look at the table in *Appendix B, SharePoint Functionality Comparison*, which illustrates the list templates that you are most likely to use on a day-to-day basis.

As your collaboration needs become more sophisticated and you become more familiar with SharePoint's functionality and user requirements, it is worth reviewing the following List Templates as these have specific functionality.

When you are creating a list, its description is displayed on the top right-hand side of the page when the list icon is selected. This is a good way to learn the functionality of the available lists.

In this section, the less intuitive functionality of lists is explained.

External list

This is a new list to SharePoint 2010 and is used to display **Line of Business (LOB)** data from an SQL database. We view this provided functionality as beyond end user activity as you will need to have knowledge of **SharePoint Designer** or **Visual Studio** to configure this kind of List to show data.

Custom list

This is a blank list with no fields or views. Use this list template if none of the built-in features of a list meet your criteria.

 It can be quicker to start a new custom list and add **site columns** and **content types**, rather than delete or change column names with an existing list template.

Import Spreadsheet

When this list is created, the columns and data from a spreadsheet are copied into it. The data import process from the spreadsheet only occurs when the list is created. Choose this list if you are migrating content from a spreadsheet into a list and all future data activity is intended to be performed in the SharePoint list.

Calendar

This is a calendar list of events. It is not a calendar of an individual's **Outlook** calendar, but a calendar that displays date values of a list. Typically, this type of list is used as a team calendar to track meeting dates or as a resource booking tool like a conference room or overhead projector. A typical business scenario of a calendar list could be for resource booking requests that require an approval process. Custom fields can be added to the list such as department and resource. With this business scenario, there can be a view to display categorized departments and a sub category of the requested resource, so there is the ability to identify which departments are making the requests and for what resources.

An advantage a calendar list has over an Outlook calendar is that different views can be created to show list items in different formats. The calendar list can also be synchronized into Outlook. This functionality is covered in more detail in *Chapter 7, Office Integration with SharePoint*. This list has calendar-formatted views.

Managing lists

To manage a list, you will need to customize it to meet your needs. The interface for most of these actions is on the Ribbon in the selected **List** tab.

The Ribbon has a lot of end user functionality and it can be confusing to users who are not familiar with it. It is important to remember that most of the functionality has been categorized into sections. If you look at the preceding screenshot, you will notice at the bottom of the ribbon there are section ribbon labels—**View Format**, **Manage Views**, **Share & Track**, **Connect & Export**, **Customize List**, and **Settings**. Often the functionality that you are looking for is within one of these sections rather than being immediately visible on the Ribbon.

Creating views

When the number of items in a list is large or there are different users groups who want to view list items different ways, custom views should be created to filter and display content to meet a criteria.

This is one of the benefits of SharePoint over simple Windows folders—many departments can have different views into data from the same location.

Technically, there is no limit to the number of views that can be created in a list. However, the more views that exist, the more confusing the navigation is to the user.

To create a view, click on **Create View** on the Ribbon and a series of view styles will be displayed.

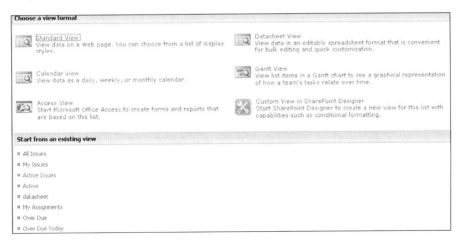

In the preceding screenshot, there is the option to choose the view format, which is the style of view that can be shown in a list.

 Many users describe a view as a defined list of items in a table that can be sorted, filtered, and edited.

Standard view

This is the typical web items style and most views created in a list are a Standard view, which is a linear list of items. To create a **Standard View**, click the **Standard View** text. This will present you with a view design template screen where the view design can be built.

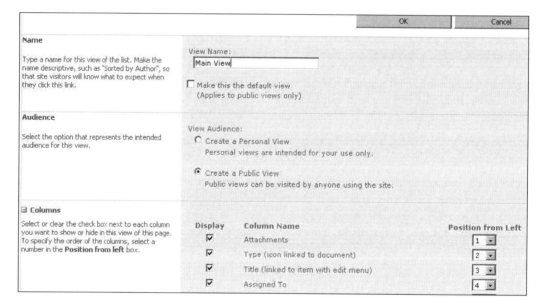

The steps to build the view are:

1. **Name the view**: Ideally, this should be named to represent the information it is displaying. The checkbox **Make this the default view** means this is the view that will be displayed when the list is first displayed when it is opened by the user.

2. **Select the audience of the view**: Personal for yourself or Public for other user(s) to use.

3. There is the ability to choose the order of the columns that are defined in the list by changing the ordering positions of the columns, and selecting the checkbox for each column name.

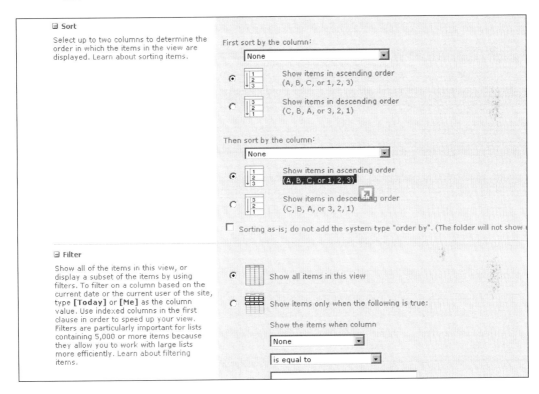

4. Select the column that the view should be sorted on.

5. **Select filter criteria**: This could be a category within a defined column on the form. There can be multiple filters applied to a view.

It is possible to filter a view to display only items that relate to the current user who is logged into SharePoint. This can be done by using the **[Me]** as the filter. For this filter to work, there must be a column type of **Person or Group** defined in the list. By using this filter technique, it may be possible to create fewer views if a view was required for different users.

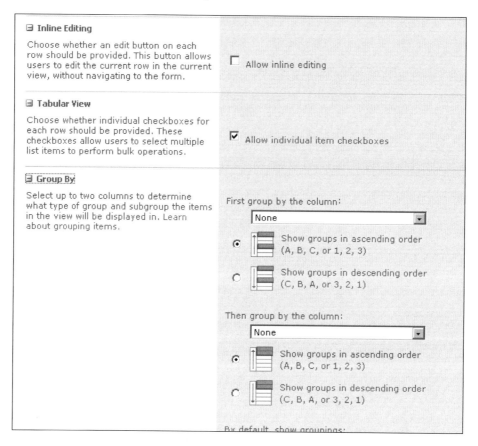

6. **Select Inline Editing**: This allows you to edit list items line by line in the standard view.

7. **Select Tabular View**: This allows you to perform a bulk operation on items in a view, such as deleting or applying an alert to items all at once.

These two features in a view are useful for data manipulation within a list as it requires fewer steps for the user to perform tasks.

8. If required, items in the view can be categorized with the **Group By** feature. This feature works best when there are **Choice field** types in the list (defined categories: New York, London, Hong Kong) so items can be categorized with a defined set of values in a field.

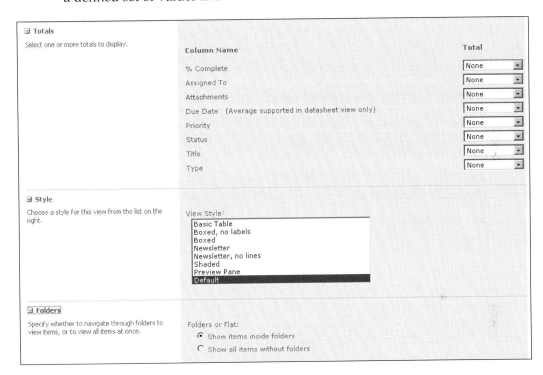

By using categorizing of data, lists that contain many items are easier for the user to read and allow navigation *drill down* to specific items that may be of interest. There can also be sub categories in a list to further drill down though list content.

9. A Total value can be added to some columns in a view. This is a useful feature in performing basic mathematical operations on particular columns: **Count, Average, Maximum, Minimum, Sum, Standard Deviation**, and **Variance**. If you want to track the total sum of active issues assigned to you, the Sum selection would be chosen under the **Assigned To** section.

Totals cannot be applied to all columns in a list, such as multiple value keyword columns.

 This can affect performance if the list is large. For example, with over 2,000 items, the view not only displays the additional information, but also calculates additional data. If performance becomes an issue and Totals are in the view then it may be worth considering the **Export to Spreadsheet** option in the view and perform calculations from within Excel.

10. **Select the style**: The default style is adequate for most views. If you are comparing a lot of information in a view, the **Shaded** style alternates colors of the rows so there is less confusion with comparing items between rows. If a list has a few columns in a view and your business requirement is to glance at the items and then view the entirety of the item, the **Preview Pane** view style is ideal as this style allows you to hover the curser over a list item in a view and all of the item's fields are displayed in the view. We have often seen this view style used when a list that is being used for technical logging activity information and this view style provides a quick navigation technique to read different list items very quickly.

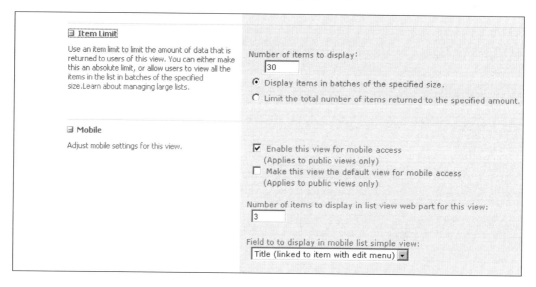

11. **Item Limit**: If the view is going to be placed on a page where there is not much room for a lot of items, limit the view. By sorting the view by the **Created** field, you can show the last items created. If the page is displaying a snapshot of list activity this may be satisfactory.

12. **Mobile**: If the SharePoint server can be accessed externally then your mobile device can access the view.

13. Click **OK** to save the view.

The standard view is now created and has field columns with a similar look and feel to a spreadsheet. By clicking on an item in the view, the entire item will open.

Calendar view

The calendar view shows list items in a web Outlook calendar format—monthly, weekly, or daily. The creation process of a calendar view is similar to the steps for a Standard view. The list will require date values to display correctly.

Certain functionalities have been removed as this is a calendar display rather than a linear list of items.

Access view

This link does not open the Access application and allow you to create SharePoint views; rather, it allows you to create Access reports of list data and Access forms to enter information into a list.

There is often a business requirement to provide reports from list data. The best graphical reporting tools for SharePoint data are Access and Excel as both these products have strong reporting capabilities, and often senior management are familiar with reports produced in these tools.

Information can be entered and submitted to a list from an Access form. An advantage of this input method is that the form's interface can be further customized than a list form, such as placing the fields in tabular table columns. This is useful if the form has a lot of fields.

Datasheet view

The creation process of a **Datasheet view** is similar to the steps for a Standard view. This view format provides you with a view that has a similar functionality to a spreadsheet where the fields in the columns are editable. This is useful for bulk editing of information where there is a lot of copying items to and from different cells.

Gantt view

The creation process of a **Gantt view** is similar to the steps for a Standard view. This view format is ideal for milestone project management activities of a list.

Existing views

It is possible to create views from existing views in the list, simply by clicking on an existing view from the list. By using an existing view, the deployment of views in a list is quicker because an existing view can act as a template for other views in the list.

This will create a new view based on an existing view in the list.

 If you have many similar views in a list, such as views assigned to multiple users, we recommend that you create a view that has all the required information, and create the other separate views from this view.

Modifying views

To modify created views, click on **List** on the Ribbon and select the **Modify View** menu, and then select **Modify View**. This will open the **Edit View** page, which is identical to the **Create View** page.

On the **Edit View** page there is a delete button. This will delete the view that is being edited.

 If the view is the default view in the list, it cannot be deleted.

How to add, view, edit, and manage content to a list

To perform these functions, the Ribbon can be the navigational method or you can click on the content itself. Either way is efficient; it is simply a personal preference.

The Ribbon method

To add a new item, click on the Items in **List Tools** and then click on the **New Item** shown in the following screenshot:

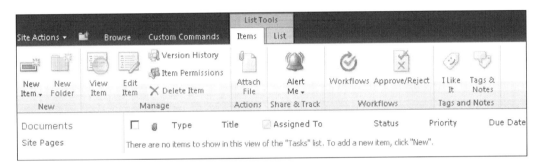

 If there is more than one content type in the list there will be additional items on the New Item on the ribbon.

To view or edit an item, click the checkbox next to the list item and then click the **View Item/Edit Item** from the ribbon.

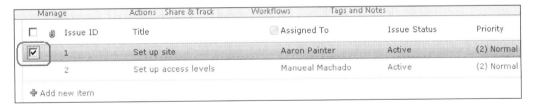

List method

To add an item, click **Add new item** located at the bottom of the list:

Both methods will open a new form.

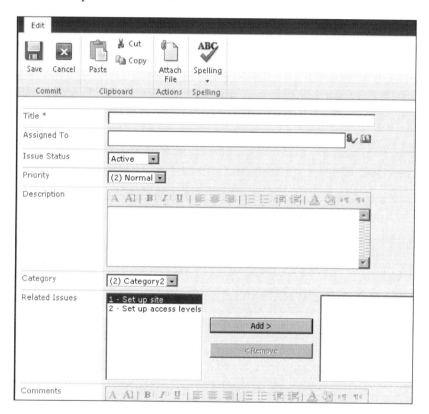

 For readers that are familiar with MOSS, the new form to edit or view an item opens as a pop up and it is not possible to obtain the URL or any parameters in the browser.

Content can be added to the fields by clicking the **Save** button on the form and saving the entered information.

To view or edit an item, click on the downward arrow on the item to display an item menu. Then, click on the **View Item/ Edit Item** to see the entire form.

 The downward arrow is only displayed when you hover your mouse over the item.

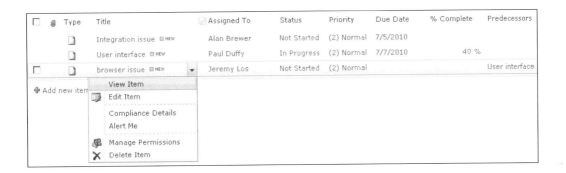

Managing content

In this section, you will learn how to manage content that is in a list. Managing content is about how to manipulate it so that it can be used for your business collaboration activities.

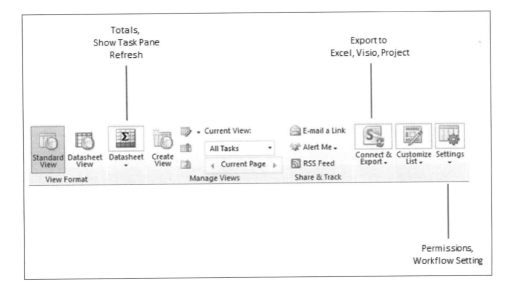

The functionality to manage content can be navigated from the Ribbon.

Alerts

Alerts are notifications on list or library items that automatically notify users when new content is added, changed, or deleted.

Alerts are useful in many business scenarios, such as:

- Content owners who are responsible for a list\library and need to unconsciously monitor user activity in it. For example, if you use a list as a bug tracker tool for a software release and have subscribed to receive alerts when a new item is created in the list and you are not receiving any alerts, the team is probably not testing the software release; so, you can proactively inquire with the team rather than wait until the next status meeting.

- An alert notification can be subscribed to on a single document, so if the requirements document changes you can be the first to know of this change.

 To avoid your e-mail inbox being inundated with alerts, create a folder in Outlook and create a rule to copy all received alerts to this folder.

This functionality is covered in more detail in *Chapter 10, Alerts and Notifications*.

E-mail a link

There is the ability to e-mail a link to the list to someone else by clicking on the **E-mail a Link** option on the Ribbon. This is often used by a user as an informal approval or review process with other team members. Rather than e-mailing an attachment, an e-mail link to the document in the library is better because the e-mail link will always link to the same file even if the file is resaved.

We have observed that sometimes users are hesitant to use this SharePoint feature because they feel users will click on the link and edit the document and resave it in the list, thus overwriting the original document. This concern can be overcome by two approaches:

- Set the permissions on the document to read-only for the rest of the team.
- Check out the document prior to sending the link. Users will only be able to view the document in read-only mode.

Managing Permissions

In *Chapter 3, SharePoint Team Sites* you were introduced to site permissions in the Site Security for your Team section. This permissions inheritance methodology is applied to lists.

By clicking on the **List Permissions** icon on the Ribbon, you have the ability to **Manage Parent Permission** and **Stop Inheriting Permissions**.

As with Site permission inheritance, there is the ability to manually break the inheritance of an item in a list.

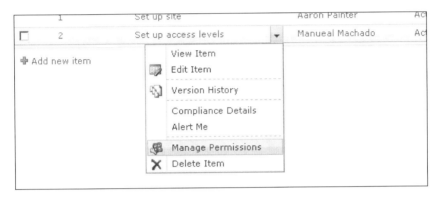

This can be done by clicking on the drop-down menu of an item and selecting **Stop Inheriting Permissions** in the Ribbon.

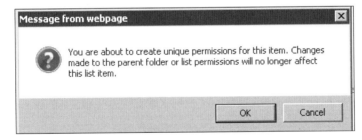

You will be prompted with an information box, alerting you with what you are about to do.

By breaking the inheritance of an item, list, or even a site, it creates a security administration overhead in which you would have to create unique permissions, and this can cause confusion with users and administrators.

You can only manage permissions on the site, list, or item level. You cannot manage the permissions on a view in the list.

RSS feeds

RSS stands for **Really Simple Syndication** and is a web feed technology from blog entries, news headlines, audio, and video in a standardized, normally timely format. The benefit is that you can subscribe to different sources of information and aggregate the feeds into a single location, such as Outlook (See *Chapter 7*) or another location on the SharePoint site (See *Chapter 13*).

To create an RSS feed from a list, click on the **RSS Feed** on the Ribbon.

Datasheet view

The Datasheet View provides the ability to edit items in a list as if the list was an online spreadsheet. You can tab across fields, paste between them, and sort and filter columns. This is useful if you need to edit multiple items at once.

To switch from a Standard view to a Datasheet view, click on the **Datasheet** icon on the Ribbon.

In the Datasheet view, there is additional functionality available, featured in the following sections:

Show Totals

You can show the totals of each column in a list by clicking on the **Show Totals** icon on the Ribbon. The totals can be defined as Average, Count, Maximum, and Minimum.

A	⓪ ▾	Issue ID ▾	Title ▾	Assigned To ▾	Issue Status ▾	Priority ▾	Due Date ▾
		1	Set up site	Aaron Painter	Active	(2) Normal	
		2	Set up access levels	Manueal Machado	Active	(2) Normal	
*							
	Total			2		2 ▾	
							✔ None
							Average
							Count
							Maximum
							Minimum

Adding columns

To add a column to a list, click on **Create Column** on the Ribbon.

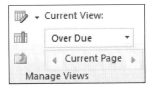

Type in the column name, and select the column type.

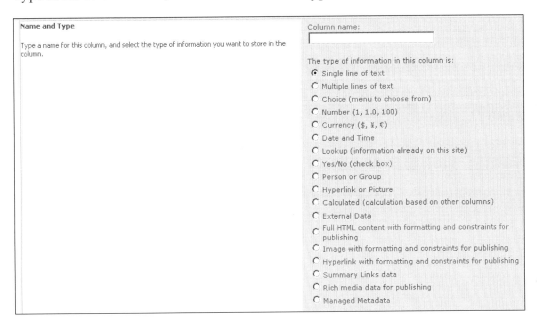

Column type	Description
Single line of text	A single value column, such as a Full Name.
Multiple lines of text	**Text Description**: This field format has rich text capabilities, such as bold, and font sizes similar to Word, so it is ideal for entries that would perhaps be in an e-mail or Word document. If version control is enabled on the list, there is also the ability to append text to a previous submission. This is useful when there is a dialog between multiple people.
Choice (menu to choose from)	**Multiple Choice values**: This is ideal when you require the fields to be predefined to the user. Also, if a view has categorized data in it, this column type should be used.

Column type	Description
Lookup (information already on this site)	**Look up information from another list on this site**: This column type can be viewed as a relationship data structure— one to many. This is also useful when there are multiple lists using the same data.
Person or Group	**User look up from Active Directory**: By using a user's name from Active Directory, additional information about the user can be obtained, such as their department and manager. Also, by using this column type, workflow notifications to the value can occur.
Hyperlink or Picture	URL address.
Calculated (calculation based on other columns)	Ability to select other columns in the list and perform calculations from these, such as the number of days between two dates.
Full HTML content with formatting and constraints for publishing	Ability for a column to display the contents of the HTML from an Editor Web Part. Snippets of HTML can be entered directly into the column.
Image with formatting and constraints for publishing	Columns that store links to images defined in the item properties. Each column displays an image, with proportional sizing. This field type renders an image to the correct size on a web page when it is loaded.
Hyperlink with formatting and constraints for publishing	Columns that store hyperlinks and display the names of hyperlinks defined in the item properties. Link formatting and constraints may apply. This field type renders an image to the correct size on a web page when it is loaded.
Rich media data for publishing	A column that can store and display media files. Ideal for video content as it is streamed in the browser that could be stored in the **Asset Library** of the site.
Managed Metadata	Centrally managed metadata to tag the item. By associating metadata to content, it is easier to search. This is discussed in *Chapter 8*.

The **Column Validation** on a column provides logic validation on a form, which can provide a more descriptive validation message to the user. This can be based on either individual column value validation or an overall item validation based on multiple columns.

Under each new column there you have the ability to make the value a required field, give it a default value, and add it to the default view.

Sync to SharePoint Workspace

SharePoint Workspace, formerly known as **Groove**, is part of the Microsoft Office Professional Plus 2010 edition. Therefore, it's important to note that SharePoint Workspace 2010 only works with SharePoint 2010. For older versions of SharePoint, the Groove software is required.

SharePoint Workspace provides the ability to use content offline on your desktop, and then synchronize into the SharePoint lists when you are back online. This functionality is ideal for those who are travelling and have limited Internet access to online information.

This functionality is covered in more detail in *Chapter 11, Enterprise Content Management*.

List Workflows

SharePoint Workflows consists of a sequence of connected steps that depict a sequence of operations performed by a person. By clicking on the workflow button on the Ribbon, you have the ability to add and review workflow settings.

The key benefits of using workflows are to facilitate business processes and improve collaboration, through managing tasks and steps and speed up decision making by helping to ensure that the appropriate information is made available to the appropriate users at the time that they need it.

Workflows also help ensure that individual workflow tasks are completed by the appropriate people and in the appropriate sequence, so users who perform these tasks can concentrate on performing the work instead of on the work processes.

A business scenario for a typical workflow could be with a document library to route a document to a group of people for approval. When the author starts this workflow, the workflow creates document approval tasks, assigns these tasks to the workflow participants, and then sends e-mail alerts to the participants.

When the workflow is in progress, the workflow owner or the workflow participants can check progress on the Workflow Status page. When the workflow participants complete their workflow tasks, the workflow ends and the workflow owner is automatically notified that the workflow has finished.

[For a workflow to work with a business process, the business process must be understood, such as how it starts and ends, and who the approvers are.]

This functionality is covered in detail in *Chapter 6, Workflows Fundamentals*.

Visio, Access, and Project

Applications such as Visio, Access, and Project have user functionality designed for certain business activity, such as Visio for process mapping, Access for reports, and Project for project management, but often this information is created centrally in a list. SharePoint has the functionality to copy list items to these desktop applications so users can work and prepare this content for another activity. By clicking on the application icons on the Ribbon, list content is made available in the Visio, Access, and Project applications.

It would be difficult for the functionality of Visio, Access, and Project to be replicated in a web-based form in SharePoint, so Microsoft has complimented these desktop applications with SharePoint by allowing information to be stored in a list and be accessed from the applications. Also, users can be very familiar with a certain application such as a project manager and Microsoft Project, and would rather work with Project and publish information to SharePoint than work in a SharePoint list to enter information.

The advantages of this approach are that information can be stored in a SharePoint list, with the benefits, such as centralization, version control, and security.

This functionality is covered in detail in *Chapter 7, Office Integration with SharePoint.*

Export to Excel

By clicking on the **Export to Excel** link on the Ribbon, the items in the view are exported to Excel. There are a number of benefits in exporting content to Excel, which include Excel's reporting capabilities such as graphs and pie charts, and if users do not have access to the list information then it can be e-mailed to them.

You may be thinking to yourself, "I thought the whole idea of SharePoint is to centrally store information in a single location where it is accessible to everyone".

Yes, it is, but there are certain scenarios where exporting data to Excel is the most appropriate approach, such as:

- Users who require to review the data are external to the organization and do not have access to SharePoint.
- It is not unknown that senior management will prefer to review the information in an Excel file, rather than clicking on a link in an e-mail. Old habits die hard!

 This is an export of data from a list, rather than another application to edit data and sync back into the list.

This functionality is covered in detail in *Chapter 7.*

View navigation

To navigate to different views in a list, click on the **View** drop-down menu on the Ribbon.

Front loading

For lists to be truly utilized you must think about your current tasks and how you want them structured in SharePoint. This is called **front loading** of information. Questions that you should think of are:

- What tasks require better collaboration and with whom?
- Which is the most appropriate out of the box list template to use?
- What other SharePoint functionalities are required? alerts, workflow, and permissions?
- What information is going to be migrated from Excel into a list, and what column types should be used and processes established such as alerts, workflows, and retention.

Advanced list features

In this section, you will be introduced to advanced features of lists.

Form Web Parts

When a list item is opened, the field columns are displayed in a form style page. There is the ability to add web parts and apply a mobile device page to the form. This functionality provides a richness to the form as list views can be added to a form page, which is useful if list information needs to be compared.

This functionality is covered in detail in *Chapter 13*.

List settings

By clicking on the **List Settings** icon on the Ribbon, you have the ability to manage the setting of a list.

General Settings	Permissions and Management	Communications
Title, description and navigation	Delete this list	RSS settings
Versioning settings	Save list as template	
Advanced settings	Permissions for this list	
Validation settings	Workflow Settings	
Rating settings	Generate file plan report	
Audience targeting settings	Information management policy settings	
Metadata navigation settings		
Per-location view settings		
Form settings		

Under **General Settings**, the following list of functionalities can be applied or changed:

Title, description, and navigation

The name, the description of the list, and the option to display the list on the **Quick Launch** is available.

Versioning settings

The versioning setting provides two main functions: the ability for content to be approved before it is visible to users, and allowing version control of items. This provides you with the ability to determine who can see **draft** content based on the **Draft Item Security** setting.

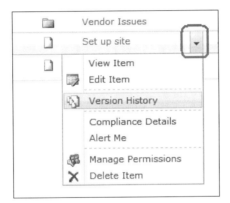

 Versioning is really rarely used in lists and is more often used in document libraries, probably because the content is being edited more often. However, it's an important functionality to mention in this context.

To view the version history of an item, click on the **downward** menu arrow.

The **Version History** setting in a list can increase the storage capacity of the SharePoint server if multiple versions of items are saved. Often, users request that they need version control for their content, but it is often viewed as a rarely used feature.

A compromise between the requested feature and actual user behavior is to select a version limit of a few items.

Advanced Settings

The **Advanced Settings** allows further customization to a list such as **Content Types** and **Permissions**.

Content Types

Content types were introduced in SharePoint 2007 and are content templates that can be reused in another list. Content types range from an expense document to a custom list, with defined fields relating to client information. When a list is defined to have multiple content types such as expense forms, contract, and URLs, there are user ability benefits as multiple contents can be stored in the same list. There is also a set of defined content types that are available. By using predefined content types, deployments of lists are quicker because fields are already defined, workflows already associated, although with information management policies, and document templates.

For example, suppose you defined a content type named Contract. This content type might include the following:

- Columns named Customer, Amount, and Final Effective Date
- An approval workflow
- A retention policy linked to the Final Effective Date field
- A Word template for a contract document

Content types are defined and managed at the site level, but they are typically defined at the root site in a site collection. In order to use a content type you must associate it with a list or a document library. You can associate a content type with multiple lists or libraries, and each list or library can host multiple content types.

This is useful in scenarios where different types of document share similar metadata—for example, you might store expenses and contracts in the same document library because both share similar fields, but might differ in terms of approval processes or retention requirements. The ability to associate behaviors with a content type, such as workflows and event receivers, is comparable to the concept of triggers on a database table.

Because the content type can be applied to multiple locations, you can use content types to define a contract, purchase order, or invoice that has the same metadata and the same behavior across the entire organization.

When you associate a content type with a list or library, the content type is attached to the list, together with the site columns, workflows, and policies for that content type. These policies and workflows will apply to any item of that content type in the list.

Content Types add huge value to a successful SharePoint implementation.

This functionality is discussed further in *Chapter 5*, *Library Management*.

E-mail Notification

This provides the ability to e-mail content into a list. This functionality is useful to allow users to forward content from their mailbox into a list, particularly if the content is generated by e-mails.

Also, external parties such as vendors and customers who do not have access to the SharePoint server or even your organization's network environment can submit content to a list via e-mail.

We have seen this functionality used for customer inquiries, where a customer submits an e-mail (`sales@CompanyName.com`) and the e-mail recipient is a list, which automatically triggers a workflow to a sales associate who re-routes the workflow to the relevant person, based on the e-mail's request.

This type of activity could be done with a sales e-mail account and a sales associate could monitor any incoming e-mail. However the value that SharePoint provides in this business process is that there is viability to see the request is in the workflow and who is assigned to the task, so e-mails do not get lost, particularly from customers.

Attachments

Attachments provide the ability to upload multiple attachments to an item.

Folders

Folders give users the ability to create folders in a list. This is useful to group items in a list, similar to files in folders on a network drive.

With MOSS 2007, the use of folders was not recommended, but with the 2010 release, they now are.

With SharePoint 2010, folders may also be configured to allow inheritance of metadata values to documents or items in that folder. This could be useful if there is a requirement to **tag** content of many files that have slightly different metadata.

It is important to understand when it is appropriate to use folders or not.

Pros

The Pros are as follows:

- Ability to apply multiple item security to items by applying security at the folder level
- Ability to apply metadata to multiple items at once
- Easier to migrate files from the network drive, to a library folder structure to a library, with a simple cut and paste approach

Cons

The Cons are as follows:

- Can have duplication of files in multiple folders.
- Can be difficult to search for contents if you do not know which folder it is in. The folder structure of storing content does not really encourage users to use SharePoint's search capabilities, which is a quicker way to find content.
- If there are sub folders within the file structure, users can become frustrated with the **drill-down** approach to finding content.

We believe the folders approach works better for the contributor of content as they can upload content more easily, but it does not benefit the receivers of the content who work with the information because content is more likely to not be stored in the correct location or have metadata applied to it, which makes it less searchable.

Folders are rarely used in lists and are most common in libraries.

Search

Search allows items to be searchable on the site. SharePoint's search feature is a powerful tool to search across an entire site.

There is the ability to set a library or list to be non-searchable, but we'd encourage you to make everything searchable in order to promote collaboration. Just because content is not searchable does not mean that it is hidden from other users as might be your motivation for doing so.

Offline client availability

This feature is related to SharePoint Workspaces. See *Chapter 11*.

Datasheet

This allows for a Datasheet view to be displayed from a Standard View. This makes it easier for users to navigate between views with fewer steps. If the information is sensitive, you may not want the datasheet option available as users will have the ability to cut and paste entire rows and columns at once.

Dialogs

Dialogs determine if the New/Edit/View Item forms will be displayed in a dialog window or the entire page. This is a personal preference in user interface aesthetics. We prefer the dialog window as when this window closes, the user is returned to the page where they opened the form.

Validation settings

When a form is saved, you will have the ability for the form to perform content verification on the form prior to it being saved. This is useful if dates or numbers need to be compared.

Rating settings

You will have the ability to rate an item in a list. By selecting this option, a rating column is displayed in the list where users can rate an item. This is a Web 2.0 feature and is discussed further in *Chapter 12, Blogs, Wikis, and Other Web 2.0 Features*.

Audience targeting settings

By selecting the checkbox, a **Target Audiences** field is added to the form in the list, and the user submitting the form can select an AD or SharePoint group, distribution list, or an individual that can view the item. This personalization feature is useful because information is targeted to users or a configured audience. It is discussed further in *Chapter 13, Pages and Web Parts*.

Metadata navigation settings

There is the ability to configure navigation of a list based on associated metadata using **Navigational Hierarchies** and **Key Filters**. This Web 2.0 navigational feature displays navigation links to users based on certain content that is stored in a list. This functionality is discussed in *Chapter 8, Managing Metadata*.

Per-location view settings

This is the ability for a view to be used to display content based on a folder level within the view or a certain Content Type. It is not uncommon for a user to navigate to a list of items and have a desire that they are displayed in a certain way from within a folder. This feature allows content to be displayed differently depending on the folder level within a view.

This feature is useful as you require users to drill-down into the folders and at a certain sub folder level only want to show certain views.

Permissions and management

Under the permissions and management there is the following list functionality that can be applied or changed:

Delete this list

Delete the list and its content.

Save list as template

Save the list and its content as a template so the defined columns can be used elsewhere in the site collection. A template can be copied to another SharePoint server.

Permissions for this list

This functionality was discussed in *Chapter 3* and earlier in this chapter.

Workflow Settings

This functionality was discussed in *Chapter 6* and earlier in this chapter.

Generate file plan report

This creates a summary of the list's design, such as content types, permissions, number of items, routing rules, and retention policies. This is useful if you need to troubleshoot between two different lists on a site, and need to compare and contrast the design. For example, if you wish to identify which content types or permission setting were in a list, this report would provide this information.

Information management policy settings

This allows rules and policies to be applied to content in a list. This is discussed in *Chapter 11*.

Under **Communications**, the RSS Setting can be applied or changed. The RSS setting provides the ability to choose which fields are displayed in an RSS feed from the list.

Summary

This chapter's focus has been on List Management and how to apply business activity to this functionality. In *Chapter 1, Where Should End Users Start with SharePoint?*, we stated SharePoint was a web-based platform where applications and business functionalities are deployed. One of the productivity and total costs of ownership benefits of SharePoint, is to migrate business functionality to the SharePoint platform. Not just from Excel, but general e-mail dialogue form Support, and Sales. This migration of business functionality should also include business processes from bit boutique (single purpose) applications to the SharePoint platform.

We recommend that you now explore the concept of webinizing information from both Word and Excel documents into lists, and identify the lists column structure, the required views to display information, and if necessary, any alert or workflow trigger events.

The next chapter explains libraries, which is where documents are stored. Document management is the other critical and vital functionality of SharePoint.

5
Library Management

In the previous chapter you were introduced to **List Management**, where non-document content is stored. This chapter explains **Library Management,** how files can be stored and managed, and how to collaborate on documents with team members. There are a lot of similarities between SharePoint lists and libraries, and where there is repetition in functionality or instructions, the List Management chapter will be referenced.

Topics covered include:

- The basics
- Creating libraries
- Managing libraries
- How to add content to libraries
- Advanced library features
- Record management
- Content types

The basics

A SharePoint library is a repository for uploaded or created files. Similar to **Lists, Libraries** are configured to filter, sort, or group files together for visualization and editing.

Libraries are based on **Library Templates**, such as **document, form**, and **picture**. You can create multiple libraries based on a single library template.

The following library features are outside the functionality scope of this book and are provided only to enhance your knowledge and awareness of SharePoint's functionalities. These include **Edit Library, Customize Form,** and **Form settings**.

Creating Libraries

To create a Library click on **Site Actions**, then **More Options...** in the **Ribbon**.

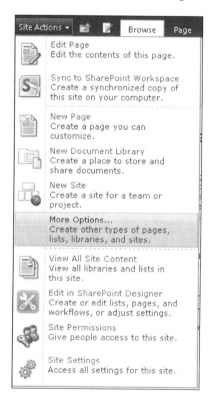

You will be presented with a series of list box templates, each of which have slightly different functionality, which is explained later in this chapter. There is the ability to filter the displayed **library templates** with the navigational menu on the left-hand side.

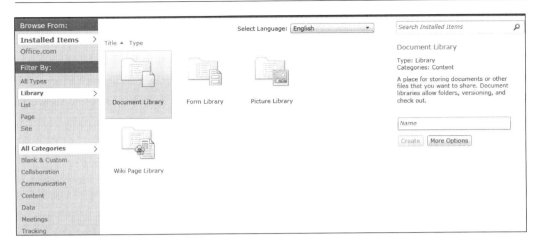

Select a library by selecting an icon.

1. Enter the name.
2. Click the **create** button.
3. The library will now be created in this site.

 From the Site Actions menu there is the ability to create a Document Library with fewer clicks by selecting the **New Document Library** option, which will direct you to the Document Library template.

Library templates

SharePoint has provided many out of the box library templates that are predefined, and will generally meet your needs with perhaps some minor enhancements by adding a few extra fields.

The SharePoint Foundation 2010 Edition has the following out of the box library templates.

Document library

These libraries store files that would normally be saved on your desktop or network drive, such as Microsoft Office Word, Excel, and PowerPoint files. There is strong integration with SharePoint and Office files, though non-Office files can be stored and collaborated on as well, such as Photoshop or CAD files.

File size upload limits can be adjusted to be unlimited, but we recommend not using files greater than 50 MB because the download time of files are too long.

Form library

This type of library stores InfoPath forms.

With the SharePoint Foundation Edition, InfoPath files can only be viewed and edited if you have the InfoPath client installed on your computer. With the SharePoint Enterprise Edition, the InfoPath form can be viewed and edited within your browser, so no software is required.

Most organizations have Office and Outlook deployed to users' desktops, but generally do not have the InfoPath client as a standard desktop deployment. If this is the case in your organization, there is little value with using the Form libraries to store data in InfoPath files.

The InfoPath technology is outside the scope of this book.

For further information on InfoPath visit this website:
`http://office.microsoft.com/en-us/infopath/`

Picture library

This type of library is ideal for storing **JPG** and **GIF** type files. Graphical files could be stored in a regular document library, but the advantage of using a Picture library is that there is additional field data that can be associated with the file, such as **Date Picture Taken, Description**, and **Keywords**.

Wiki page library

This library type allows users to freely create and edit web page content within their browser. The wiki pages support hyperlinks to both internal wiki and external pages.

Wikis are an excellent and very useful tool for webinizing content, such as policies that would normally reside in a large Word document. By default, they show version history with the last time the information was updated rather than the entire document, and whether the page has outgoing links from other wiki pages that can be quickly referenced.

The SharePoint Server Enterprise Edition has the following out of the box library templates.

Report library

This library will create, manage, and share information contained in business data Web Parts, **Key Performance Indicator (KPI)** Web Parts, and Excel Web Access Web Parts used for business intelligence purposes.

 This library can even be used to create new versions of reports for special events or milestones, and later revert to a previous report. This is useful for dash-boarding and project management activities.

Data connection library

This library type stores data connection files that other Office applications are allowed to access, such as Excel.

A real world example of this functionality might be an Excel file displaying live data from the **Customer Relationship Management (CRM)** database. A data connection to the CRM database such as server name, database name, and authentication credentials are entered and published into this library.

The sales report (Excel file) has the connection reference in it, which is associated with the CRM database.

This library type should be viewed as a central configuration repository with the permissions set so that general users have read-only access to connection information, and power users and IT have editor permissions to enter and publish connections to data sources.

The benefit of this data connection integration approach is that if a database moves or is updated, the connection information is only changed in a single entry, and the information does not need to be redeployed to business users' Excel files.

 Data connection libraries are of value when you are accessing external data sources to SharePoint.

From a security standpoint, this is very good because this library can be restricted, so only authorized users can add and change data connections.

From a maintenance standpoint, there is a single reference to an external data source, rather than multiple.

Also, connections can be reused with multiple sources and can be secured in a single data connection entry.

Data connection libraries are part of the SharePoint Server functionality.

Slide library

The purpose of this library is to store PowerPoint file information so it is accessible to different PowerPoint files.

It is common within organizations that PowerPoint files use the same template format and slides, yet information is stored separately in each file. A slide library allows sharing of this information among the various PowerPoint slides.

Asset library

This library allows storing of media type files such as `.mpeg` and `.wav` files. The file types can be either audio or video and the content is streamed to you, rather than a download.

It is important to know which library templates are available on which sites as this can affect deployment timelines and chosen site templates. The following table illustrates this:

Library Temple	Site Temple
Asset Library	Team Site, Document Workspace, Group Work Site, Visio Process Repository, All Meeting Workspace, Document/Record Center, Business Intelligence Center, Personalization Site, Enterprise Search Center, FAST Search Center, Enterprise Wiki, Publishing Portal, and Publishing Site with Workflow
Data Connection Library	Team Site, Blank Site, Document Workspace, Blog, Group Work Site, Visio Process Repository, Business Intelligence Center, Personalization Site, Enterprise Search Center, Basic Search Center, and Publishing Site
Document Library	Central Administration, Blank Site, Document Workspace, Blog, Group Work Site, Visio Process Repository, All Meeting Workspace, Document/Record Center, Business Intelligence Center, My Site Host, Personalization Site, Enterprise Search Center, Basic Search Center, FAST Search Center, Enterprise Wiki, Publishing Portal, Publishing Site, and Publishing Site with Workflow
Form Library	Central Administration, Team Site, Blank Site, Document Workspace, Blog, Group Work Site, Visio Process Repository, All Meeting Workspace, Document/Record Center, My Site Host, Personalization Site, Enterprise Search Center, Basic Search Center, FAST Search Center, Enterprise Wiki, and Publishing Site

Library Temple	Site Temple
Picture Library	Central Administration, Team Site, Blank Site, Document Workspace, Blog, Group Work Site, Visio Process Repository, All Meeting Workspace, Document/Record Center, My Site Host, Personalization Site, Enterprise Search Center, Publishing Portal, Publishing Site, and Publishing Site with Workflow
Slide Library	Team Site, Blank Site, Document Workspace, Blog, Group Work Site, Visio Process Repository, All Meeting Workspace, Document/Record Center, Business Intelligence Center, My Site Host, Personalization Site, Enterprise Search Center, and Publishing Site
Wiki Page Library	Team Site, Blank Site, Document Workspace, Blog, Group Work Site, Visio Process Repository, All Meeting Workspace, Document/Record Center, My Site Host, Personalization Site, Enterprise Search Center, Basic Search Center, FAST Search Center, and Publishing Site

Managing libraries

To manage a library is very similar to lists, and most of the actions required to customize it to meet your needs are on the libraries **Ribbon** in the selected **Library** tab.

Identical list and library functionality such as creating, managing, and modifying views will not be discussed in this chapter, and we recommend instead that you refer to *Chapter 4*, *List Management*.

Adding, viewing, editing, and managing Library content

The major difference between adding content to a library and to a list is that the content can be created outside the SharePoint environment and then uploaded into the library for SharePoint functionality to be applied, such as workflows, version control, and notifications.

We do not think there is one correct approach for creating a document inside or outside SharePoint. Typically, the approach depends on the individual and the content of the document. However, the team collaboration benefits of SharePoint can only be achieved by storing the document in a library.

Document libraries

There are a number of ways to upload documents to a library; each way has its benefits.

To upload a document or create a document within a library you can navigate using the Ribbon, or you can click on the **Add document** link. Either way is efficient; it is simply a personal preference.

Adding documents

There are a number of ways that documents can be created in a library, including from the **Ribbon** and the **Explorer view**. The type of document that is available to create is dependent on the template used on the list. To create a new Word document with the ribbon, the following steps should be applied:

1. Click the **Document** tab in **Library Tools** and then click on **New Document**.
2. This will open up a Windows Internet Explorer warning window.
3. Click **OK**.
4. The associated application such as Word opens and you can work on the newly created document.
5. To save the document into the library, click **Save** and you will be able to name the document. The file will automatically be saved into the library.
6. To upload a document, click **Add Document** located at the bottom of the list.

The instructions stated above are for a Word document library. This library type could be an Excel or PowerPoint file. If the library allows multiple content types, it could allow multiple files to be created from the ribbon interface.

7. This will display an **Upload dialog** Window.

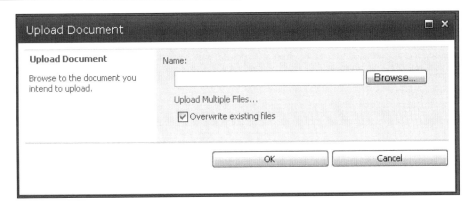

8. Click on the **Browse…** button and select the file that you want to upload.
    The file will be uploaded to the library.

9. In the preceding screenshot is the text **Upload Multiple Files**. This displays
    the following figure:

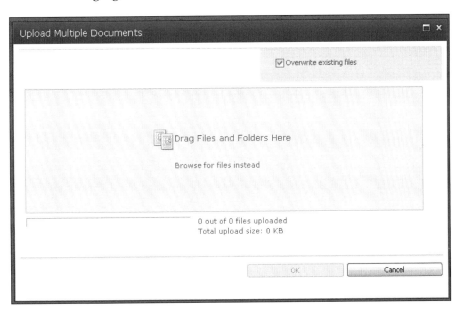

You now have the ability to drag files from your desktop onto this window and click
OK to upload the files to the Library.

For multiple uploads, there may be PC configurations that prevent the user from uploading multiple files. These could be settings in the browser that disable Active X controls or JavaScript running. These setting are in the **Tools | Internet Options** of your browser.

You can also select individual files to be uploaded at once by clicking on **Browse for files** instead.

Documents can also be uploaded by clicking the **Upload Document** icon on the Ribbon or by clicking on the **Open with Explorer** icon on the Ribbon.

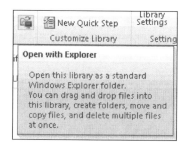

Editing documents

There are four ways to edit an uploaded document in a library; each leaves you with a different user experience.

Option 1 – Check mark

Click on the **check mark** of the document in the view and click on the **Edit Document** icon on the Ribbon.

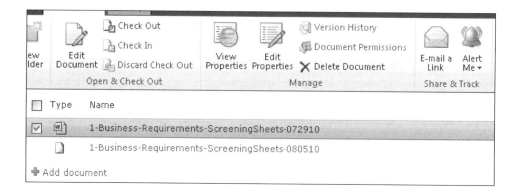

This will open the document in edit mode.

Option 2 – Downward arrow menu

Click on the **downward arrow** menu of the document in the view and select **Edit In Microsoft Word**.

With this method you have the ability to Edit and view the document in the browser. This functionality is discussed further in *Chapter 7, Office Integration with SharePoint*.

Option 3 – Browser

You can click on the **document** and the following figure is displayed. Then, choose either to **Open in Word** or **Edit in browser**.

 Office Web Apps needs to be installed within the company's SharePoint environment.

Option 4 – Explorer view

Click on the **Open with Explorer** icon on the Ribbon.

This will open your browser in an Explorer view and you can click on the **document** to open it.

In some corporate environments the Explorer view may not be supported. This could be because of security, server setup, or PC configuration.

Managing content

Managing content in a library is very similar to managing content in a list. Libraries includes alerts, the ability to e-mail a link of the document library to someone else, Permissions Datasheets, RRS feeds, changing views, and workflows. Main functionalities in a library that are not in a list include:

Send To

The **Send To** functionality allow you to copy or link a document in a library to another destination. To use this feature, click on the **downward arrow** of an item in the library.

Other Location

Select the **Other Location** to copy the file to another SharePoint library.

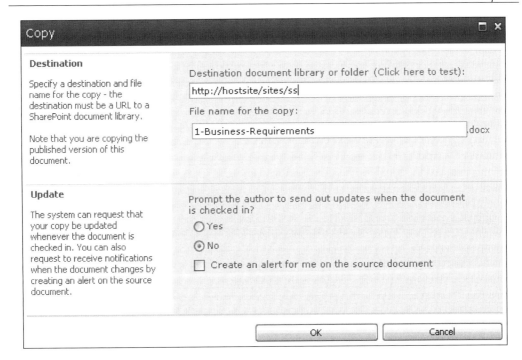

Type in the URL of the library and click **OK**.

There is an option to remind the author to send a copy of this file to the other locations when it is checked in.

 The **Send To | Other Location** feature is useful when there is a single document such as a policy document that has been copied to multiple sites, so when a change to this document occurs, the change is replicated in the other locations.

For this activity to occur, you will need access to the destination location.

 A useful feature of the **Send To | Other Location** functionality can be employed when you need to copy a file to another site collection, such as a public-facing SharePoint site. The scenario would be that a document is approved in the intranet site collection and then copied to another site collection that is public-facing using the **Send To | Other Location**.

E-mail a link

If you want to e-mail a link to the document, select **E-Mail a Link** and your e-mail client will open a new memo with the document URL link pasted into the memo's body. This can be sent to any user that has access to this library.

 In your browser, there is an e-mail client setting that may be required to be set; it identifies your e-mail client.

The advantages of this method of sending files to a team member rather than as an attachment is that the link will always open the latest version of the file in the document library. Alternatively, with attaching a document to an e-mail approach, if there are any changes to the document after the memo is sent, another e-mail needs to be sent out.

 A way to prevent users from editing the document in the library is to **Check Out** the document that the e-mail link points to, so only reader access is available to other users. This is useful if you do not have access rights to change the permissions of a document.

This functionality is also available via the Ribbon by selecting the **checkbox** of the document in the view and selecting **E-mail a Link** on the Ribbon.

Download a Copy

To download a file to another location, click on **Download a Copy**. This will create a separate copy of the file from the document library.

Document Workspaces

In a document library there is the ability to create a site from a document within a library. This is useful with collaboration activity performing tasks that only relate to this particular document. To create a document workspace:

1. Click on the **dropdown** menu on the document.
2. Point to **Send To**, and then click **Create Document Workspace**.
3. Click **OK**.

If the **Create Document Workspace** option is not available, you do not have permission to create a workspace on that site. Ask the site owner to give this permission to you or to create the workspace site for you.

Picture libraries

For the most part, Picture libraries are very similar to document libraries' functionality with the ability to upload pictures, create, and modify view and alert subscriptions. However, there are a few subtle differences:

- You cannot create a picture in the library; you can only upload and edit.
- There is no Ribbon interface. In fact, there are four menu options:
  - **New**
  - **Upload**
  - **Actions**
  - **Settings**

- A picture library has three different view formats:

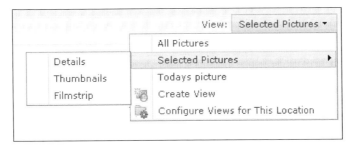

  - **Details**: Displays the file like a standard view with the file icon and columns
  - **Thumbnails**: A thumbnail version of the picture is displayed in the library
  - **Filmstrip**: Displays a row of all the images in the library, and when you click on an image the full-sized image is displayed

There are checkboxes next to each image; if you select these and leave the library (or even the site) and return to this library and select the **Selected Pictures** view, the previously selected images are displayed.

 This is a nice feature for personalizing your activity on this library.

Managing pictures

From the **Actions** menu on the library, pictures can be managed.

These activities are explained in the following sections.

Editing a picture

This functionality allows you to edit a picture using the **Microsoft Picture Manager** software installed on your computer. The types of editing that can be done include cropping, rotating, and resizing the image.

To edit a picture, checkmark the **checkbox** to the corresponding picture and click the **Edit Link** on the **Actions** menu on the toolbar, and Microsoft Picture Manager will open with the selected images.

The picture can be saved back into the library by selecting **File** and **Save** in the application.

Delete

The delete function will delete the image. The image is moved to the recycle bin that can be found on the **Quick Launch** navigation, where it can be recovered if necessary.

Download

The Picture Libraries download function allows you to download the image **Full Size, Preview**, or **Thumbnail** size.

If you click on the **Set Advanced** download options, there is the ability to save the file in different file formats and ratio sizes.

Send To

The **Send To** functionality of a Picture Library is unique when compared to other libraries as it allows you to copy the selected image(s) to an e-mail, Word, Excel, or PowerPoint document.

View Slide Show

This functionality launches Windows Explorer and allows you to click through images like a slideshow with the ability to pause, rewind, and fast forward.

The other actions of the picture library such as folders, Windows Explorer, Connect to Outlook, Alert Me, and View RSS Feedback are the same as a Document Library.

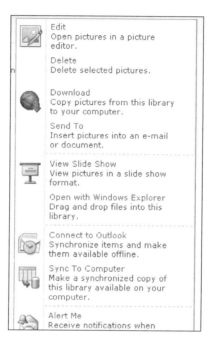

Wiki libraries

Wiki libraries are different to other libraries because files cannot be stored in them, files cannot be uploaded into them, and views are more for editing of content rather than navigational. When a wiki library is created, it is populated with two wiki pages. These are for presentational purposes.

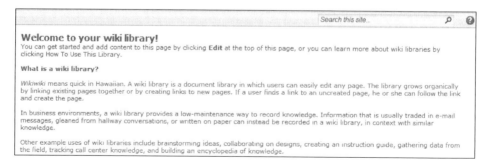

For a short overview of how to use a wiki in SharePoint, click on the **How To Use This Library** link on the Quick launch. This link to a wiki page in the library explains how to create and edit pages and create wiki links.

One of the advantages of a wiki is that it keeps a version history of previously entered content, and because the information is centrally stored, multiple user collaboration is easy. This is useful for knowledge base activity because in order to understand a final version of a page, there is often a need to see previous releases of content and who created these versions.

Adding pages

There are two ways to add a wiki page.

Option 1

1. Edit an existing page by clicking on the **Edit** icon on the Page Ribbon.

2. On the wiki page, type the name of the new wiki page inside double brackets, for example `[[Agenda Items]]`.

3. Click on the **Save & Close** icon on the Ribbon.

The wiki page Agenda Items will create the next item when the link on this page is clicked. It is possible to see that the page has not been created yet because the Agenda Items text has dashed underlines.

Option 2

1. On the Page Ribbon in the **Page Group**, click on **View all Pages**.

2. You will be presented with a library of existing wiki pages.

3. Click on **Add new page**.

4. Type the name of the new wiki page and click the **Create** button.

5. The newly created page can be edited and saved.

The second way of creating pages does not link the page to other pages. This has to be done by typing in the page name inside double square brackets. We recommend the first way when creating wiki pages.

It is possible to confirm if a page is linked to other pages by clicking the **Incoming Links** icon on the Page Ribbon. This will display any pages that link to the open page.

Editing pages

Wiki pages can be edited either while the page is being displayed, or by clicking on the **View All Pages** icon on the Page Ribbon that will then display all the pages in the wiki library.

Managing pages

Because the purpose of a wiki is to allow multiple people to contribute to the content of the library, there may be situations where a previous version of a wiki page is required to be restored to the published page.

This can be done when you:

1. Open a wiki page that you wish to view previous page versions.
2. Click on the **Page History** icon on the Page Ribbon.
3. View a list of previous versions of this page displayed by the Quick launch.
4. Select the page that you wish to restore.
5. Click on **Restore this version** on the top of the page.

6. This page will now be restored.

Throughout the previously described navigation steps you have the ability to delete and view the version history of pages.

A wiki library has other library functions associated with it, such as data sheet, alerts, workflow, and permissions. These are discussed in *Chapter 3, SharePoint Team Sites, Chapter 6, Workflows Fundamentals*, and *Chapter 10, Alerts and Notifications*.

Report libraries

There are two content types in this library.

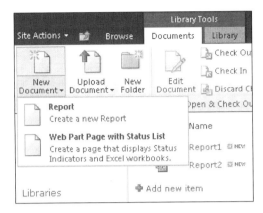

Both of these content types are available from the **New Document** icon on the Ribbon, but in the library on the **Add new item** link the Report is the only option.

Adding a content type

Report

This content type stores Excel files that can be published as a web page. This function is discussed in *Chapter 7, Office Integration with SharePoint* and *Chapter 13, Pages and Web Parts*.

Web Part Page with Status List

This content type is discussed further in *Chapter 15, Applying Functionality for Business Initiatives*.

Editing content types

Both these content types can be edited using the Ribbon interface.

Managing content types

The Report Library has three defined views:

- **Current Reports** — All reports
- **Dashboards** — All Web Part Pages
- **All Reports and Dashboards** — All content in the library

Alerts, workflow, and creating and modifying view can be managed in this library as if this was any other library or list.

Data Connection Libraries

A Data Connection Library contains two kinds of data connections: an **Office Data Connection (ODC)** file or a **Universal Data Connection (UDC)** file. Excel 2010 uses data connections that comply with the ODC file schema and typically have the *.xml file name extension. Data sources described by these data connections are stored on the server and can be used with Excel 2010.

Adding a connection to an Excel file

The instructions below list the steps for creating a data connection file to an established data source, which in this case is an Excel file:

1. Open Excel 2010, click on the **Data** tab, click **Connections**, and then click **Add**.

2. In the **Data Connection Wizard**, click **Create a new connection to | Receive data | Next**.

3. Choose the **SharePoint library** as the data source that you are connecting to and then click **Next**.

4. Complete the remaining steps in the **Data Connection Wizard** to configure your data connection and then click **Finish** to return to the **Data Connections** dialog box.

5. In the **Data Connections** dialog box, click **Convert to Connection File**.

6. In the **Convert Data Connection** dialog box, enter the URL of the data connection library that you previously copied (delete `Forms/AllItems.aspx` and anything following it from the URL), enter a name for the data connection file at the end of the URL, and then click **OK**. It will take a few moments to convert and save the data connection file to the library.

7. Confirm that the data connection was converted successfully by examining the **Details** section of the **Data Connections** dialog box while the name of the converted data connection is selected.

8. Browse to the SharePoint data connection library, click the drop-down next to the name of the data connection, click **Approve/Reject**, click **Approved**, and then click **OK to enable the data connection**.

Using a data connection in an Excel file

1. Open Excel 2010 and then click **Data menu** on the **Ribbon | Data Connections | Add**.

2. Click on one of the SharePoint Data Connection Libraries listed.

3. Select the SharePoint data source.

4. Select the Excel Use.

5. Click **OK**.

6. Save the Excel file.

Every time this Excel file opens a connection is established to the data source and data from the source is displayed in the Excel file.

 If multiple users are creating different reports from the same data connection, the data connection can be simplified further by creating an Excel document library and using the Excel file that is connecting to the source file as the library template.

Data connections can be edited and managed like any other SharePoint list item.

Slide Libraries

To use this functionality you must have PowerPoint 2007 or a later edition installed on your computer.

Adding slides

To add slides from a PowerPoint presentation to the slide library, the following steps should be applied:

1. From the library select the **Publish Slide** menu option from the **Upload** toolbar menu.

2. The PowerPoint application will open. Select a saved **PowerPoint** file that is saved on your desktop or network drive.

3. In a dialog box, each slide of the PowerPoint deck is displayed.

4. Next to each slide is a checkbox. Check the slides that you want to copy into the library and click **Publish**. Each selected slide will be saved into the library. You do need to refresh the browser for the uploaded slides to be displayed.

 The above steps can be performed from PowerPoint, with the Publish slides functionality in the **Save & Send** category.

To copy slides in a library to a presentation:

1. Select the slides that you wish to use in a presentation by checking the slides checkbox and click the **Copy Slides to Presentation** button on the menu. This will display the following prompt box:

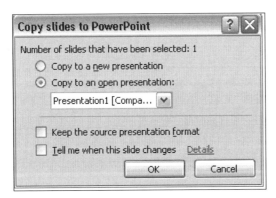

2. You can either copy the slides to a new presentation or an existing one.

3. If you want the slides to maintain their current theme and formatting, select **Keep the source presentation format**. If you are adding slides to an existing presentation, this option may not be required because you may only want to copy the content of the slide.

4. If you wish to be notified if there is a change to the slides in the library that now reside in your PowerPoint deck, select **Tell me when this slide changes**. Each time you open a PowerPoint file that has had Slides copied to it you are prompted to check for updates.

Editing slides

Slides can be edited just like any uploaded file in a library or list. For editing purposes, you should view each slide as a unique single slide presentation.

Managing slides and presentations

Slide Libraries have the same functionality as other libraries, such as check in, version control, and views.

Using folders in a Slide Library can be a good method to organize slides of presentations into categories. However, if you require slides from different folders to be copied into a presentation, you will need to perform the **Copy Slide to Presentation** process multiple times because this copy method only works on a per view basis. A better method of organizing data is to create a keyword column in the library so you can filter on keywords to perform the copy action in a single click.

Asset libraries

The Asset Library is similar to the Picture Library with the ability to store video and audio files and do not have the non-2007 Ribbon interface.

Both libraries have the same column names in the views — **Title, Preview, Keywords, Comments, Date Picture Taken, Picture Size fields**, and **Show Thumb Nails in Views**.

The differences between the Asset and Picture library are as follows:

- The Picture Library uses the Picture Content Type, which has the Preview Image URL ability, and the Asset Library uses the Image Content Type that has the Author and Copyright field additions.
- To preview media in the asset Libraries you will need Microsoft Silverlight and Windows Media Player installed on your PC. Both of these are free to download from the Microsoft site.

All media files, such as MPEG, should be stored in the Asset Library.

Adding files

Files can be uploaded by clicking on the **Upload Picture** menu from the **Upload** menu on the toolbar.

Editing files

Uploaded files can be edited the same way as the picture library.

Managing files

Asset Libraries have the same functionality as other libraries, such as check in, version control, and views.

Libraries best practices

The functionality of a library can be very broad, so it is difficult to specify exact best practices that can apply for every situation. However, the following points should be considered and understood:

- If multiple users are editing documents, require **Check Out** to be enforced in the library setting. This will prevent users overwriting different versions of files.

- Add the **Checked Out By** column to the default view of the library so users can see who has a document checked out. If you hover over the **Checked Out** icon, the person's username who has checked out the document is displayed.

- Decide whether versioning is appropriate for the functionality of the library. Remember that the more versions you have, the greater the disk space required. The decision as to whether versioning is appropriate will depend on the value of the content.

    ○ If it is an important report that has multiple users editing it, or a document that requires auditing and compliance, then versioning is appropriate.

    ○ If the library contains documents that are of interest, but not essential, then versioning may not be appropriate.

    ○ As a half-way house approach, versioning can be limited to a set amount of documents.

- Use folders only if you need to scope unique permissions on documents or if you are required to make a subset of documents easily available offline in Microsoft Outlook.

- If a library has more than 2,000 items, remove the out of the box default view, which shows all items. The default view should be filtered so the page can load in a reasonable amount of time.

- Content Types for documents are an excellent way to have multiple file types in the same library. There are several scenarios that this is useful in:

    ○ **Business reports**: If there is a report library that contains multiple reports, each report should be a separate content type in the list. This will keep reports together in a single library.

    ○ **Centralization Management**: Because content types can be centrally managed, if the report changes, only the content type changes in a single instance, not in each library where the report is being used.

- ○ **Multiple contents sources**: Often there is a requirement to store multiple content types; not just as a document, but as a contact or a link. If the library contains vendor information then it would be useful to have a link to their site, a document on their terms, and contact information all in the same library. The content types in this scenario might be a Word document, URL link, or a contact.

Train users on the above library functionalities — check out, workflows, and versions. This is not a best practice; rather an adoption approach to functionality of practices.

Advanced library features

In this section you will be introduced to advanced features of libraries. The advanced List settings are covered in detail in *Chapter 4*.

Document IDs

With previous versions of SharePoint, an underlying complaint with document management was that there was a lack of unique identifiers for documents, and that if a document was moved to another location, any reference to it would not work.

In SharePoint 2010, there is a unique numbering in documents and content as well as the ability to create a unique document ID.

To enable the Document ID Feature, go to the **Site Collection Features** in the site **Collection Administration** and activate the **Document ID Service**.

In the site **Collection Administration** menu there is a **Document ID Service** item.

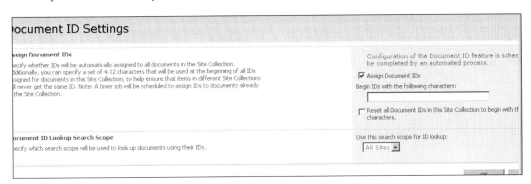

Site Collection Administration

- Search settings
- Search scopes
- Search keywords
- Recycle bin
- Site collection features
- Site hierarchy
- Site collection navigation
- Site collection audit settings
- Portal site connection
- Site collection policies
- Content type publishing
- Site collection output cache
- Site collection object cache
- Site collection cache profiles
- Variations
- Variation labels
- Variation logs
- Translatable columns
- Suggested Content Browser Locations
- Document ID settings
- SharePoint Designer Settings
- Visual Upgrade
- Help settings

When you click on this you will see the following options available:

Document ID Settings

Assign Document IDs
Specify whether IDs will be automatically assigned to all documents in the Site Collection.
Additionally, you can specify a set of 4-12 characters that will be used at the beginning of all IDs assigned for documents in this Site Collection, to help ensure that items in different Site Collections will never get the same ID. Note: A timer job will be scheduled to assign IDs to documents already in the Site Collection.

Configuration of the Document ID feature is sched be completed by an automated process.

☑ Assign Document IDs
Begin IDs with the following characters:

☐ Reset all Document IDs in this Site Collection to begin with th characters.

Document ID Lookup Search Scope
Specify which search scope will be used to look up documents using their IDs.

Use this search scope for ID lookup:
All Sites ▾

Assigning Document IDs

To assign Document IDs the following steps should be applied:

1. **Assign Document IDs**: All existing documents and new documents will get an ID.

2. **Begin IDs with the following characters**: This is the 4-12 document ID that you can configure. All that SharePoint will do is adding a - *number* to the end of this like -1, -2, and so forth.

Document ID Look up Search Scope

Use this search scope for ID Lookup: You can create a scope, and if a user enters in a document ID then it will directly open up instead of going to the results page.

Content types

Document libraries and lists can contain multiple content types. For example, a library can contain both the documents and the graphics related to a project. When a list or library contains multiple content types, creating a new document from the Ribbon in a library can look like this:

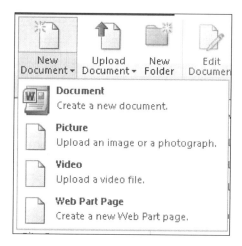

The columns associated with all available content types are displayed.

You can define custom content types in a site's content type gallery. A custom content type must be derived, directly or indirectly, from a core content type such as Document or Item. After it is defined in a site, a custom content type is available in that site and in all sites below that site. To make a content type most broadly available within a site collection, define it in the content type gallery of the top-level site. You can also create a custom content type in a content type hub that is defined in a managed metadata service instance. When it is created in a **content type hub**, the content type will be available to other site collections that are part of web applications associated with that managed metadata service instance.

To allow a library to have multiple content types:

1. Click the **Advanced Settings** in the library or list's settings.

2. Select **Yes to All management of content types**

3. Click the **OK** button.

To add multiple content types to the library/list, follow these steps:

1. In the library or list setting click the **Add from existing site content types**.

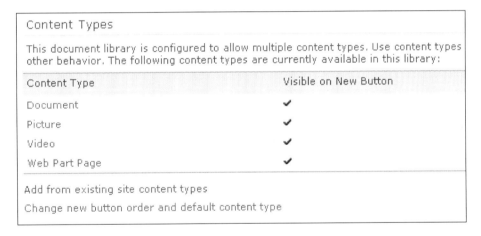

2. Select **Available Site Content Types** and click **Add**.

3. Click **OK** button.

These core content type definitions are starting points, and new content types based on existing ones can be added by modifying existing core types. If you want to use a particular content type, it should be created in the content type gallery of the top-level site, in a site collection. You can create a content type that defines the metadata for:

- That contract
- The contract's template
- Workflows required to review and complete the contract
- Policies that enforce auditing of actions related to the contract
- A retention period for retaining the contract
- Labels to include in printed versions of the contract

Then, any document library in your site collection to which you associate the contract content type will include all of these features and will enable authors to create new contracts based on the template.

Content types are organized into a hierarchy that allows one content type to inherit its characteristics from another content type. This inheritance allows classes of documents to share characteristics across an organization, and it allows teams to tailor these characteristics for particular sites or lists.

For example, all customer-deliverable documents in an enterprise might require a set of metadata, such as account number, project number, and project manager. By creating a top-level Customer Deliverable content type from which all other customer-deliverable document types inherit, you ensure that required information, such as account numbers and project numbers, will be associated with all variants of customer-deliverable documents in your organization.

 If the content type owner adds another required column to the top-level Customer Deliverable content type, the content type owner can propagate the changes to all content types that inherit from it, which will add the new column to all customer deliverable documents. Content Types can also have specific workflows associated with them.

Properties integration with the 2010 Office release

In Microsoft Office, when a user is editing a document saved in SharePoint, a **Document Information Panel** is shown at the top of the document. The Document Information Panel, which is displayed in Word, Excel, and PowerPoint documents, enables users to view and change the properties for an individual file, or for a content type that is saved to a document management server such as a Document Workspace site or a library based on SharePoint Foundation. These properties, also known as metadata, are details about a file that describe or identify it. Users can use these properties to organize, identify, and search for documents.

The Document Information Panel displays an editable form of the document's properties on the server.

Along with editing properties in the Document Information Panel, authors who are using Microsoft Word 2010 can insert properties that are defined on the server into their documents. For example, if the document properties include a project manager name, this name can be inserted into the title page, the footer, or anywhere else the name is used in the document. If a new project manager is assigned to a project, the Project Manager property can be updated on the document management server; this updated project manager name will be reflected in every instance of this property that has been inserted into a document.

Using metadata with content types

Metadata or columns is information about a document that is used to categorize and classify your content. Metadata is associated with a content type as a column. Metadata can provide contextual information about your documents by associating it with an author, subject, audience, language, and so on. Unlike properties, metadata is stored as columns and can be indexed and searched on by SharePoint's search engine.

Metadata added at the site collection level can be associated with content types. Using metadata with content types allows all subsequent content types to inherit some or all of its metadata from the parent content type at the site collection level. Additional metadata can then be added at a lower level such as a document.

Column templates

Each item of metadata that is associated with a content type is a column, which is a location in a list to store information. Lists or libraries are often displayed graphically as columns of information. However, depending on the view associated with the list, the columns can appear in other forms, such as days in a calendar display. In forms associated with a list or library, columns are displayed as fields.

You can define columns for use in multiple content types. To do this, create them in a Column Templates gallery. There is a Column Templates gallery in each site in a site collection. As with content types, columns defined in the Column Templates gallery of a site are available in that site and in all sites below it.

Folder content types

Folder content types define the metadata that is associated with a folder in a list or library. When you apply a folder content type to a list or library, the new command in that list or library will include the folder content type, which makes it possible for users to create folders of that type.

 Another use of folders is that they can be configured to apply default metadata values to data stored within the folder. This is often used to automatically categorize information when it is created/ uploaded into the folder, without the user having to enter metadata values.

You can define views in a list or library that are available only in folders of a particular content type. This is useful when you want a folder to contain a particular type of document and you want views in that folder to only display columns that are relevant to the document type contained in that folder.

Document sets

These are a new feature of SharePoint 2010 and are basically a container for multiple documents to which you can assign certain metadata, and treat as a single entity in many ways. Therefore, you can manage work products that span multiple documents.

Document sets are special types of folders. To create a Document Set:

1. Click on the Library Setting page, **Advanced Settings**.
2. Set **Allow management of content types?** to be **Yes**.
3. Click **Add from existing content type**.
4. Select **Document Set Content Type**.

5. Click the **Add** button.

6. Click the **OK** button.

You can now add a document set to the library through the **New Document Menu** in the **New Group** on the **Library Tools** Ribbon.

Document sets also include version control, which makes it possible for you to capture the state of the entire document set at various points in its life cycle.

Summary

This chapter's focus has been on Library Management and how to integrate both Office documents and other types of files with the SharePoint technology and to begin to collaborate with other team members. You are now familiar with Sites, List, and Libraries, and you should have the knowledge to start architecting content and start using the basic functions for your day-to-day tasks.

The next chapter focuses on workflow functionality of Lists, Libraries, and Sites that enables you to apply more SharePoint functionality to your day-to-day activities.

6
Workflows Fundamentals

The SharePoint 2010 releases continue to build and improve the workflow functionality introduced in previous versions. Workflow development and implementation have become major forces in the business world, both in terms of streamlining office functions as well as cutting costs. Organizations that have adopted the SharePoint technology are slowly transitioning from manual unstructured processes to carefully structured, monitored functions. Knowing this inevitable transition is looming should be reason enough to get you interested in workflows and the benefits gained by this transition. The implementation of correctly designed workflows can give an organization many significant advantages. For one, they can give an organization the opportunity to restructure and reorganize common business processes. Workflows can modernize and automate these same business processes. Additionally, workflows create a chain of custody and an audit trail of all of the activities involved in the process. The purpose of this chapter is to make you aware of the significance of workflows and where they could be implemented in your organization.

This chapter examines the concept of workflows, how SharePoint 2010 enables workflow development, and deployment and security considerations. You will learn basic workflow concepts and be introduced to all of the workflow tools and features available to you as a SharePoint end-user, and how to use these tools to create basic and advanced workflows. Topics covered include:

- Workflow basics
- Creating workflows
- Managing workflows
- Workflow types
- Workflow authoring tools
- Workflow visualization

Workflow basics

Before we get any further, it is important to understand what a workflow is and how it can impact a business. A workflow can be loosely defined as a sequence of connected steps performed by a person, a group of persons, an organization of staff, or one or more simple or complex mechanisms. It is used to describe the operations, procedural steps, organizations or people involved, and required input and output information, all included as part of a structured or unstructured business process.

We can better illustrate the concept of a workflow with an example of a common approval-type business process. Company Alpha has the following process for requisition requests.

This is illustrated as follows: A requisition form is filled out by an employee, which includes a description of the requested item, costs, details, and so on. This requisition form must then be approved by the head of the department that the employee belongs to. Once it is approved by the required department head, it must be approved by the organization's purchase manager.

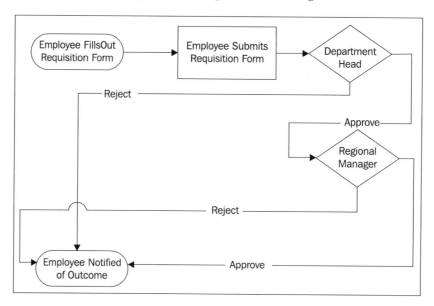

This rather simple example can be broken down into the following workflow components.

Participants

The employee that submits a requisition form, the department head that approves or rejects the request, and the purchase manager that approves or rejects the request are all known participants in this business process. These participants form a chain of custody for the business process as data flows sequentially from one participant to the next.

Input data

The input data is the requisition form that is being filled out by the requesting employee. This form will contain the initial data (such as a description of the desired items, details, costs, required dates, and so on) that will be used in the tasks by the department head and the purchase manager.

Tasks

In this case, there are two decision-making tasks associated with this workflow. The department head will have to decide whether to approve or reject the request. If rejected, the initiator will need to be notified and the workflow will terminate. If approved, the workflow will move to the next workflow step and the purchase manager will have to decide whether to approve or reject the requisition request.

Output data

In this example, the output data consists of notification of the requisition request's approval or rejection. Once the workflow reaches one of its four conclusions, the employee that initially submitted the request will need to be notified as to whether or not his request was approved or rejected, as well as perhaps a reason if it is rejected.

The components described previously are typical of almost all workflows, so when you are designing and deploying a workflow it is important that these are understood.

 We estimate that 80 percent of a workflow deployment initiative is requirement gathering, rather than the point-click experience with the SharePoint interface.

SharePoint workflows are based on the **Windows Workflow Foundation (WF)** and part of the **.NET 3.5 Framework** that essentially consists of three components:

- **Runtime engine**: This provides the workflow execution environment, transactions, persistence, state management, and tracking capabilities.

- **Hosting application**: This provides the execution context for the runtime engine as well as any application-specific services that may be required to support the workflows, such as the SharePoint **library or list**.

- **Activities**: These are based on the WF framework's base activity library; they are the building blocks of the workflow.

This was a brief architectural understanding description of the foundation of SharePoint workflows. These three components are always working behind the scenes when you are creating and executing workflows.

A more in-depth examination is outside the scope of this book and can be found in a variety of published materials dealing with SharePoint 2010 development.

Workflow types

There are basically two kinds of workflows: sequential and state-machine.

Sequential

These perform their actions in sequence, one after another from start to finish. Although they might seem rigid, these workflows can be made more flexible by adding, looping, branching, and other flow control mechanisms. Additionally, branching decisions can be made based on values that are passed in from outside sources, or based on actions made by end users. Processes that can be easily automated make good candidates for state machine workflows, because steps can be easily added. A few examples may include an employee performance review, a company travel system, and the requisition request form described in the beginning of this section.

State-machine

These can be broken down into states and state transitions. They perform different actions based on specific events, which can be simple or complex. Instead of defining a sequential path from start to finish, the workflow goes through many potential states before reaching completion. For example, the workflow can transition from state A to state B, or skip state B and transition to state C based on the event received in the workflow. Good candidates for state-machine workflows include help desk systems, employee onboarding systems, purchasing systems, and so on.

Now that you have had a basic introduction into workflows and the different types of workflows, we will see how they apply to the different versions and editions of SharePoint 2010.

Creating workflows

Workflows are associated with either a document in a library, a list item in a list, or a **Site workflow**. The steps to create these workflows are the same.

In this section, we are going to look at creating pre-built workflows with libraries, lists, and sites.

Scenario: A user creates a document, and then that document is routed to the appropriate parties for some type of approval prior to being accepted as an authentic organizational artifact. It usually contains an approval/rejection decision, along with a comments section indicating why the particular decision was made.

The **approval workflow** is typically the most common workflow found in an organization as most simple approvals only require a *'Yes, this is fine'* level of approval.

 The approval workflow functionality is not available with SharePoint Foundation.

To create an approval workflow, the following steps should be applied:

1. Open a document library.
2. Select the **Library** tab and look to the right-hand corner of the Ribbon.
3. Select the **Workflow Settings** drop-down and select **Add a Workflow**.

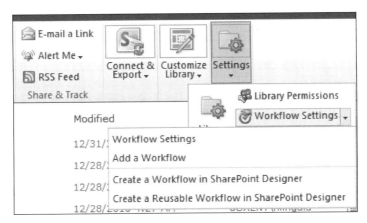

4. Select **Approval – SharePoint 2010** workflow. Give the workflow a name.

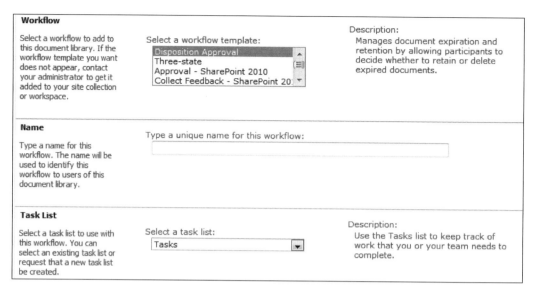

5. Keep the **Task List** and **History List** default settings.

6. Uncheck the selected checkbox under **Start Options**, and select the checkbox for **Start this workflow when a new item is created**. The workflow will start automatically each time a new document is created in this library.

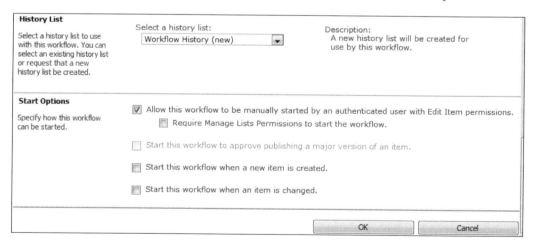

7. Click **Next**.

8. Select an approver for the document (you can select one or more serial approvers). These approvers will always be the approvers for this workflow in this library.

9. Type in a message for the approver(s).

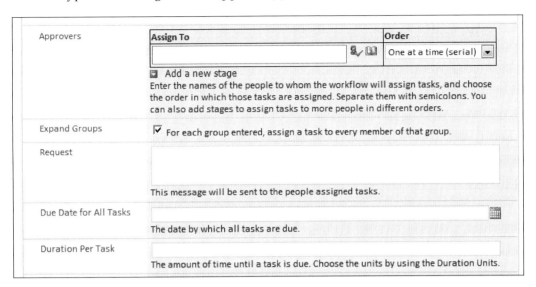

10. Enter an appropriate due date for the approval task.

11. Enter an appropriate duration for the approval task.

 The due date and duration should be set so approvers can approve the item without reminders being sent out to them. Obviously, the workflow is a priority to the submitter, but this does not mean it is for the approvers.

12. Select the duration units.

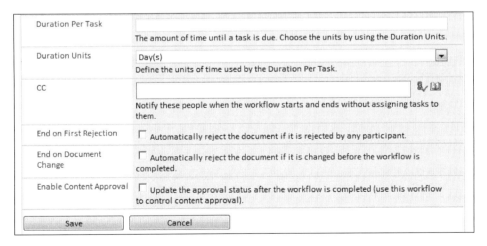

13. Decide whether or not to **CC** anyone during the approval process.

14. Select options for **First Rejection**, **Document Change**, and **Content Approval**.

15. Click **Save**.

The next time that a document is created in this document library this workflow will start an approval task for the approver(s) you specified. The workflow will continue, based on all of the options you selected previously, until it reaches its logical conclusion: Approved or Rejected.

The instructions stated previously define the workflow to be started when the item is created in a library or list. In step 6, there was an option to start a workflow manually. This workflow trigger is useful when a workflow process is more ad hoc. To start a workflow manually:

1. Click the downward menu arrow on the document/item.

2. Select **Workflows**

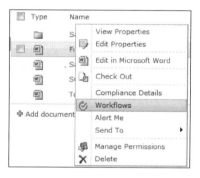

3. Choose a workflow associated with the list.

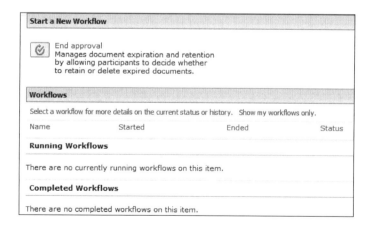

The other predefined workflows can be created by following the steps of the preceding instructions. These workflows are discussed later in this chapter.

Workflow architecture

A workflow is associated with a library or list, but the user approves/rejects **tasks** in a **Task List** in the **Team Site**. This task list will list all the approval tasks of all associated initiations of a workflow.

Managing workflows

The workflow settings page gives users with the appropriate permissions rudimentary management functions for the workflows associated to their respective document libraries.

By clicking on the Workflow Setting icon on the Ribbon and the **Workflow Setting** option, you are presented with the workflow information associated with this library/list.

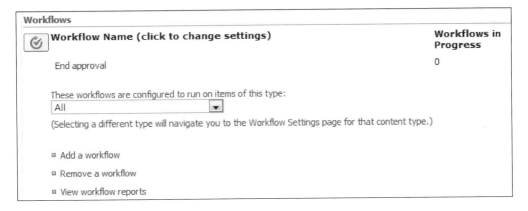

This information includes:

* The names of the workflows in the library or list
* Ability to remove a workflow
* Current workflow processes that are running

Workflow types

All of the predefined workflows can be created by following the steps outlined previously in this chapter. The predefined workflows are stated in the following table:

Workflow Name	Brief Description	SharePoint Edition
Three-state	Designed to track the status of a list item through three states (phases).	Foundation
Collect feedback	Routes a document or item to a group of people for feedback.	SharePoint Server
Approval	Routes a document or item to a group of people for approval.	SharePoint Server
Disposition approval	Manages document expiration and retention by letting participants decide whether to keep or delete expired documents.	SharePoint Server
Collect signatures	Routes a document that was created in a Microsoft application to a group of people to collect their digital signatures.	SharePoint Server
Translation management	Manages manual document translation by creating copies of the document to be translated and by assigning translation tasks to translators.	SharePoint Server
Issue tracking	Routes an issue to team members for resolution.	SharePoint Server
Collect signatures	Routes a document that was created in a Microsoft application to a group of people to collect their digital signatures.	SharePoint Server

Three-state

This workflow is specifically designed to track the status of a list item through three states or phases. It can be used to manage business processes in which organizations need to track a high volume of issues or items. For example, this workflow can be used to track a document through three different states: New, Pending Review, and Completed.

This workflow is only supported on lists and any other workflows will need to be manually developed and deployed using custom code.

SharePoint Foundation only supports the predefined **Three-state workflow** template.

SharePoint Server 2010 includes the following three-state predefined workflow templates that can address common business scenarios. These are described as follows.

Collect feedback

This workflow routes a document or item to a group of people that have been selected to provide feedback. The reviewers can provide feedback, which is then consolidated and sent to the initiator of the workflow in an e-mail. This workflow type is useful for document review and collecting feedback from co-workers. Instead of individual e-mails from each reviewer, it is all consolidated. By default, this workflow is associated with the Document content type and therefore it is automatically available in all document libraries.

Approval

This predefined workflow routes a document or item to a group of people that have been selected as approvers. The Approval workflow is sequential in nature. The first set of approvers can undergo the review and approval process, then the next set of approvers, and so on until completion. Each stage or approval set can also have its own specific behavior. For example, members of the first group of approvers can do their review in serial order (one after the other), members of the second group can do their review in parallel (in any order), and so on.

By default, this workflow is also associated with the document content type and therefore it is automatically available in all document libraries. A variation of the approval workflow is also associated with the pages library on a publishing site, and can be used to manage the approval process for the publication of web pages.

The employee requisition form described at the beginning of the chapter can be created and deployed in minutes with this predefined workflow.

Disposition approval

This workflow manages document retention and expiration by letting participants decide whether or not they want to keep or delete expired documents.

The disposition approval workflow supports record management processes. It is primarily intended for use in a records center site. This workflow can be started automatically, manually, or when an item changes and the approver is presented with the following screen, with the options to either delete or retain the document.

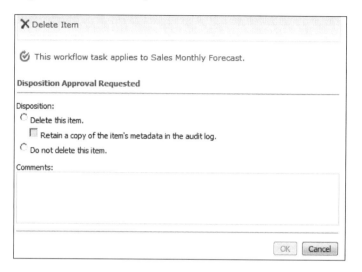

Collect signatures

This workflow allows you to route a document that was created in a Microsoft application to a group of people to collect their digital signatures. This workflow must be started in applications in the 2007/2010 Microsoft Office suites such as Microsoft Word. The participants must complete their signature tasks by adding their digital signatures (login) to the documents in the respective client programs. By default, the Collect Signatures workflow is associated with the Document content type, and therefore is automatically available in all document libraries. However, the Collect Signatures workflow appears for a document in the document library only if that document contains one or more Microsoft Office Signature Lines.

Translation management

This workflow manages manual document translations by creating copies of the document to be translated and by assigning translation tasks to translators.

This workflow is only available for Translation Management libraries.

Issue tracking

This workflow routes an issue to team members for resolution. It presents a web page to the user who is then able to enter new issues as they arise. As an issue progresses through the different workflow states, the web page that the user sees will change to reflect appropriate events.

Workflow authoring tools

SharePoint 2010 workflows basically consist of two elements: a form the workflow uses to interface with its users, and the logic associated with the workflow. Both of these elements are designed by you, the end user.

Forms can be automatically created using the pre-built workflows. Additionally, they can be designed using the InfoPath client, or they can be directly created through the workflow authoring tools. Whatever method you choose, forms are essential in communicating with the end user through the duration of the workflow lifecycle. A workflow can potentially display forms at four points throughout its lifecycle:

- **Association**: This stage is the binding of a workflow to an object such as a document library. At this stage, an administrator would be able to set options that apply to every workflow instance based on this binding.

- **Initiation**: This stage represents the creation of a workflow instance. At this stage, specific values can be set that will determine the flow of the data in the workflow. A workflow author would need to provide a form so the workflow initiator can enter these values. These values could then potentially determine the next step in the workflow.

- **Modification**: The stage represents the potential modification of a workflow that is currently in progress. For example, additional individuals may need to be added to a workflow, submitted values may need to be changed, and so on.

- **Task Completion**: The current workflow instance must present its participants a form where they can complete the currently assigned task so the workflow can move to the next phase or to completion.

The logic behind a workflow is always defined by a group of activities, as you learned in a previous introductory section regarding Workflow Foundation in .NET 3.5. Microsoft provides two tools to let you create the forms and logic for a workflow: SharePoint Designer 2010 and Visual Studio 2010 with **Workflow Foundation (WF)** Workflow Designer. Each of these tools is designed to target a specific audience. Visual Studio 2010 with Windows with WF Workflow Designer is intended for software developers, who can run the tool directly from within the Visual Studio environment using the professional edition of Visual Studio 2010. SharePoint Designer 2010 is intended for information workers who have less technical expertise than software developers, but can understand the business process as well as programming and logic fundamentals.

SharePoint Designer 2010

SharePoint Designer (SPD) 2010 is a free desktop application from Microsoft that enables users to develop and deploy rules-based wizards workflows for SharePoint sites without the involvement of the IT department. The details of the program are outside the scope of this book and it is mentioned only to inform you of another workflow tool for SharePoint. **SPD** is designed to be very difficult for the user to destabilize the SharePoint server environment, and although we are primarily concerned with its use as a workflow authoring environment, it has many more capabilities.

The following screenshot shows the landing page for the SPD application:

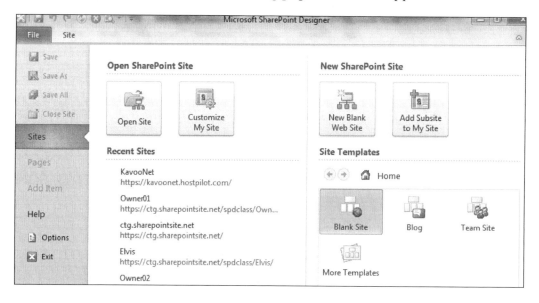

Workflows in SPD 2010 are divided into steps similar to the Outlook rules engine. Each step can have a condition and an action. The condition will determine whether the action will be executed. Actions can be run serially, in parallel, or a combination of both.

SharePoint Designer limitations

There are some limitations that should be noted. These are:

- Workflows designed using SPD 2010 cannot be modified while they are running
- Only sequential and parallel workflows can be created
- State-machine workflows are not supported

Additionally, only two of the four workflow states, initiation and task-completion, can be used with these types of workflows.

Visual Studio 2010 with WF Workflow Designer

To develop more advanced and robust workflows, software developers can use the SharePoint workflow tools provided in Visual Studio 2010 Professional. This authoring environment provides support for sequential, parallel, and state-machine workflows, and for all four phases of the workflow lifecycle. Unlike SPD, it is a graphical authoring tool that helps developers visualize the logic being coded. The following screenshot shows a sample portion of a workflow designed with Visual Studio 2010:

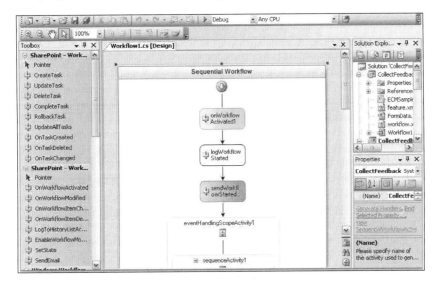

Visio 2010 does have workflow import and export capabilities to SharePoint.

Tool comparison

The following table compares the different available functionality to create workflows with SharePoint Designer and WF Workflow Designer in Visual Studio 2010:

Feature	SharePoint Designer	Visual Studio 2010 with WF Workflow Designer
Additional activities (other than those provided by SharePoint Foundation) are provided?	No	Yes
Can be made available across the farm?	No	Yes
Can be scoped to a site collection?	Yes	Yes
Can create custom activities?	No	Yes
Can use Microsoft Visio Professional to create workflow logic?	Yes	No
Need to write code?	No	Yes
One-click publishing of workflows?	Yes	Yes
Workflows can be created using only actions that are approved by site administrators?	Yes	No
Workflow can be modified while it is running?	No	Yes
Workflow lifecycle phases all available?	No	Yes
Workflows can be deployed remotely?	Yes	No
Workflows are accessible in client applications (other than the browser)?	Yes	Yes

For further information, please visit this link:

```
http://technet.microsoft.com/en-us/library/cc263308.aspx
```

Workflow visualization

Workflows can streamline and automate ordered portions of business processes, but it is very important to be able to identify where and how you can adapt workflows to meet your organization's requirements. One element to consider is whether your identified business processes generate a lot of e-mail or paper. If this is the case, they may be a great candidate for conversion to electronic forms and workflows.

The requirements gathering phase is by far the most important portion of workflow design; it can also be the most time-consuming. Often, outside consultants such as business analysts are hired to evaluate your business processes and participants to see where time is lost and where improvements can be made. Regardless of your budget and the approach you choose, the most important and essential stage is documenting the actual business process accurately before considering transitioning it into a SharePoint workflow.

[

Remember, a visual diagram of the process is worth a thousand words.
]

The next step is to appropriately match the technology to the business requirements that you have gathered. SharePoint 2010 comes with a myriad of built-in partial workflow features, besides the ones we have mentioned in the previous sections. These include approvals, content expiration, publishing, feedback, and the pre-defined workflow templates. It is conceivable that you would be able to meet business needs using these out of the box features, without ever even having to design or develop custom workflows using the authoring tools mentioned in the previous sections. Ultimately, the tools that you choose will depend on the degree of workflow complexity. Additional workflow components to consider when determining the complexity of your workflow include the following:

- **History List**: The history list maintains an audit trail of each step in the workflow, including approvals, updates, and errors.
- **Task List**: The task list maintains the list of tasks assigned to the participants in the workflow.
- **Start Options**: These options dictate whether workflows are started automatically, or are manually triggered by a user with the appropriate permissions. Users can manually kick-off a workflow directly from an item.
- **Tasks**: These actions can be run serially or un-parallel; they can also be reassigned if needed.
- **Completion Activities**: This setting defines what actions complete or cancel the workflow instance.
- **Post-Completion Activities**: This setting gives you the option to perform an activity after the workflow has been completed.

Along with requirements gathering comes the visualization of the workflow. SharePoint 2010 has added new capabilities with regards to workflow modeling and visualization. The most notable is the new, long-sought after integration with Visio 2010. Visio has been the tool of choice for users and business analysts who model business operations. However, until this release there has been no direct integration between the workflow models constructed in Visio and their realization in SPD. However, Visio 2010 Premium changes all of this and introduces a brand new template just for SharePoint workflow called Microsoft SharePoint Workflow. The following screenshot shows the template available in Visio 2010. This template is available in the flowcharts template gallery in Visio 2010 Premium.

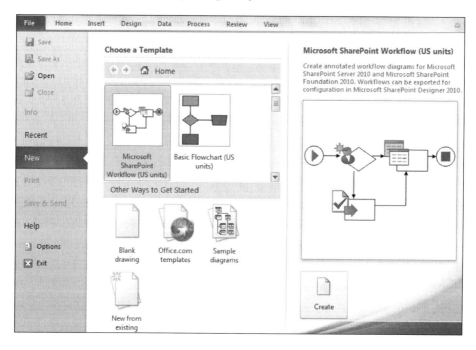

The Microsoft SharePoint Workflow template exposes key SharePoint activities that business analysts can use to draft functional SharePoint workflows. The following screenshot shows the SharePoint workflow activities available in Visio 2010. These activities are subdivided into three categories: SharePoint Workflow Actions, SharePoint Workflow Conditions, and SharePoint Workflow Terminators. They are activated just by dragging and dropping from the toolbar onto the canvas. Please note that every SharePoint activity maps directly to its counterpart activity in SPD.

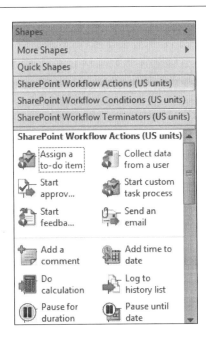

Once you have finished designing your workflow in Visio, you can export it directly to SharePoint Designer. The following screenshot shows the exporting functionality in Visio 2010:

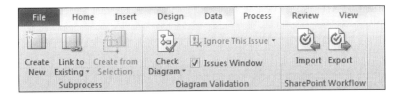

The reverse of this process also holds true. A workflow designed in SharePoint Designer 2010 can be exported to Visio 2010 for business analysts to review before the workflow is published to the SharePoint Server.

Summary

This chapter's focus has been on SharePoint 2010 workflows, the basics behind workflow design, and the authoring tools available to you for SharePoint 2010 workflow development. This chapter has explained the comparisons of the authoring tools and options available to you in the different SharePoint versions, and how to integrate workflow modeling using Visio 2010 with SPD. Workflow design is a vast and complex topic, the nuances of which are mostly outside the scope of this book. However, you should be familiar enough with the basic principles to be able to start architecting workflow solutions for your organization's simpler business processes.

The next chapter discusses Office 2010 integration to SharePoint and the benefits of documents stored in SharePoint.

7

Office Integration with SharePoint

The Microsoft Office 2010 Suite includes Outlook, Word, Excel, and PowerPoint among other applications. While the products can be used standalone, they can also function as client applications for SharePoint.

In this chapter, we will look at how the Microsoft Office 2010 client applications integrate tightly with SharePoint 2010. You will see how you can work in Word, for example, and access information from SharePoint without leaving your document. You can easily save files from the client application directly to SharePoint. You can broadcast a PowerPoint presentation over the web for impromptu meetings. These are just some of the new capabilities offered by the integration between Office and SharePoint with the 2010 releases.

The functionality that provides this improved integration includes:

- Ribbon Interface
- Office Web Apps
- Co-Authoring
- Social Computing
- Backstage
- Slide Show Broadcasting
- Visio Web Services

So, in addition to a browser, you can also use these applications to directly access documents stored in SharePoint. The Office 2010 clients give you access not only to the documents themselves, but also to information stored with the documents, called metadata. From Word, you can create, view, and edit files stored in SharePoint, and access and change the metadata stored with the document in SharePoint.

The software requirements to perform these functions are listed as follows:

- SharePoint 2010 Server with Office Web Apps installed
- Office 2010
- Browser (Internet Explorer 7 and above, Firefox 3.5 and above, or Safari 4.x)
- Optional: Office Communication Server

Ribbon

The **Ribbon** interface, also referred to as the **Fluent UI**, was introduced in Microsoft applications with Office 2007. Microsoft found that much of the functionality in previous versions of Office was difficult for users to find. The Ribbon was introduced to surface the functionality to where users could easily access it and quickly apply it.

Office 2010 continues the use of the Ribbon interface and indeed expands it. Where Office 2007 introduced the Ribbon only in products such as Word, Excel, and PowerPoint, Office 2010 has the Ribbon in all products included in the suite. In Office 2010, the Ribbon is new to InfoPath, SharePoint Workspace (formerly Groove), Visio, and Project for example. Outlook 2007 had the Ribbon for creating and editing messages and invitations; Outlook 2010 adds the interface throughout the product, even in the e-mail navigation and calendar views. Not only is the Ribbon pervasive throughout Office 2010, but SharePoint 2010 also uses the Ribbon in the browser interface.

> The Ribbon interface enhances the user's experience by providing a familiar and consistent way of working across products. The consistent experience reduces the time it takes to learn a product and to complete tasks.

The Ribbon provides a graphical display of the functionality available to users in a given product. So, instead of choosing text commands from pull-down menus, a user can see a graphical representation of what a command will do, click it once, and immediately apply the functionality.

The Ribbon represents the culmination of a **Graphical User Interface** (**GUI**), where *what you see* truly is *what you get*. This interface eliminates the need for searching for commands through several layers of menus or in complicated dialogue and property boxes — often with multiple tabs.

Commands are grouped logically in the Ribbon. Contextual Ribbons will appear at times to provide functionality specific to a selected object. So, for example, a **Table Tools** menu appears when a table is selected in a Word document.

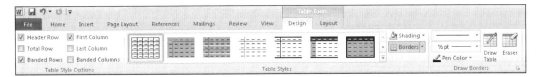

The Ribbon interface was introduced in Outlook 2007. Unlike in Word or Excel 2007, in Outlook 2007 the Ribbon only appeared when you were creating or editing a message or a meeting invitation.

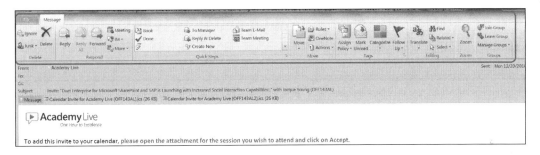

Outlook 2010 extends the use of the Ribbon throughout the product, even when you are navigating your mail, calendar, or tasks. The Ribbon dynamically changes depending on the item selected, and the user immediately has access to the commands appropriate to the context.

The following screenshot shows the Ribbon interface in the e-mail navigation view:

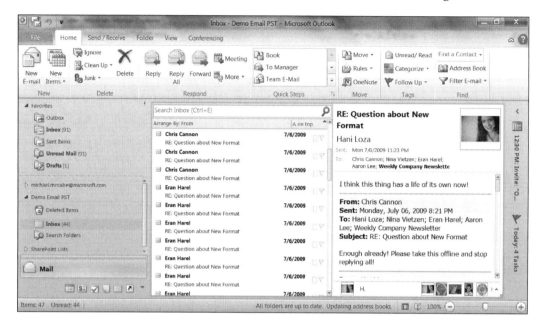

 Using the conversation view:
Outlook 2010 offers a new conversation view to make it easier to follow the thread of an e-mail exchange.

To change to the conversation view, follow these steps:

1. Right-click on the **Arrange By** header above your list of e-mails.
2. Click on **Show as Conversations**.

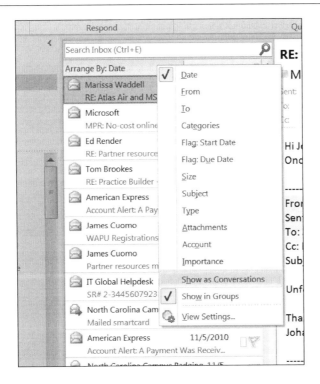

Your e-mails then appear listed in easy-to-follow conversational threads:

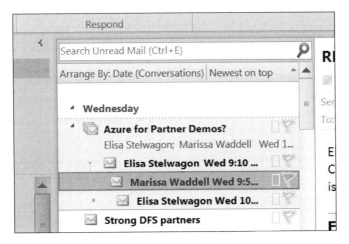

While we have seen here how the ribbon provides a consistent **user interface (UI)** across the Office applications, in the next sections, we will also see how that same UI is part of the SharePoint 2010 experience.

Office Web Apps

Have you ever needed to work on information in a Word document or an Excel spreadsheet, but did not have access to those applications? If traveling, or working outside your office at a customer's site, you may only have access to a kiosk or machine with only a browser installed. In those instances, you will be able to view and edit your documents that are stored on a SharePoint 2010 Server.

Microsoft Office Web Apps give users the ability to view, create, and edit documents, presentations, and spreadsheets using a browser when the full Office application is not installed on the computer.

[Office Web Apps need to be installed in the SharePoint 2010 server.]

This shows a Word 2010 document being viewed using the Office Web App:

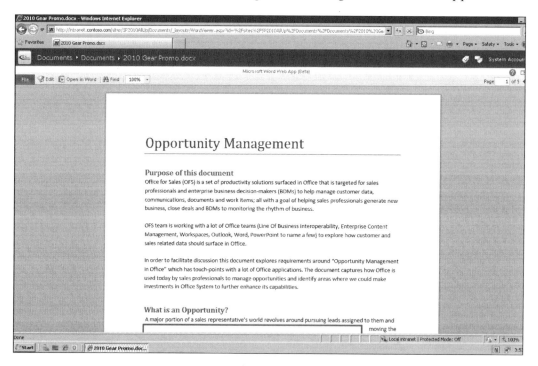

The document in View Mode shows the formatting and layout of the printed document. In View Mode, the Office Web App includes charts and images as well.

When editing a document using the Office Web App, however, formatting is not shown; charts and images are indicated with a placeholder, but are not shown.

The following screenshot shows the Word 2010 Web App in Edit Mode with the abbreviated Ribbon:

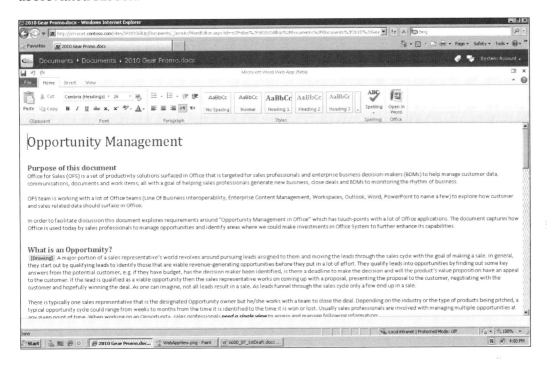

The tools for editing in the Office Web Apps are a lighter and scaled-down set compared to those available in the full Word, PowerPoint, Excel, or OneNote clients. In the preceding screenshot, for example, note that there are only four tabs: **File**, **Home**, **Insert**, and **View**. The full Word 2010 client would have at least eight tabs.

Functionality not available in the Word Web App includes:

- Page Layout (margins, page orientation, and so on)
- References (for example footnotes)
- Mailings (mail merge, labels, envelopes)
- Review (spell check, track changes)

All of these would be available in the full Word 2010 client.

In order to use Office Web Apps to view and edit documents, they must be saved to a SharePoint site. Microsoft Office Web Apps are compatible with most browsers, including Internet Explorer, Firefox, and Safari.

Microsoft classifies browsers into three levels:

- Level 1: Supported - includes Internet Explorer and Firefox
- Level 2: Supported with known limitations - Safari is included here
- Level 3: Not Tested

In certain circumstances, Level 2 browsers may deliver a somewhat different user experience depending on the operating system.

For example, a Level 2 browser would not allow you to use the **copy** and **paste** commands from the ribbon. Instead, you would need to use the keyboard commands, *Ctrl+C* and *Ctrl+V*.

Co-authoring

If you have ever collaborated with others to write a document, you know what chaos can ensue as you try to control versions and manage the time and sequence of edits.

In Microsoft Office 2010, co-authoring enables two or more people to edit a document simultaneously. Sections of the document are simply blocked off for each author to have exclusive control of a part of the document.

You can work on a document while others edit other parts of the same document at the same time. This saves having to wait until you have made your additions and edits before they can make their changes.

This increases everyone's productivity because all contributors can access the document when they want to. Multiple users can be making changes to different parts of the document without having to wait for it to be saved and checked before getting access, thus speeding up the process of collaboratively completing a document.

Co-authoring in SharePoint and Office 2010 represents a major improvement over 2007. The 2007 Office suite included Groove, a peer-to-peer collaboration application that enabled you to work simultaneously on a document with another user. Both users needed to have Groove installed on their PCs, however. With SharePoint and Office 2010, you can co-author simultaneously with another user by simply using a browser. The document, of course, must be stored on SharePoint 2010, and both users must be using Office 2010.

In order for co-authors to work on a document simultaneously, each author must select a portion of the document and block other authors from editing it. This is done by following these steps:

1.   Select the text you want to edit.

2.   Click on the **Review** tab.

3.   In the **Protect** group, click on **Block Authors**.

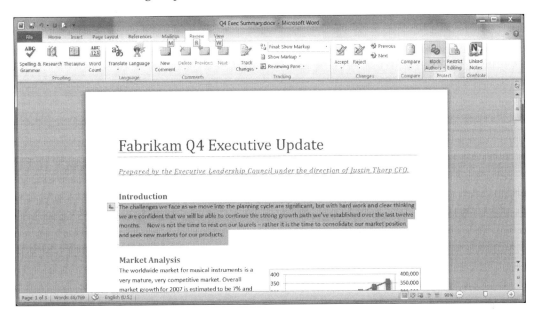

The selected text will appear with an icon in the left margin indicating that the section has been blocked to keep others from editing it.

In order to make the section available again, you must save the document and upload it to SharePoint. But, while the section is blocked, other authors can block other available text and edit while you are making your changes.

When changes are saved and uploaded to SharePoint, they become available to other users as well.

Unified Communications

When **instant messaging (IM)** with **Microsoft Lync Server** is available, you will be able to see the availability of other authors in the document by the color indicator to the left of the name.

Phyllis Harris

By hovering over a user's availability indicator, you will expose an action box. From there, you can select one of the icons to start an IM conversation, send an e-mail, or even call the person on the phone.

The integration of UC into SharePoint and the Office applications saves you time. You don't have to switch to another application to collaborate with another author; for example, with a single click you can call the other person, send an e-mail, or start a chat conversation using IM.

Microsoft Exchange integration provides e-mail integration, while **Microsoft Lync Server** provides presence information, instant messaging, click-to-call, and **Voice over IP (VoIP)**. When you use Microsoft Lync Server with VoIP, you do not need a physical phone; you can use your computer as a *soft-phone*.

A soft-phone is your computer giving you the capabilities of a telephone by using software and your PC. As long as you have speakers and a microphone on your PC, the Microsoft Office Communicator software will allow you to make and receive calls over the Internet.

The Microsoft Lync Server is not required by SharePoint, but adds these rich communication capabilities to a user's experience in SharePoint and in the Office applications. The preceding screenshot shows these features in a SharePoint My Site, but the same features of Presence, IM, and Telephony show up in Outlook, Word, and Excel, for example when you have Microsoft Lync Server installed.

 Microsoft Lync Server is not a requirement of SharePoint 2010. The Presence, IM, Web Conferencing, and Voice capabilities provided by Microsoft Lync Server work with SharePoint 2007 and 2010.

Social computing

With the **Outlook Social Connector (OSC)**, you can connect to people and their resources residing in SharePoint 2010. The OSC connector for SharePoint is available out-of-the-box with Outlook 2010.

Connectors are available for third-party business and social networks such as MySpace, LinkedIn, Facebook, and Windows Live.

In Outlook 2010, contacts will appear in the **People Pane** at the bottom of a mail message.

Click on the pictures of other addressees and you'll see their picture highlighted with related information, such as recent e-mail, out-of-office messages, messages with attached files, and calendar information.

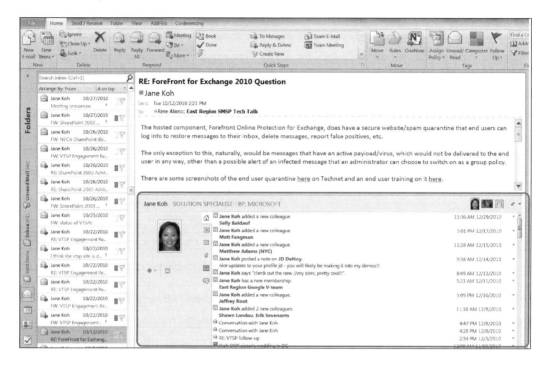

By selecting the icons to the right of the person's picture, you can see all items or filter by RSS feeds, unread messages, messages with attachments, calendar invitations, or IM conversations.

With OSC, you can synchronize data from networking sites. You will receive updates in one manageable view. It's an easy way to track all the ways you communicate with contacts in your business and social networks—in one place. So, for example, you could see information about everyone copied in an e-mail whether you use SharePoint, LinkedIn, or MySpace to connect with them.

Let's take a look at how you set up an OSC connection.

First of all, Microsoft has made the specifications and **Software Developer Kit (SDK)** for creating connectors available. Using the SDK, third-party developers of social and business networks can develop and make their connectors available.

You will need to download the connector from the site you use, and then set up the connection in Outlook 2010.

To set up the OSC connector for Windows Live Messenger, for example, follow these steps:

1. On the Ribbon in Outlook 2010, click on the **View** tab, and in the **People Pane** group, click on **People Pane** and then **Account Settings**.

2. Check the **Windows Live Messenger** box, enter your **User Name** and **Password**, and click on **Finish**.

Now, updates about your contacts from Windows Live Messenger will appear in the People Pane.

Backstage

You can think of Backstage as a vastly expanded File menu. In Office 2003 and earlier, you will recall the main menu with File, Edit, Insert, and so on. With Office 2007 and the introduction of the Ribbon, most of the functionality from the old File menu was accessed by clicking the Office logo in the upper left-hand corner of the screen. With Office 2010, you will find the functionality by clicking the first tab, appropriately named **File**.

> In Office 2007, the Office Logo icon that appeared above the Ribbon is referred to as the **Office Pearl**. Similarly, in Windows 7, the Windows Logo that replaced the word **Start** on the toolbar is referred to as the **Windows Pearl**.

To view Backstage in all Office 2010 applications, click on the **File** tab. This opens Backstage, and you quickly realize it has gone beyond what was available in the earlier File menu.

In this view, you can see the full range of information about the document, including authors' profiles, metadata, and workflows. Most of the information is stored with the document in SharePoint. Backstage makes it easier to access because you can see it in Word, for example, without having to switch between the application and SharePoint.

It is like having a window right into SharePoint. Not only is the information accessible, but you can interact with it, making it easier to get your work done faster.

The Backstage view can also be extended; that is, you can add custom actions to meet specific business requirements, though this requires custom code and is outside the scope of our discussion in this book.

In Office 2010, the **File** menu has been expanded to include a range of options for printing, saving, sharing, and controlling a document.

Commands familiar from earlier versions of the File menu can be found here, such as **Save**, **Open**, **Close**, and **Exit**. With Office 2010, choices such as **Info**, **Print**, and **Save & Send** expand what you can do with a document from this one location, especially when working with a document stored in SharePoint.

> Backstage's tabbed design gives an easier way of managing all the expanded functionality that has become available with Office 2010 and the deeper integration with SharePoint Server 2010.

Let's take a closer look at the **Info** and **Save & Send** sections.

Info

In this section, you can check documents in and out of SharePoint.

 The **Info** section in Backstage is only available for documents stored on SharePoint 2010 servers.

You can leave notes for others on the **Note Board**.

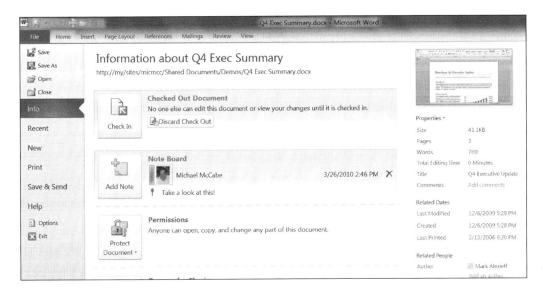

This note will also appear in an information bar just below the Ribbon and above the document:

The Note will also appear on the author's My Site on the Note Board, under Tags and Notes:

Permissions allow you to restrict access to a document and to encrypt documents with a password. You can also restrict what a user can do with the document, such as print, copy, or edit.

You can control the permissions to the document by clicking on **Protect Document**.

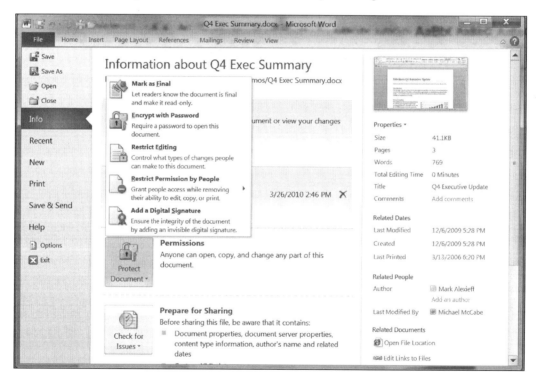

In SharePoint 2007, managing permissions could only be done in a SharePoint library. Now, it can be done right from the application where the document is edited.

You can prepare the document for sharing by deleting personal information or slide notes; to do this, click on **Check for Issues**.

The **Info** section of Backstage is also where you can control the versions of the document stored on SharePoint by clicking on **Manage Versions**.

Save & Send

This section is the most important for working on documents stored on SharePoint and collaborating with others.

Backstage **Save & Send** allows you to:

- Save and Send
- Send Using e-mail

 With this choice, you can attach the document in an e-mail message, or send a link to where the document is stored on SharePoint.

- Save to Web
- Save to SharePoint
- Publish as Blog Post
- Manage File Types
- Change File Type to an earlier version of Word, for example, or to a format used in other applications
- Create PDF/XPS Document

- Manage Workflows

  When workflows are available in the SharePoint document library, where the document being edited resides, they will be available here. You can start a workflow here, or if one is already in progress you can check its status.

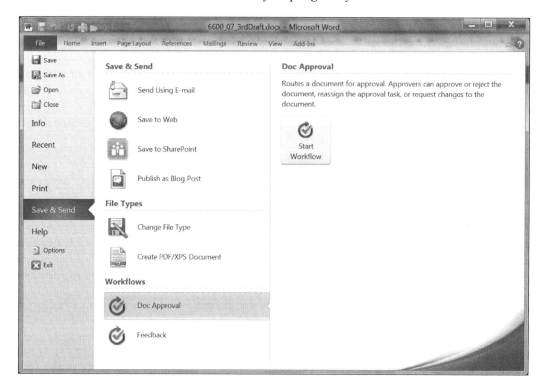

Publishing as a blog post

Publishing blogs is one of the new Social Computing features of SharePoint 2010. Blogging and tagging are what are often referred to as Web 2.0 features. We will discuss more about these capabilities in *Chapter 12, Blogs, Wikis, and Other Web 2.0 Features*, but here we can see how Backstage facilitates blogging.

This option, within the Save & Send section of Backstage, makes it easy for you to author blog contributions in Word and then publish them to the web. To publish a blog from Word 2010 directly to a SharePoint site, follow these steps:

1. Create your blog in Word 2010.
2. Click on the **File** tab to open Backstage.
3. Click on **Save & Send**.

4. Click on **Publish as Blog Post**, and Word 2010 will convert the document to a blog.

5. On the Ribbon, click on **Publish**.

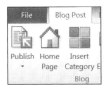

6. Enter the URL where your Blog is located (usually on your SharePoint My Site) and it will be published:

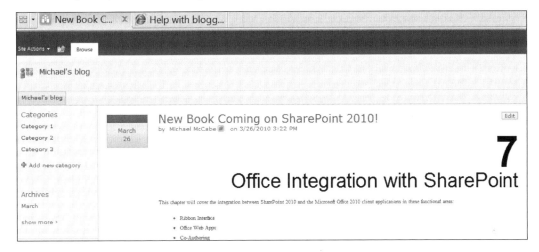

In this section, we have seen how Backstage provides a point of central control over the various ways an Office document can interact with SharePoint. From Backstage you can view information about your document, whether that information is stored in the document itself or on SharePoint. You can save your document to SharePoint, as well as publish it as a blog on a SharePoint site. Backstage allows you to interact with SharePoint without having to leave the application. You stay where you can work on your content without having to jump back-and-forth to a browser in order to access SharePoint functionality.

Slideshow broadcasting

Have you ever had the spontaneous need, while you are in the middle of a phone conversation with a person at another location, to show them a presentation you have on your PC? You did not anticipate it, and so you did not set up a web conference in advance.

Now, you will be able to do just that. The integration of PowerPoint 2010 and SharePoint 2010 provides the ability to share slideshows easily with others in less than a minute, allowing you to present information whenever the need arises.

The viewers can be at remote locations and do not require PowerPoint on their computers. They simply click a link that you send them and the Slideshow is presented in their browser.

A presentation can be delivered ad hoc; there is no need to set up a web conference in advance. It is the simplest and quickest way to share PowerPoint content with a live audience.

These are the steps for broadcasting a slideshow in PowerPoint 2010:

1. Open the presentation you want to share.

2. In the **Slide Show** tab, in the **Start Slide Show** group, click on **Broadcast Slide Show**:

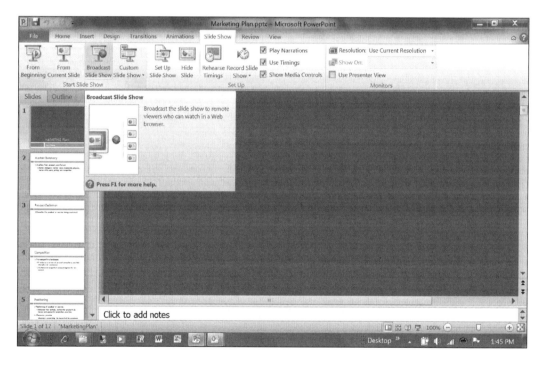

3. Choose a broadcast service, for example:

   ○ **Internal Broadcast** site (hosted on SharePoint)

   ○ **PowerPoint Broadcast** (hosted on Windows Live)

   ○ **Add a new service** (not yet listed; provide URL)

4. Click on **Start Broadcast**:

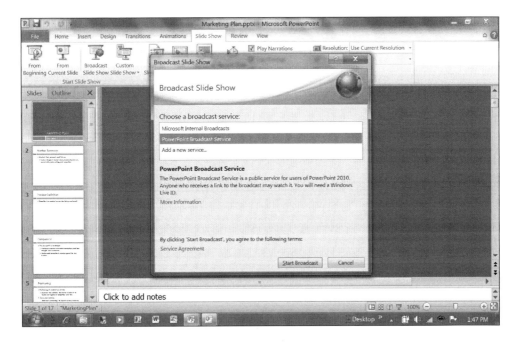

5. Share the link with remote views and click on **Start Slide Show**:

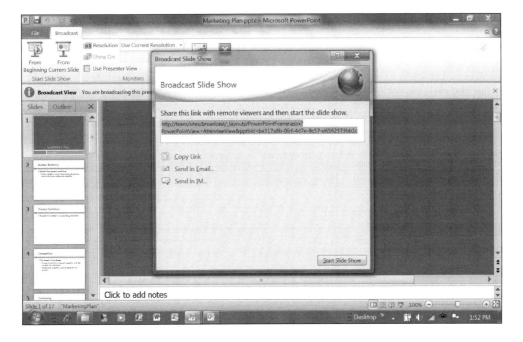

The remote viewers will receive the link you e-mail or copy and paste into an invitation. The remote viewer clicks on the link you sent to join the broadcast:

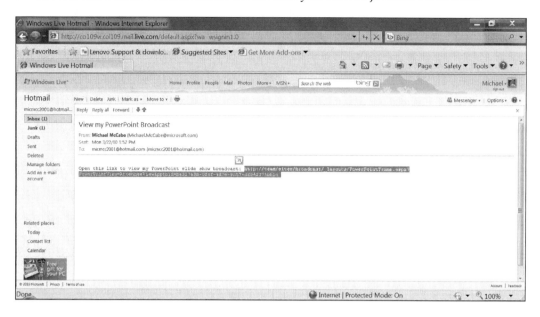

This is what the person who is broadcasting will see:

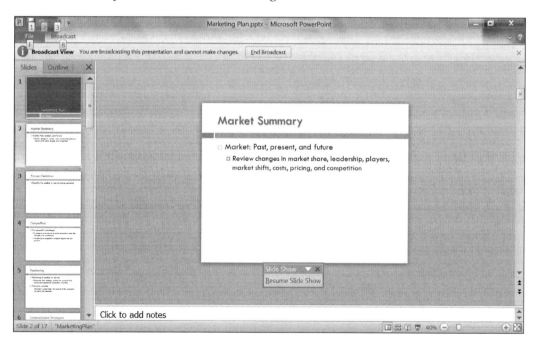

This is what those viewing the broadcast will see:

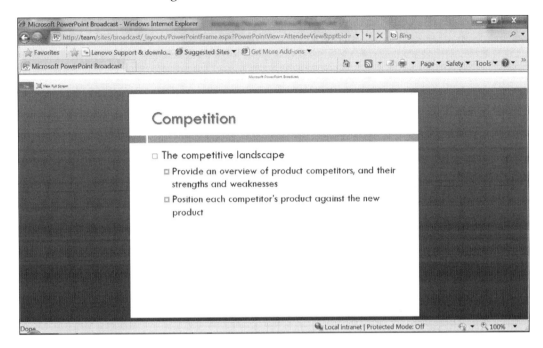

 The presentation that is being broadcast has to be hosted on a SharePoint 2010 site. The broadcaster must be using PowerPoint 2010. The viewer needs only a browser to see and follow the presentation.

Visio Web Services

In SharePoint 2007, Microsoft introduced Excel Web Services, allowing a SharePoint Server to serve up an Excel spreadsheet that could be viewed in a browser. Visio Web Services provide similar capability for Visio diagrams.

Visio Web Services allow users to view a Visio diagram in a web browser. Viewers do not need Visio installed on their computers.

The Visio Web Service is part of SharePoint Server 2010, and the shared diagram is a .vdw file that is created in Visio 2010. Authors of the files need the full Visio 2010 client installed on their computers. The file must be stored on a SharePoint 2010 site with the Visio Web Service running.

To share a Visio 2010 diagram using the Visio Web service, follow these steps:

1. Open the diagram in Visio 2010.

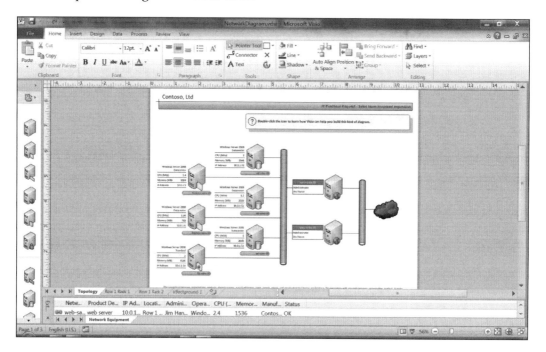

2. Click on the **File** tab, and choose **Save to SharePoint**.
3. Under File **Types**, choose **Web Drawing (*.vdw)**.
4. Click on **Save As**.
5. Name the file and click **Save**.

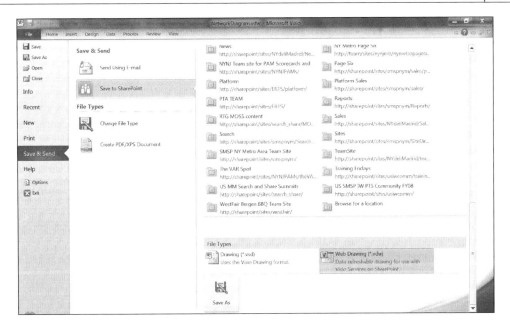

The file will be converted to *.vdw format and saved on the SharePoint site selected. When a viewer opens the file, it will be viewable in a browser:

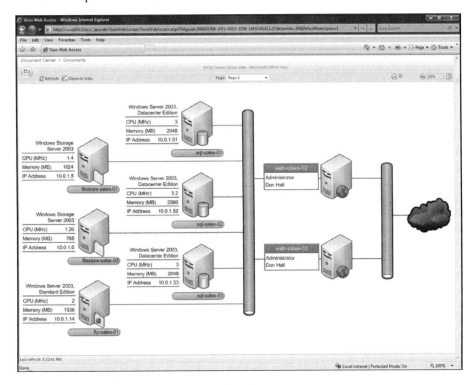

When a diagram is connected to data sources, online users can see your real-time information in the diagram using their browsers. They can drill down into the data, even if they do not have Visio installed on their computers. They can pan and zoom in the diagram, follow hyperlinks in objects, and refresh data using the Ribbon tools.

Limitations of Office integration with SharePoint

The Office 2010 integration with SharePoint makes it much easier to create your documents in applications such as Word, Excel, and PowerPoint, and then share them on SharePoint. However, there are some limitations to be aware of:

- Broadcasting slideshows does not offer the full collaborative capabilities of web conferencing that are available with Lync or Live Meeting. Those viewing the broadcast, for example, would not be able to make changes or download the slides during the broadcast.
- The features described in this chapter all require you to run Office 2010.

Summary

SharePoint 2010 integrates tightly with Office 2010. This is significant because it saves users time by putting the capabilities of SharePoint in the applications where people do most of their work.

So, we have taken a look at some of the most useful points of integration between Office 2010 and SharePoint 2010, including:

- Ribbon interface
- Office Web Apps
- Co-authoring
- Social Computing
- Backstage
- Slide Show Broadcasting
- Visio Web Services

In the next chapter, we will explore how SharePoint can help you capture information called **Metadata** to make it easier to categorize documents uniformly. **Metadata** enables you to navigate document libraries more efficiently. It will also relate to improving Search in SharePoint, which we will discuss in *Chapter 9, Getting better search results with SharePoint 2010*.

8

Managing Metadata

In this chapter, we will describe the basic terminology and concepts of metadata, and where and how to apply it. We will take a look at how metadata is managed with the **Term Store Management Tool** console and how it is applied using the SharePoint and Office 2010 **User Interface (UI)**.

We will cover:

- What is metadata?
- Benefits of metadata
- Taxonomies
- Folksonomies
- When to use managed vs. normal metadata?
- How to apply metadata to content?
- Searching and navigating with metadata

What is metadata?

While the search engine in SharePoint can do full-text search on the contents of a document, you often want to base your search on information about the document, such as its creator, the last person to modify the document, or the dates of creation or edits. This information *about* a document is called **metadata**.

For documents where the content is not searchable, such as audio and video, metadata becomes even more important for providing users with richer search results.

Metadata is everywhere in Microsoft SharePoint Server 2010. For example, metadata helps you navigate SharePoint document libraries, add tags to wikis and blogs, and apply terms to documents stored on SharePoint from within the document or from Backstage.

The following images (clockwise from upper left) illustrate using metadata to navigate a document library, applying metadata in Word 2010, viewing metadata in Office 2010 Backstage, and applying tags on a SharePoint 2010 website:

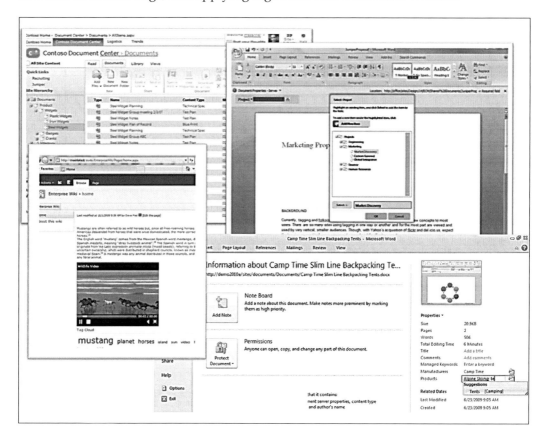

For most organizations, SharePoint has become a mission-critical content repository to store documents, customer information, employees' skills, and areas of expertise.

So, it is vital that users have a quick and easy way to retrieve the information stored in SharePoint. Whether that requires finding a customer-ready presentation about a product, a spreadsheet with pricing information for a distribution partner, or a contract to be signed by a client, being able to find the most accurate and up-to-date information using SharePoint's search tools is critical.

The most important advantage of using managed metadata is that it makes it easier and faster to find information stored in SharePoint. Using managed metadata in SharePoint 2010 improves search results, reducing multiple search iterations and consequently the time it takes to find what you are looking for.

Another important benefit of managed metadata is that it can be used as a navigation tool in libraries and lists. Instead of investing time and effort in creating and naming folders, and then moving documents into folders, you can take advantage of the managed metadata hierarchy as a navigational tool with much less effort. By simply adding managed metadata to documents as you create them, you are fitting them into the hierarchy. Unlike using folders, the managed metadata hierarchy is shared, and will be consistent across SharePoint sites and site collections.

When documents are stored in SharePoint, metadata can be applied in a systematic way using the Managed Metadata tool. This tool is the vehicle for defining a taxonomy, or hierarchical list of the terms that can be applied to documents.

 Normal metadata, of course, can always be applied in non-managed fields for adding dates, usernames, and calculated values, for example.

Consider that before tools such as SharePoint, we tried in a very primitive way to include metadata about files on our hard drives or in file shares. But, the tools in that environment, namely the filename and the directory folder name where the file was saved, were clearly very limited. The obvious problems with those tools were and still are:

- Size limitation (after all, how big a file or folder name do you really want?)
- Inconsistencies in naming
- The lack of a robust search facility to retrieve information (even if you can squeeze it into the file or folder name)

In general, metadata refers to terms applied to documents to provide information about those documents beyond their actual contents. Full-text search tools can help you find information in a document, while providing metadata terms to identify attributes of documents enhances the results that can be provided by search.

In SharePoint, metadata refers to the information about an item other than the content of the item itself. Metadata can be stored with a document in SharePoint. The document properties stored with Office files are examples of metadata, but SharePoint can store information about a file beyond what may already be captured with document properties.

For Microsoft Office documents, many properties are automatically saved with the file. However, you may have additional keywords or descriptive items you want to save with the document to give an easier way for people to find it when searching.

For example, if you are working on a customer proposal for a law firm, you might want to add metadata indicating that it has to do with legal services. You may also want to include information about other people working on the proposal, or the type of area of legal service the proposal relates to by including terms such as *real estate law* or *contracts*. The metadata management capabilities of SharePoint 2010 allow you to easily include such metadata with a document file stored on SharePoint.

This is important for non-Office files that may not contain their own fields for document properties. SharePoint can store many different items or file types: a Word file, a PowerPoint presentation, an Excel spreadsheet, but also PDF files, photographs, and even videos.

 Besides Microsoft Office files, the file formats supported by SharePoint 2010 include: `.pdf`, `.rtf`, `.tif`, `.txt`, `.ascx`, `.asp`, `.cmd`, `.css`, `.eml`, `.exch`, `.html`, `.msg`, `.nsf`, `.odc`, `.php`, `.url`, and `.xml`.

The disadvantages of not having managed metadata become obvious once you begin to apply it. Without managed metadata, users had to create their own ways of classifying documents. The tools for doing this were document names, folders, and moving documents into folders. That was more time-consuming, inconsistent across libraries and sites, and did nothing to improve search results or navigation.

Managing metadata

Users normally supply metadata using the document properties of the file, or keyword fields in SharePoint. With SharePoint 2010, users can also **tag** documents or add their own **ratings**. This metadata is unmanaged in the sense that it is not pre-defined. Users can add new terms. Unmanaged metadata is often inconsistent, with multiple synonyms for a similar term.

Managed metadata refers to a hierarchical collection of centrally managed terms that you can define and use as attributes for items in Microsoft SharePoint Server 2010. The main difference between managed and unmanaged metadata is that managed metadata provides a way to standardize terms and provide a consistency across documents. The advantage is that users can then search and navigate with the standardized terms.

In Microsoft SharePoint 2010, enterprise metadata management is a set of features that enable taxonomists, librarians, and administrators to create and manage terms and sets of terms across an organization.

Taxonomies

A **taxonomy** is essentially a system of classifying things. A taxonomy provides a standard set of terms that users can apply consistently across documents.

A manufacturing company, for example, might classify their products this way:

- Metals
  - Brass
  - Aluminum
  - Copper
  - Nickel
  - Silver

- Plastics
  - Polyurethane
  - Vinyl

- Fabrics
  - Leather
    - Calfskin
    - Cowhide
  - Cloth
    - Cotton
    - Wool
  - Synthetic
    - Rayon
    - Nylon
    - Dacron

 Note the hierarchical nature of the taxonomy with its terms and sub-terms.

In order to provide consistency in the terms used across an organization, taxonomies are set up. These taxonomies are usually carefully planned and designed by a group within the organization that is familiar with various aspects of a business. They define the terms that will most frequently be assigned to documents as metadata to provide identifiers that will, in turn, give users more useful results when searching. The taxonomies are defined hierarchically so that terms can be logically grouped together in a nested hierarchy.

Hierarchical taxonomies are not only useful when used for retrieving documents because they provide consistency across the organization, but they make the user's job of assigning metadata quick and easy as well. In an Office 2010 document that is stored on SharePoint 2010, for example, a user will have access to the defined taxonomy and could simply pull down a list of terms and select those to be applied to the document.

Enterprise metadata management in SharePoint and Office 2010 provides the infrastructure and tools for managing and applying metadata. Administrators and taxonomists employ the Metadata Manager to create flat or hierarchical lists of terms, kept in term stores. Metadata management tools in SharePoint and Office also allow users to easily apply the terms to documents.

Term store management tool

The term store management tool is used to create and manage terms and term sets. With the appropriate permissions you can use the tool to create, add, modify, and delete terms and term sets.

 Normally, end users will not have access to the SharePoint central administration tools to manage terms sets, but it helps to see how the term store is set up so you will understand the advantages for end users.

You can manage terms in a hierarchy within a term set. You can also turn keywords into managed terms. In this way, keywords that users contribute to a SharePoint site with social tagging can become part of the managed metadata hierarchy.

To access the Term Store Management Tool:

1. Open the SharePoint Central Administration Console.
2. Under **Application Management**, select **Managed service applications**.

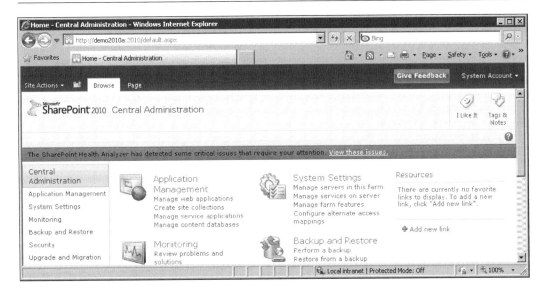

Managing Metadata Service

By selecting **Managed Metadata Service** on the left, an administrator can give others permission to manage the service in the **PROPERTIES** tab on the right. Other settings such as **Default Language** and **Working Languages** can be set here.

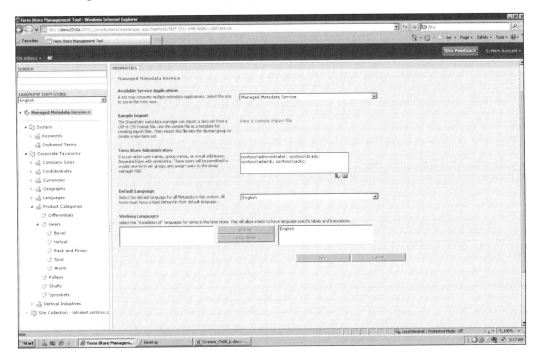

Groups, Term Sets, and Terms

Under **Managed Metadata Service** you will see **Groups** listed. In the view above, for example, the groups are System and **Corporate Taxonomy**.

The groups are divided hierarchically into **Term Sets** (**Product Categories** in the preceding example) and **Terms**. Term sets contain terms (in the preceding example **Differentials, Gears,** and so on are terms within the term set **Product Categories**).

Terms can be further nested in the hierarchy into **parent** and **child** terms. In this example, **Gears** is the parent term for **Bevel, Helical,** and **Worm**.

> The **System Group** is provided by default. **Term Sets** for **Keywords** and **Orphaned Terms** are stored there. These **Term Sets** are flat; that is, not hierarchical.

Corporate Taxonomy in the preceding screenshot is a group that has been set up by those responsible for creating the managed metadata taxonomy. To access and manage the taxonomy, those users require appropriate permissions.

Metadata managers, librarians, and taxonomists will be the primary users of the **Term Store Management Tool**. The tool provides an easy way to create, manage, and share metadata.

Here, you see the properties for **Rack and Pinion**. Taxonomists add and modify the properties with this part of the tool. By pulling down an action menu for a selected term, users can **create** new terms, as well as **copy** and **move** terms. They can also **delete terms** or **merge** them to eliminate ambiguities. To **deprecate** a term means to take it out of use without deleting it.

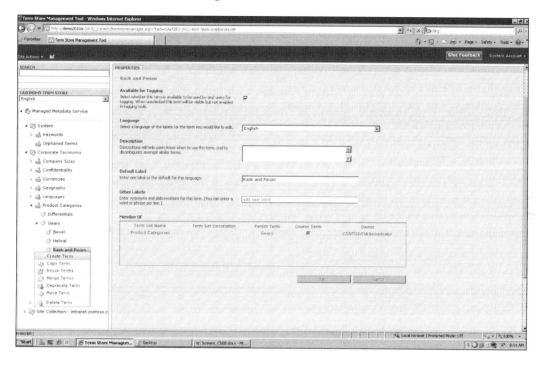

Keywords

Keywords are unmanaged metadata that are not hierarchically arranged. They are kept as a flat list. **Keywords** include the tags and properties users can add outside of the managed metadata structure of a taxonomy. Social tagging on My Sites, blogs, and wikis would be an example of applying **Keywords**.

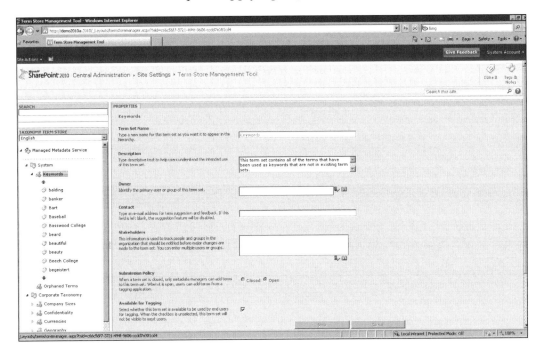

Folksonomies

A **Folksonomy** is an informal flat list of terms. Folksonomies are collected by social tagging in SharePoint, and a user can assign terms to documents, blogs, wikis, or in fact most of the information in SharePoint.

Social tags are metadata that is applied to items in the social networking features that are available in Microsoft Office 2010. For example, you might want to apply one or more descriptive tags to a blog entry.

In some ways, social tags behave similarly to terms in a taxonomy term set; if the value requested is not an existing term or you do not want to use an existing term, Microsoft SharePoint Server 2010 adds a new entry to the keywords in the **Group**.

Social tags, unlike managed metadata terms, give you more flexibility. Managed metadata can require permission, or an approval process, to add a new term. Unmanaged metadata can be applied more quickly because no approval process is required. Folksonomies do not have the rigid structure or tight control by a select group that taxonomies do, nor do they have the consistency of an organizationally defined taxonomy. They do, however, provide users with the ability to introduce new terms that could enhance the ability to search for and quickly find the best information available on a given topic.

Folksonomies can also inform taxonomies when terms introduced via a folksonomy become incorporated into the organization's taxonomy after appropriate review. In that respect, the taxonomy does not remain static, but can grow and become more current as new terms emerge out of a folksonomy.

When to use managed metadata and normal metadata

Managed metadata is useful in situations where there is the need for consistent application of terms across an organization. This is often the case in professional services organizations. For example, a large, globally dispersed consulting organization might want to track projects and consultant skills so that expertise can be shared and reused across the organization. Managed metadata applied from an authoritative taxonomy allows them to ensure consistency across the organization.

Managed metadata makes it easier to find information about their projects and expertise because it improves the search results they will get, as well as providing the taxonomy's structure for navigation in document libraries. Additionally, managed metadata can be shared across SharePoint site collections in large organizations.

Industries such as financial services, legal, pharmaceutical, and health care would also typically be able to benefit from managed metadata infrastructures, as would organizations subject to government or industry regulatory requirements.

Normal metadata that is applied with unmanaged keyword fields, tags, ratings, or notes is more appropriate in situations where flexibility is more important. For example, in product development or media organizations, new terms might need to be incorporated easily. In those situations, the more rigid structure of managed metadata would be a hindrance to adding new terms and ultimately being able to find information based on them.

Unmanaged keyword fields allow you to enter other data types such as date and time, calculated fields, and usernames that would not be available with managed metadata.

Managed metadata, on the other hand, provides greater security. Entering new terms can be restricted to specific groups of users or roles. The display of some metadata may also be restricted. For example, human resources may want to restrict metadata that relates to salary grades so that only managers or HR personnel have access.

Applying metadata to content

The greatest benefits of applying metadata are the improved search results and easier navigation in libraries and lists. In order to realize those benefits it was important to make it much easier to enter metadata. SharePoint and Office 2010 do that by providing the tools to enter metadata wherever you are working with information. Whether you are in a SharePoint library or in Word, you can enter the metadata by choosing keywords from a drop-down list. Here, we will look at entering metadata both from SharePoint using a browser and from within an Office application such as Word.

In the past, most users had to use folders and filenames as substitutes for the tools that are now available for applying managed metadata in SharePoint and Office 2010. So, the metadata is not only consistent, but easier and less time-consuming for users to enter.

We will look here at applying metadata from within SharePoint and from within an Office application.

Working directly in SharePoint

Using a web browser and working directly in SharePoint libraries, items can be tagged by using the **Edit Item** from the drop-down menu.

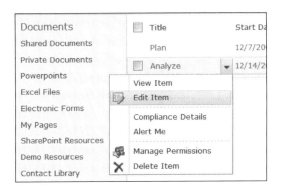

Metadata can be applied manually, or automatically using a workflow. By creating a column in a SharePoint library, and defining the column as managed metadata, users will be required to complete the field for that column when they create a new document or upload an existing document to the library.

When using document sets in SharePoint 2010, all documents in the set will inherit metadata that is applied to the parent document.

As the user types, matching keywords will appear in the list and can easily be selected.

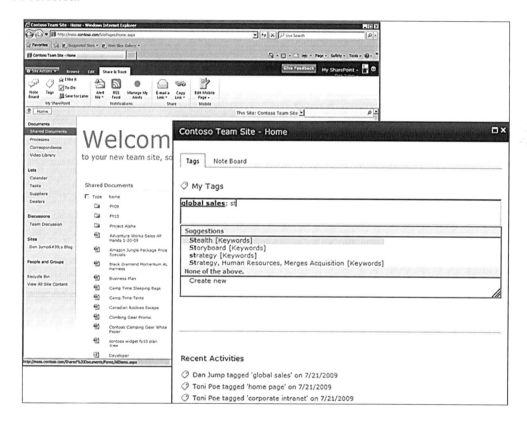

To add metadata to a list, you first need to add a managed metadata field by following these steps:

1. Open the list and click on **List Settings** in the **List Tools/List** tab.

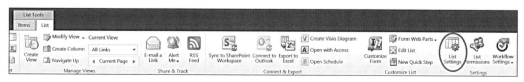

2. Under **Columns**, click **Add from existing site columns**.

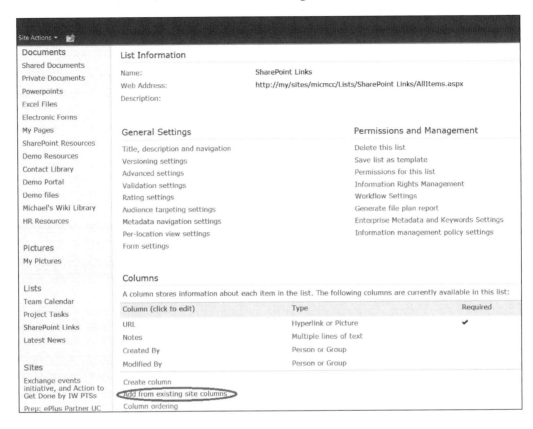

3. Add the column from a group you know contains managed metadata fields. In the following example, this is a field called **Enterprise Keywords**:

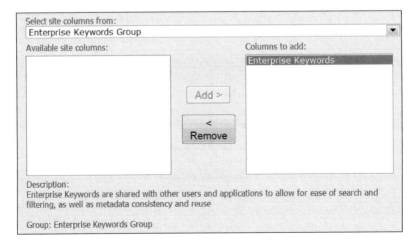

When editing an item from the list, you will now be able to apply managed metadata to the item from the taxonomy, as in the following example. When you begin typing a keyword, the taxonomy will show terms and term subsets available from the taxonomy's hierarchy.

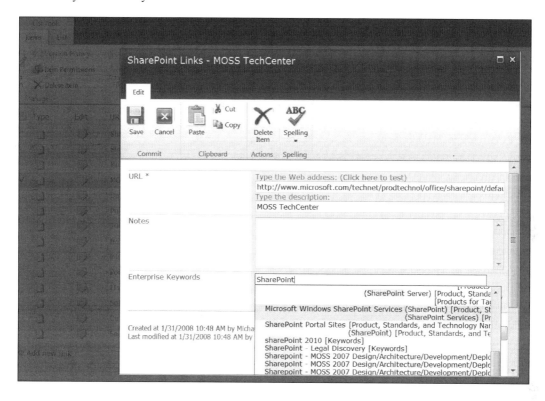

You can also include a default value in a managed metadata field. In **list settings**, select a managed term set from the managed metadata taxonomy, as illustrated in the following screenshot:

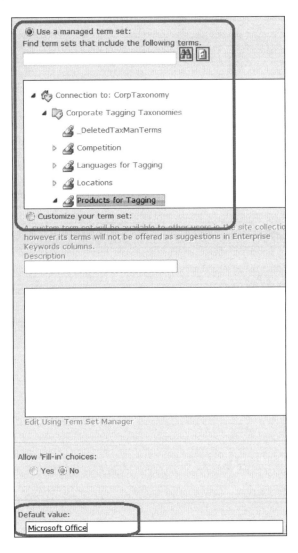

Chapter 8

The **Default value** is selected from a list of the valid terms in the selected set.

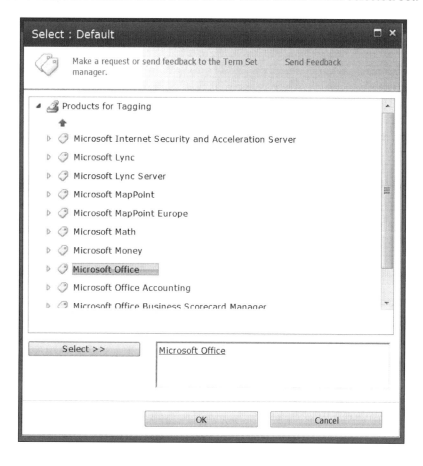

Working in Office client applications

The Document Information Panel allows for tagging in the authoring interface of the Office client.

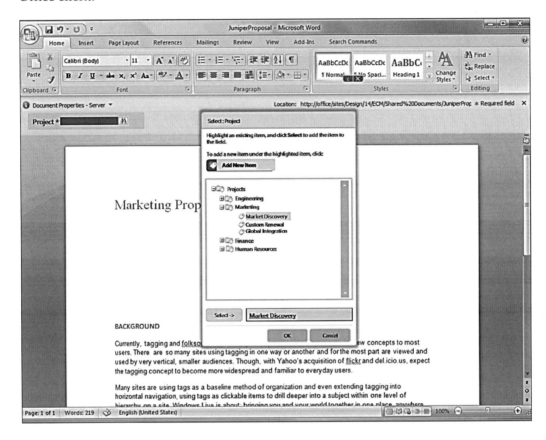

Backstage in all Office 2010 applications provides full access to managed metadata controls. Here, the **Info** tab in **Backstage** shows properties associated with the document that can be edited using the metadata management tools.

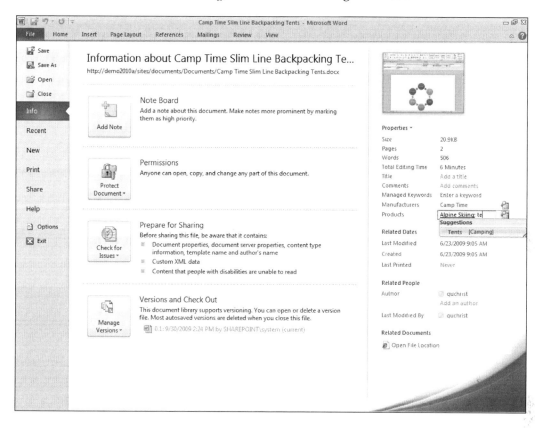

Navigating with metadata

Finding information becomes much easier with metadata-driven navigation in SharePoint 2010. Instead of having to create and name folders, and organize documents one-by-one into folders, metadata applied to the documents becomes the navigational tree for finding documents.

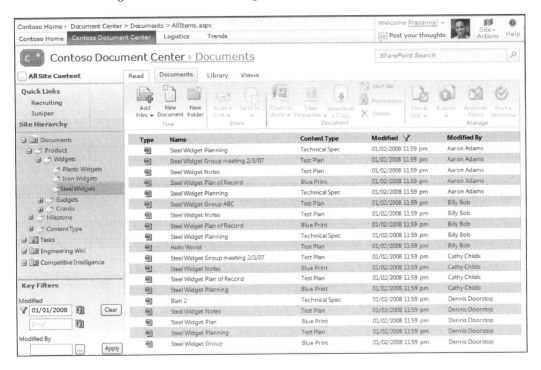

Navigating through documents using the managed metadata hierarchy, as shown in the preceding screenshot, is much more useful than folder tree navigation. Folder trees are an unmanaged and more cumbersome way of applying metadata.

Folder structures may vary from one library or list to another. Folders do not provide a standardized and consistent way of categorizing documents across sites and site collections the way managed metadata does.

The folder structure requires that you create and name the folders and place documents into them. You are already doing work to classify content, so you should not be reluctant to use managed metadata instead of folders. It will be less work for you and better results for navigating and searching content.

It makes much more sense to apply metadata from a taxonomy that has already been set up. The same terms from the taxonomy can be applied to documents in whatever library, site, or site collection they reside. And, the navigation is easier because it is provided automatically by the metadata hierarchy.

Applying metadata has become much easier with Office 2010 documents and SharePoint 2010. Metadata from SharePoint can be applied when working in a document. Libraries and lists in SharePoint 2010 can be set up to apply default metadata to documents saved there.

In the following screenshot, the metadata hierarchy appears when inserting a video into a PowerPoint presentation, making it easier to find the item and quickly complete the process:

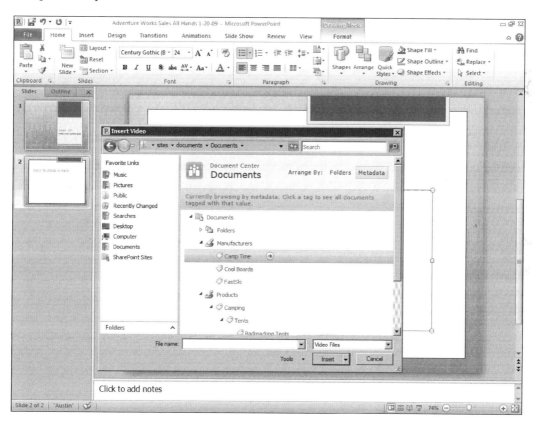

Subscriptions to tags enable users to receive updates and discover new information on content, people, projects, and much more, directly within their My Site.

The tools that SharePoint 2010 offers for creating, managing, and applying metadata provide a wide range of flexibility in terms of flexibility and scope.

The following image is a visualization of how metadata can be applied along those continuums:

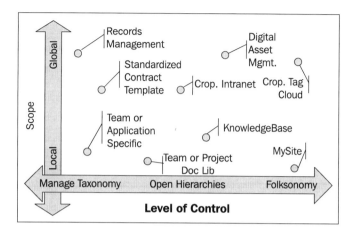

Managed taxonomies provide the control to maintain consistency and uniformity in applying metadata. Folksonomies, on the other hand, are more open and allow users to easily introduce new terms into the organization. Managed taxonomies can make it easier to find and manage standardized documents, while Folksonomies work better in the social relationships in SharePoint.

Discovery and action

Metadata in SharePoint 2010 enhances the user's ability to navigate, search, and interact with information more quickly and easily. They can find the information faster and take the steps required to complete a job.

Improving business processes

The presence of metadata can automate processes. Instead of having to create and name folders in a library, metadata can automatically build that navigational structure to guide users.

The experience becomes simpler and more intuitive with a logical structure to retrieve and take action on content.

Summary

In this chapter, we have taken a look at the types of metadata that can be applied in SharePoint 2010, ranging from hierarchical taxonomies to unstructured folksonomies. We have reviewed the administrative tools for managing hierarchical taxonomies. We have demonstrated the advantages users gain from taxonomies, especially when navigating document libraries with a large number of documents. And, finally, we have shown the range of applications where using different types of metadata can be applied appropriately.

The most important reason for using managed metadata is to have better search results when retrieving information. Not having metadata is an issue because it may require multiple searches and more time to find relevant information. You may even miss information that is related to your search.

Managed metadata makes it easier to navigate document libraries than with folders. You should use metadata instead of folders because the metadata navigational hierarchy is built dynamically from the information stored in your documents. You do not need to spend time building your own folder hierarchy-naming folders and placing documents into folders. The metadata hierarchy provides consistency across libraries. You do not need to create a folder structure for each library.

In the section on applying metadata, we have seen how easy it is to apply metadata from within SharePoint or in the Office applications. So, there is no need to dread adding metadata to documents. You would actually be doing this anyway when naming folders and placing content there. You can even set default metadata for specific libraries or lists, saving you more time and improving your search results.

The advantages that metadata provide will be discussed further in the next chapter where we explore the search capabilities in SharePoint 2010. We will also see the benefit of metadata as it applies to social networking when we talk about tagging and ratings in *Chapter 12, Blogs, Wikis, and Other Web 2.0 Features.*

9
Getting Better Search Results with SharePoint 2010

For as long as companies have been doing business, they have been looking for ways to find information quicker, and not just in one system, but across systems. This is especially true in a *knowledge economy* where information, ideas, and execution are what separate winners from losers.

In this chapter, we will look at how you can access information stored in SharePoint using the search tools provided by SharePoint 2010. We will look first at the query interface that you use to tell SharePoint what you are looking for.

Next, we will show how search results are presented and how you can refine a search using advanced search tools. You will see how you can uncover not only information in documents, but also expertise from colleagues' My Site profiles. Finally, we will explore the rich guidance that comes with search results.

The topics we will cover in this chapter are:

- Search basics
- Benefits of SharePoint 2010 search
- Search interface
- Search results
- People search
- Search guidance
- Search scenario

Search basics

There are some simple questions users frequently ask about SharePoint's search capabilities:

Question	Answer
Are the contents of a document searchable?	Yes.
Can a document be searched if a user does not have access rights to it?	No, search results will not display items for which the user does not have access rights. This is called **security trimming**.
Is all content searchable?	Yes, this includes documents, list items, URL links, and keywords.
Is search the quickest way to find information on a SharePoint site?	Yes. If you do not already know where the information is stored on SharePoint, search is the fastest way to find information.
Sometimes I upload a document, but it does not show up in search results. Why?	There may be a delay depending on how the SharePoint site's indexers are configured. This may take a few minutes or longer depending on when **incremental search crawls** are scheduled and how much content needs to be crawled.

> A search crawl is a process to examine content on a site for indexing. An incremental crawl examines only content that has been added to a site since the last crawl.

Question	Answer
Why do I get search results different than those of a colleague when we both use the same search criteria?	You and your colleague may have different access rights to content on a SharePoint site. If you do not have access rights to an item, the item will not display on the search results page.

Benefits of SharePoint 2010 Search

Microsoft has invested heavily in SharePoint 2010. These are some of the improvements in search with SharePoint 2010:

Feature	Description
Index limit	No longer a limit of 50 million items.
Query syntax	Can use **AND, OR, NOT** keywords in search query.
Wildcard search	Using * in search query.
Refiners	Refiners are shown in the panel on the search results page so you can filter the results (using metadata and tags). This functionality is supported in all SharePoint editions.
Social people search	Phonetic name matching (returns names that sound similar to what the user has typed as a query and all variations of common names, including nicknames); exploring results by name, title, and expertise; real-time presence awareness with Microsoft Lync server.
Social distance	SharePoint builds a model of your regular interactions based on e-mail conversations and group memberships that it uses to organize people search results based on social distance, where, for example, a direct colleague appears before someone three degrees removed.

SharePoint 2010 can index and query data sources not only stored on SharePoint itself, but also on sites and databases outside of SharePoint. SharePoint can index:

- SharePoint sites
- File shares
- Websites
- Microsoft Exchange public folders
- Databases
- **Line-of-business (LOB)** applications

Having access to multiple sources of information available in one place can be a competitive advantage to companies providing professional services. Their consultants can access and repurpose intellectual property held within the firm, and at the same time integrate it with information available externally. While the maximum number of indexed documents has increased, performance has also been improved. So, even though SharePoint 2010 can search for more documents, the time it takes to return your search results has been reduced.

The benefits of many of the improvements are richer results that arrive faster.

For example, when searching for expertise, the people search results will display more information from each person's My Site profile than was the case with SharePoint 2007. The following example shows the person's description, areas of expertise, and project experience. This information can often eliminate the need to click through to the My Site itself.

Christine Koch
Managing Director
Engineering
(206) 555-2987
Seattle, WA
christk@contoso.com

» Browse in organizational chart
» By Christine Koch

My Colleague

About Me:
The Target **Market Research** project provided me Web Methods experience. I enjoy projects involving Wireless Server. My past projects here at Contoso include Target **Market Research** , working with our client company, Litware, Inc.. I grew up on the West Coast, and went to PawPaw College. In my spare time, I enjoy ping pong.

Ask Me About:
Enterprise Revenue.0::Spreadsheets::Industry Best Practices::Enterprise Architecture:: Lean Six Sigma ...

Past Projects:
Target **Market Research**

Another example is the **View in Browser** link. With the optional installation of Office Web Apps, SharePoint 2010 offers the ability to view Microsoft Office files in the browser. This gives you an easier and faster way to evaluate the relevance of the search result to your needs. You can quickly view the contents of the document without waiting to launch the file's application.

In this chapter, we will take a look at the new and improved features in SharePoint 2010 Search from the user's point of view.

Search interface

You can search in SharePoint using the search box (on the right in the following screenshot) to enter your keyword or search term. The search box appears on most sites and pages in SharePoint out of the box.

 If you create custom pages, you can add the search box web part to them. *Chapter 13, Pages and Web Parts* discusses how to add web parts to a page on a SharePoint site.

Search box

The **search center** is another option. The search center is a site in itself and can be accessed from a tab on a parent site (on the left of the preceding screenshot).

Search Center

The search center interface is simple and clean with just a search box on the page. The search center is useful as a central place, usually at the top level of a SharePoint portal hierarchy, where users can search content stored across sites rather than just the content on an individual team site, for example.

You can select a specific scope to focus your search. In the following example, the default scopes **All Sites** and **People** are shown:

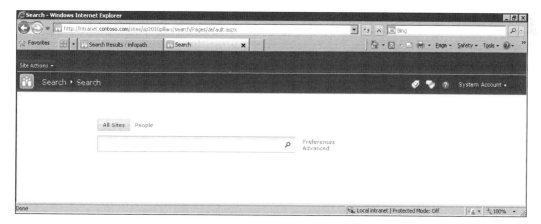

> **Scopes** define specific sites or data repositories for your search. **All Sites** and **People** are default scopes in SharePoint. Administrators can define custom scopes. For example, a scope could be defined for the legal department that only shows results from a site where contracts are stored. By selecting that scope, they reduce the search results to those documents they work with most often.

Advanced search

With SharePoint 2010 you can enter complex criteria for searches that were not possible in SharePoint 2007. You can use combinations with connectors such as **AND**, **OR**, or **NOT**. For example, you could do a search using (**Finance** AND **Legal**), or (**SharePoint Search** OR **Windows Search**).

But, an easier way to enter multiple criteria for your search is to use the **advanced search interface**. On the search center page (as shown previously) next to the search box, click the **Advanced** link and you will see the advanced search interface as shown in the following screenshot:

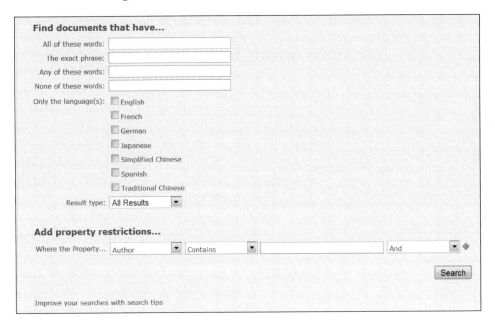

The advanced search form allows to you search for multiple terms, exact phrases, or exclude terms. You can specify languages or the type of result you are looking for, such as Word, Excel, or PowerPoint files. You can even restrict your results to criteria based on properties of the results, such as **author** or **modified date**. By clicking the + sign after the first **Property**, you add more fields and criteria.

Entering your criteria is the most convenient way to combine multiple criteria. You can visualize them in the form, and avoid errors when typing them as one long string.

Prefix matching

The * character can be used as a wildcard at the end of a string you use in your search criterion.

 The wildcard character can only be used at the end of a string; therefore, in SharePoint terms its use is referred to as **prefix matching** instead of **wildcard**.

Entering com* could return **company**, **communications**, or **computer**, for example.

Name matching

SharePoint 2010 search will return phonetic matches and nicknames when you search for a name. For example, searching for **John** will return **Jon**, or **Jean**. Searching for **Jeffrey** will return **Geoffrey**, but also **Jeff** and **Geoff**.

This can be especially useful in a global company, where employee names are often long and difficult to remember.

Search results

The search results page lists the matching items with icons to indicate the type of result. You will know from the icon what the file type is, or if it is a SharePoint portal or Internet site, for example.

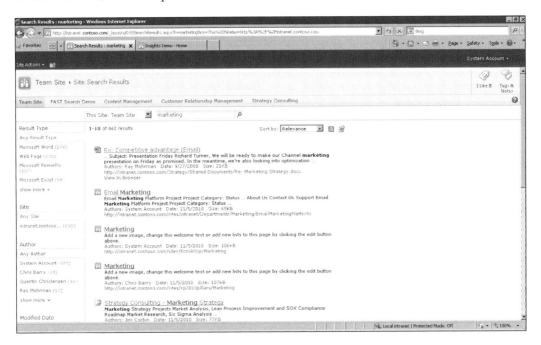

In addition to the actual results, the page displays several tools for narrowing your search. These include the contextual information, links, and the sorting tool.

Context

Your search results will show the matching word or phrase in a brief section of text from the document where it was found. You can then better decide from the context whether the item is actually something useful to you.

The actual matching text is highlighted in the result so you can easily see where it appears.

Document properties, such as **Authors**, **Date**, and **Size** also appear in the result:

> Re: Competitive advantage (Email)
> ... Subject: Presentation Friday Richard Turner, We will be ready to make our Channel **marketing** presentation on Friday as promised. In the meantime, we're also looking into optimization ...
> Authors: Ray Mohrman   Date: 9/27/2008   Size: 21KB
> http://intranet.contoso.com/Strategy/Shared Documents/Re- Marketing Strategy.docx
> View In Browser

Link

A link appears below the text with the URL of the item. You can retrieve the item by clicking the URL link.

If you are using Office Web Apps, you will also see a link to **View in browser**. This allows you to view the document in the browser without launching its full application, such as Word or Excel.

If you have **FAST** for SharePoint installed, you will also see a thumbnail showing the contents of Microsoft Office files. Clicking on the thumbnail allows you to scroll through the entire file right from within the search results page. You will not have to launch the application, or even open another browser window.

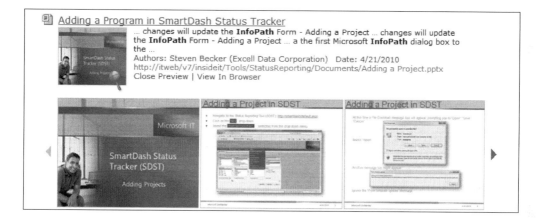

Sorting

By default, SharePoint lists your search results by relevance. Relevance is determined by a number of factors. A document becomes more relevant the more your search team appears in the document. The more often a document has been opened by others in previous searches, the more relevance it has.

The **sort by** drop-down menu allows you to choose how to list your search results. The default sort order is **Relevance**. You also have the option to sort by **Date (Newest)** or **Date (Oldest)**.

People search

The People search is a scope that shows results matching your criteria from individual My Sites and profile information contained there.

The results for People search in SharePoint 2010 provide more information from a person's profile than was the case in SharePoint 2007. This saves time because you no longer have to click through to the profile for basic information about the person.

The results page shows contact details and links to the person's organizational chart. The **About Me** and **Responsibilities** sections from the person's profile are included as a part of the result, as shown in the following screenshot:

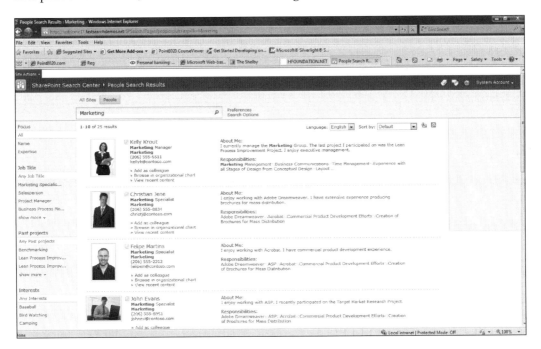

Social distance

The default sort order for the People scope is **Social Distance**. People closer to you on the organizational chart will be listed first. People designated as colleagues by you will be listed next. Then, colleagues of colleagues will show.

This way you will know if people with whom you already have a relationship can help you find what you are looking for, or have the expertise you need.

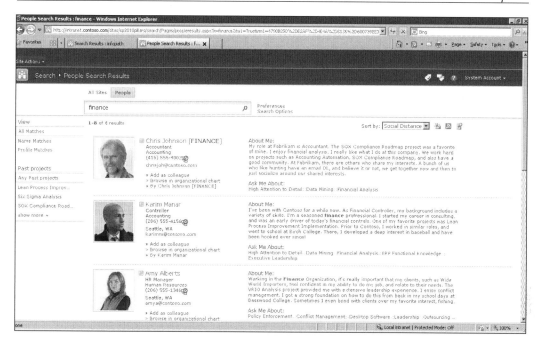

You can easily change the sort order to list the people by name instead of by social distance.

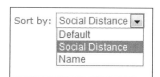

Search guidance

As you search with SharePoint 2010 you will see guidance along the way to help uncover relevant information, and focus on results of the highest value to you. The guidance tools we will look at include:

- Best Bets.
- Refiners.
- Did you mean?
- Suggestions for related searches.

Best Bets

Best Bets appear at the top of a search results page. The Best Bets are designated by an administrator. By associating keywords to the Best Bet, they will appear at the top of the list when the keyword or term is used to search.

Best Bets are chosen based on the frequency that users select the site within search results. Best Bets help users distinguish the sites that may provide the most information related to their search.

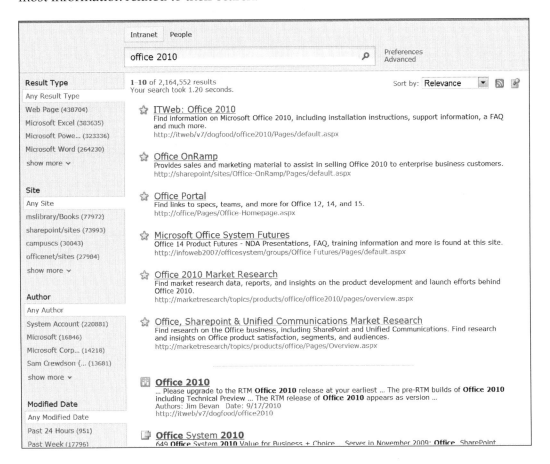

Refiners

Refiners will appear along the left-hand side of the search results page. The refiners list is built dynamically from the search results. They sort the results by type, such as **Web Page**, **Microsoft Excel**, or **Microsoft PowerPoint**. Other refiner categories may be **Site**, **Author**, or **Modified Date**, depending on properties from the search results.

You may be looking for a presentation on *marketing*. After searching for results, you can narrow down the list to just PowerPoint files by clicking the refiner for that result type.

Or, once you see the results you may decide that you only want to see results by a certain author. Refiners enable this so that you can quickly focus in on the information that is most valuable to you.

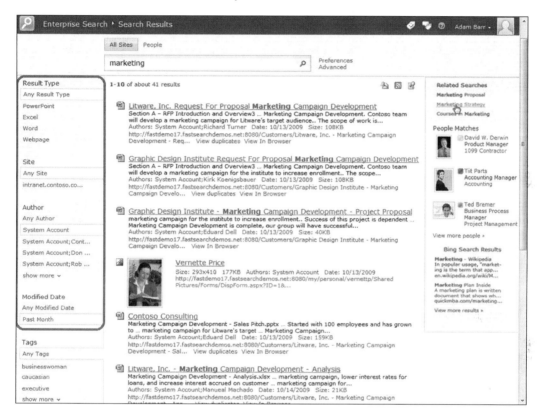

Did you mean?

The **Did you mean?** prompt will appear below the search box when you mistype your search criteria. You may make a typographical error, or misspell a word. *Did you mean?* will alert you to the error and offer a suggestion to correct it. By clicking on the suggested correction, you can immediately rerun the search to get to your desired results.

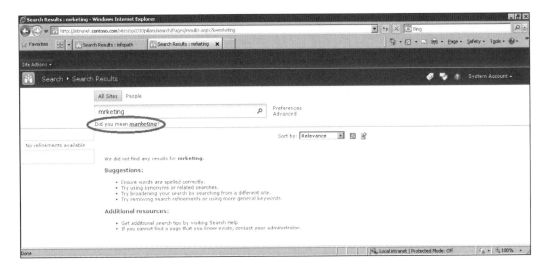

Suggestions for related searches

The SharePoint results page will often suggest searches that have been done by others that may be related to your search. A list of these related searches appears in the upper-right of the search results page. The list is built from previous searches done on the site, and is based on the frequency of the search. The more often a search has been done, the more likely it is to appear on the list.

These suggested searches are one more way that SharePoint 2010 will guide you to results that may be of greater value to you, based on others' experience.

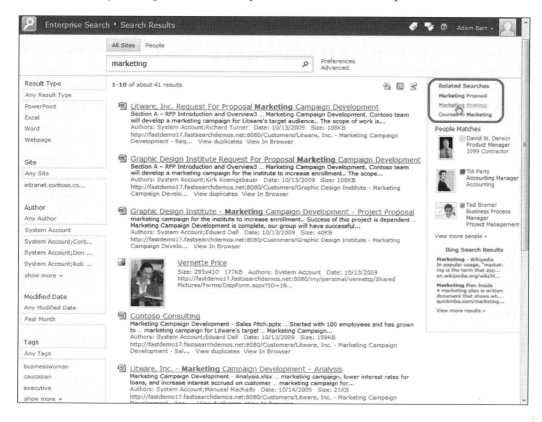

Search scenario

Let's look at a business scenario that puts SharePoint 2010 search capabilities to use.

Brad is a product manager looking for market feedback on a new product. He goes to his intranet search center and enters `market research`.

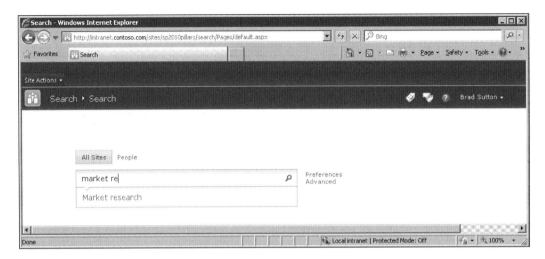

Notice that as he types, a suggestion appears. He can click to accept it, and the search results will appear.

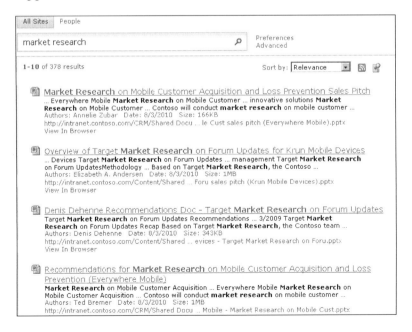

Because Brad has Office Web Apps installed, he can click **View in Browser** to see the PowerPoint file in the first search result.

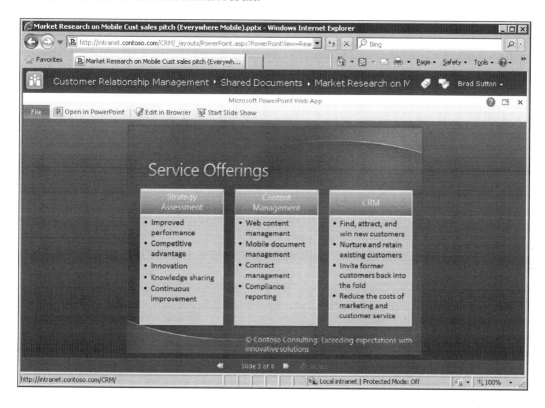

This saves Brad time because he sees the file contents displayed in the browser. He does not have to wait for PowerPoint to load. He can page through the slides to review the content. From here he could also open the file in PowerPoint, edit it in the browser, or launch it as a slideshow.

Brad, however, decides this is not the material he needs. He goes back to the previous page showing his results. He decides to look for expertise on the topic and clicks the **People** tab.

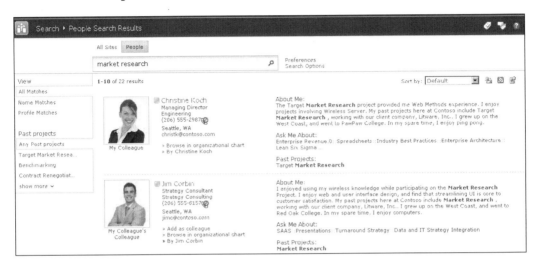

He sees his manager, **Christine Koch**, at the top of the results because the default sort order is by social relevance. Those closest to Brad on the organization chart will appear at the top of the list.

Brad decides to use the **Browse in organization chart** link on Christine's profile to find colleagues who may be able to help him find what he needs.

There, Brad views a graphical presentation of the organization showing managers, peers, and direct reports. He sees John Evans from the marketing team who has helped him before. He clicks on John's name and views content from John's **My Site**.

He finds there the customer satisfaction data and product information he is looking for. Brad's search has taken him to the data and the people he needs to do his job.

In this scenario, we have seen Brad use SharePoint search to find relevant information from documents and expertise from people. He uses tools such as **View in Browser** to evaluate the relevance of content to his search. He extends his search to people with expertise related to his search. He finds what he needs using tools such as organizational browsing and the content section of a colleague's My Site.

Summary

In this chapter, we have seen how SharePoint 2010 has improved the search interface with such capabilities as the advanced search screen, wildcards (or **prefix matching**), and name matching (including phonetic searches and nickname searches).

SharePoint 2010 search results provide more information on the initial results page. The people search, for example, surfaces more information directly onto the results page from the profile on each person's My Site. Evaluating the content in a search result becomes faster and easier with the **View in Browser** capability.

We have taken a look at the guidance SharePoint 2010 provides as you conduct a search. This includes suggestions for related searches, best bets, and even alternatives when you misspell or make a typographical error.

In the next chapter, we will look at how you can automate the process of checking for new results for searches you have saved.

10
Alerts and Notifications

Alerts and notifications are important tools for automatically keeping track of information stored in lists and libraries, as discussed in *Chapter 4, List Management*. They also keep you in touch with workflow processes (*Chapter 6, Workflows Fundamentals*), whether you need to manage the workflow or are being requested to complete tasks assigned in the workflow.

In this chapter, you will learn how **alerts** work and how they send **notifications** with links to actions you can take.

We will discuss how to set up these alerts and the selections you can make to define how an alert will operate. We will show how to manage alerts; that is, how to modify, delete, and add new alerts.

We will describe the notifications you receive as e-mail messages about what has changed, and the actions you can take based on the changes.

What is an alert?

Alerts notify you automatically when things change in SharePoint. When someone adds to, edits, or deletes a document from a library, for example, you can automatically receive a notification that the change has taken place. Alerts save you from having to continually go back to your libraries and lists to check for changes.

You can set up your alerts with several options. For example, you can choose to have the alert sent as soon as the change takes place, or have a summary of all changes in a day or at the end of a week.

You can also filter alerts by choosing only to be notified of deletions, or only edits, or only new documents.

You can set alerts for:

- Lists
- Libraries
- Documents
- List items
- Pages
- Task lists
- Calendars
- Searches
- Discussions

Creating alerts

To create an alert, select the drop-down menu next to your name on your SharePoint site, as shown in the following screenshot, and choose **My Settings**:

On the screen that appears, you will see your user information for the site with three links:

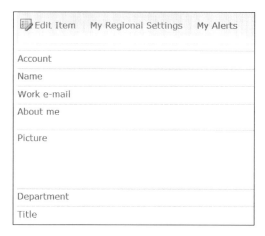

Selecting **My Alerts** will list any alerts you have already created. On that page, you will see two options:

- **Add Alert**
- **Delete Selected Alerts**

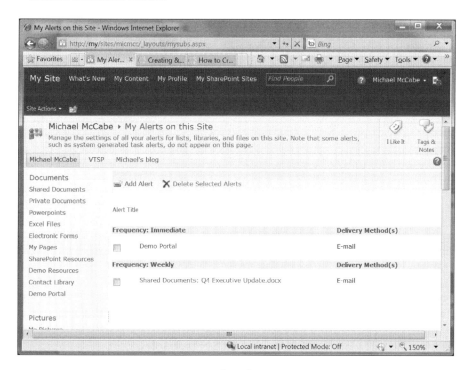

By choosing **Add Alert** and selecting the list or document library for which you want to create an alert, you open a page where you can select settings for the alert.

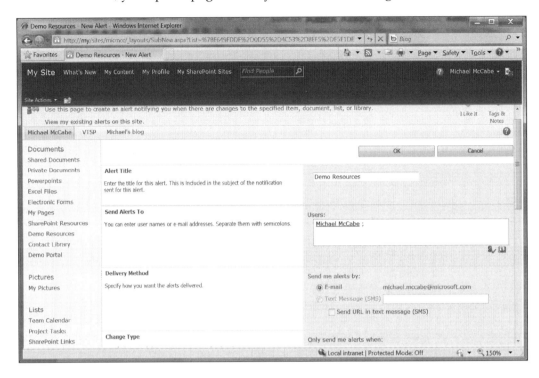

These settings include:

- **Alert Title**: By default, this will be pre-populated with the name of the document, list, or library for which you are creating the alert.

  It is a good practice to change this so that the **Alert Title** clearly indicates the subject of the alert for others to easily understand when receiving alert notification. So, for example, change a default title such as **Demo Resources** to **Alert: Changes to 'Demo Resources' library**.

- **Delivery Method**: Choose e-mail (**Text message (SMS)** requires administrator setup).

- **Change Type**: Addition, modifications, deletions.

- **Send Alerts for These Changes**: Any changes, changes to documents created by you or last modified by you.

Alerts can only be sent to known users; that is, users listed in Active Directory or a SharePoint user.

- **When to Send Alerts**: Immediately, daily, weekly.

To add an alert to an individual document:

1. Select the document in the list.
2. On the ribbon, select **Alert me** and then **set alert on this document**.

 You can click the dropdown next to the document and then select **Alert Me**.

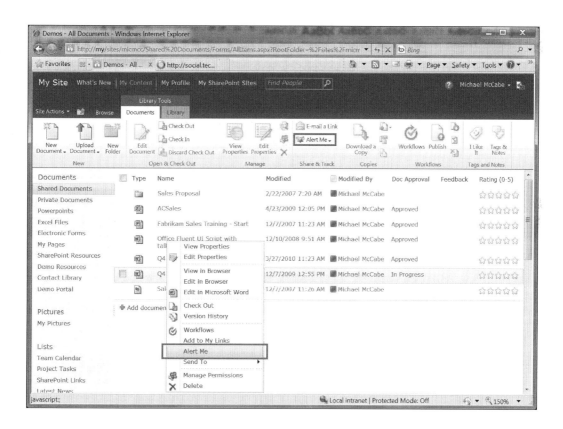

Then the dialog box to enter alert properties appears:

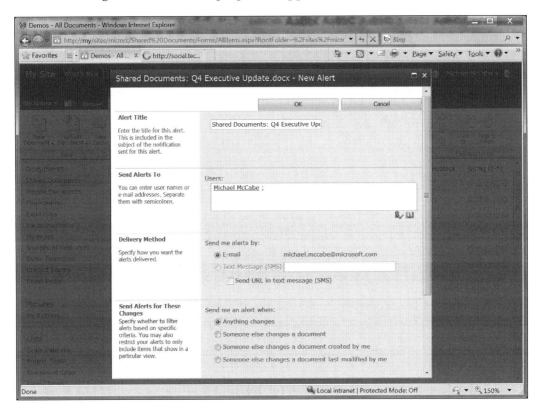

Notice the alert properties page opens as an overlay when you add an alert for an individual document, rather than opening a separate web page as is the case when you add an alert to a library or list.

The overlay opens quicker and provides the underlying view of the library or list where the document is stored.

Enter your selections with the options, as we described them previously for libraries. In this case, the alert will only apply to the individual document, not the entire library.

Alert notifications

Notifications will appear in your e-mail. For example, in the following screenshot you see the notification you receive when you create a new alert:

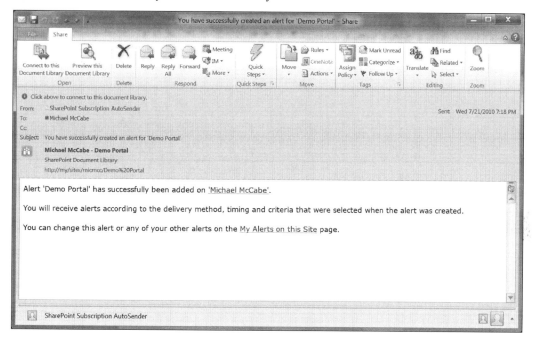

From that e-mail, you can:

- Link to the site
- Link to **My Alerts on this Site**

This example shows the notification sent when a change has occurred to a document:

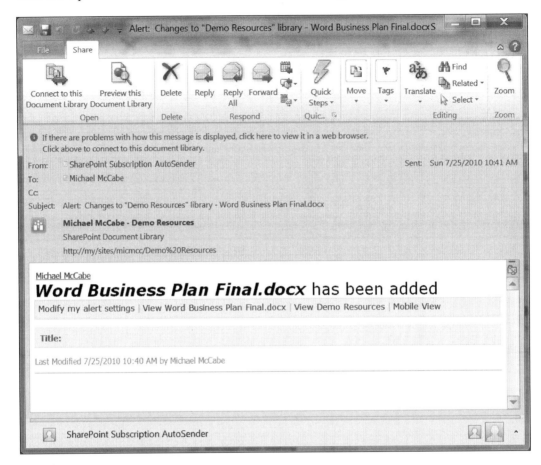

Search alerts

Alerts for saved search result sets are one of the most useful ways to keep track of changes to information you need to follow. By subscribing to an alert for your searches, SharePoint will automatically notify you by e-mail when an item is added or changed.

To set up a search alert:

1. Perform a search.
2. On the search results page, click on the **Alert Me** icon.
3. Enter a title for the alert and specify the options as described earlier.
4. Enter the settings for your alert and click on **OK**.

You will receive an e-mail whenever the results for your search change.

Task notifications

Task lists can be set up to notify a person of an assigned task.

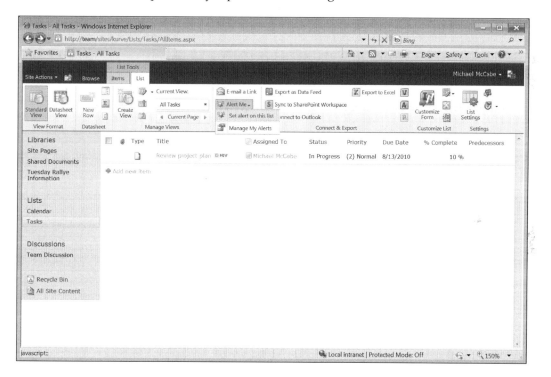

To enable a task list to send e-mail notifications, configure the list on the **Advanced**

Settings page by selecting **Yes** for **E-mail Notification**:

The person to whom the task is assigned will receive a notification with a link to the document.

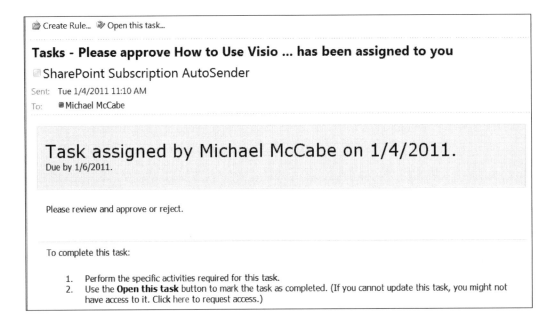

The person assigned the task receives an e-mail notification like the preceding one. When clicked, the link in the notification opens the task to be completed.

RSS feeds

To subscribe to RSS feeds for search results, follow these steps:

1. Perform a search.
2. On the search results page, click on the **RSS** feeds button, which is the orange icon just to the right of the **Sort by** field.

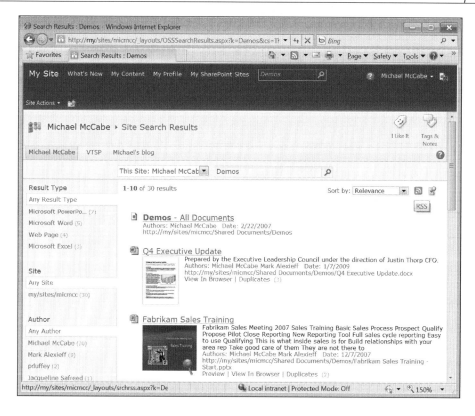

3. Click on **Subscribe to this feed**.

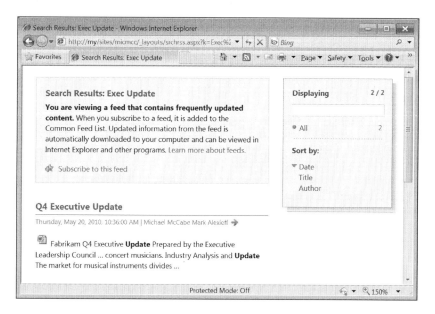

4. Type a title for the RSS feed.

5. In the **Create in** folder list, select **Feeds**.
6. Click on **Subscribe**.

A link to the new RSS feed will appear in the **Feeds** list in your web browser.

Summary

Alerts provide a powerful tool to automate the process of keeping current with changes to information in SharePoint.

We have taken a look at how to set up alerts, the notifications they generate, and the actions you can take when you receive a notification.

In the next chapter, we will discuss Enterprise Content Management, a tool for working on information from your sites even when you are not connected to the Internet.

11
Enterprise Content Management

In *Chapter 4*, *List Management* and *Chapter 5*, *Library Management*, we discussed SharePoint's functionality in adding content to **Lists** and **Libraries**, and how **Content Types** provide reusable functionality within a site; and in *Chapter 8*, *Managing Metadata*, we discussed how to add document-bound information such as **metadata**, **taxonomies**, and **folksonomies** to documents and list items. While these chapters relate to adding and managing, this chapter discusses SharePoint's functionality in managing content with procedures to ensure accurate, up-to-date, and compliant content.

In this chapter, we will cover:

- Record Management
- Content Types
- Information Management Policies
- Overview of Enterprise Content Management planning

Record Management and Information Management functionality is not available with SharePoint Foundation, and if you are creating Record Management or policies, you will need Site collection permissions.

Record management

Record Management is the practice of maintaining and tracking records within an organization. This process is normally determined based on an organization's internal and external legal compliance requirements. Generally, regulated industries such as financial and health care services require some form of record management, and the larger the organization, the greater the record management requirements. The consequences of the information not being accurate, up-to-date, or available are dire.

In a nutshell, record management involves establishing a record, setting policies and procedures, and auditing the records.

SharePoint 2010's Record Management allows **In-Place Records** management, which is the ability to declare the document as a record, and it will be viewed as a record in the site it was created in. In SharePoint 2007, the document had to reside in the specific Record Center site template for policies to be applied. The Record Center Site was introduced to you in *Chapter 3, SharePoint Team Sites*. After the document is declared as a record, it can have different **policies** and **restrictions** from when it was a document.

Records and documents (a non-policy item) can now reside side-by-side, in the same library they were created in with different policies such as retention or deletion schedules applied to individual items.

Records are both documents **and** list items and can be declared as records either manually or automatically. This includes wiki pages, blog posts, and article pages. Organizations are increasingly using SharePoint to communicate company policies and other important information such as health and safety that could be time-sensitive.

Applying Record Management to these items improves the value of the contents as content owners can be notified when content is due to expire, or the contents can be unpublished. When content is perceived to be out-of-date or static on a SharePoint portal, the user base can lose confidence in its accuracy. Record Management can prevent this happening.

Policies can be added to a Content Type, Library/List, or Folder.

Manual record declaration can be configured on Site Collection level and overridden in each document library.

In SharePoint 2007, Record Management functionality was only in the Record Center of a Site collection. With SharePoint 2010, **In-Place Records Management** can be in any site. This is beneficial as its functionality is available to be used by more users. However, from a compliance standpoint, it is important to know where these policies are being used.

Record declaration

The first step with record management is to create a record. This should be created at the site collection level, and just like security inheritance, the record can be applied to sites and sub sites.

Site collection

To configure a site collection for records, the In-Place record management needs to be enabled. Once this is done, follow these steps:

1. On the top site of the site collection, click the **Site Settings** link on the **Site Actions** menu.

2. On the **Site Settings** page, in the **Site Collection Administration** section, click the **Record Declaration Setting** link.

3. On the **Record Retention** page, in the **Record Restrictions** section, select **Block Edit** and **Delete**.

   This selection specifies the kind of restrictions that will be placed on an item when it is declared a record. This setting does not affect items already declared as records.

   The available options are:

   ° **No Additional Restrictions**: This restriction is useful if you want records to have a separate retention policy than non-records, but don't want to block the records from being deleted or edited.

   ° **Block Delete**: This is the default restriction for the Records Center.

   ° **Block Edit and Delete**: If you want to completely lock a document so that it cannot be edited or deleted. A *padlock* icon is associated with the document to visually show that the item is locked.

Record Restrictions	

Specify restrictions to place on a document or item once it has been declared as a record. Changing this setting will not affect items which have already been declared records. Note: The information management policy settings can also specify different policies for records and non-records.	○ No Additional Restrictions
	   Records are no more restricted than non-records.
	○ Block Delete
	   Records can be edited but not deleted.
	◉ Block Edit and Delete
	   Records cannot be edited or deleted. Any changes will require the record declaration to be revoked.

Record Declaration Availability	
Specify whether all lists and libraries in this site should make the manual declaration of records available by default. When manual record declaration is unavailable, records can only be declared through a policy or workflow.	Manual record declaration in lists and libraries should be: ○ Available in all locations by default ◉ Not available in all locations by default
Declaration Roles	
Specify which user roles can declare and undeclare record status manually.	The declaration of records can be performed by: ◉ All list contributors and administrators ○ Only list administrators ○ Only policy actions Undeclaring a record can be performed by: ○ All list contributors and administrators ◉ Only list administrators ○ Only policy actions

4. In the **Record Declaration Availability** section, select the option that specifies whether or not items can be manually declared as records in lists and libraries by default. If the **Not available** in all locations by default option is selected, items can be declared as records only through a policy or workflow.

    The options in this section let you define for the entire site collection whether or not the **Declare Record** and **Undeclare Record** buttons appear on the Ribbon. If the buttons appear on the Ribbon, only users with the proper permissions can declare a document as a record. Each list or library has its own **Record Declaration Settings** page that allows them to *break off* from the site collection setting to show or hide the records declaration buttons on the Ribbon.

    If record declaration settings are not set at the list or library level, they will use the site collection setting by default.

5. In the **Declaration Roles** section, specify the types of users who can declare or undeclare items as records (detailed as follows) and click **OK**.

The types of users are:

*   **All list contributors and administrators**: Any user with the *edit items* permissions to a list can declare and undeclare items as records.

*   **Only list administrators:** Only users with *manage list* permissions to a list can declare and undeclare items as records.

*   **Only policy actions**: Only policy actions or custom code running as the System Account can declare and undeclare items as records.

List or library

You can also configure lists and libraries so that all items added to them will automatically be declared as records.

To configure in-place records management for a list or library, follow these steps:

1. Go to the list or library that you want to configure for records management.

2. On the Library/List Ribbon, click **Library/List Settings**.

3. In the Permissions and Management section, select **Record declaration settings**.

4. In the **Manual Record Declaration Availability** section, do one of the following:

   ○ Select whether you want to use the site collection default setting

   ○ Allow for the manual declaration of records for this list or library

   ○ Never allow for the manual declaration of records for this list or library

5. In the **Automatic Declaration** section, select whether or not you want items that are added to this list or library to be automatically declared as records.

6. Click **OK**.

Managing records

To apply a record manually, these steps need to be applied:

1. In the library or list select the document that you want a Record applied to.

2. Click the **Declare Record** icon on the toolbar.

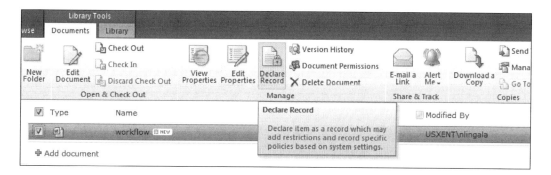

3. You will be prompted with a message **Are you sure you want to declare the selected documents as records?**

4. Click **OK**.

There is now a column called **Declared Record**, which denotes the date and time of when the document or item becomes a record.

To undeclare a record:

1. Select **Compliance Details** from the drop-down menu on the record.

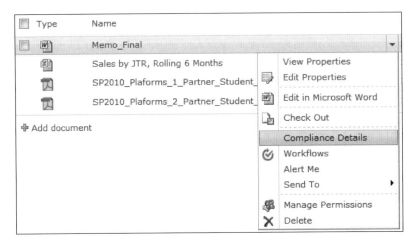

2. Select **Undeclare record**.

If this menu is disabled, the document library is set to automatic declaration mode. This will need to be deselected.

By the menu being on a document, users can see if an item is a record and if other policies are associated with it.

Content types

A content type can be viewed as the metadata and behavior template for a particular document or item. Each content type contains references to one or more site columns. You can also associate workflows, information management policies, and document templates with content types. Content types should be used when content structure such as document format needs to be repeated across a single site collection. If a content type is required to be used across multiple site collections, the Content Type Hub feature is required.

Suppose you define a content type as a Contract, the metadata and actions associated with a contract might include:

- Columns named Customer, Amount, and Final Effective Date
- An approval workflow
- A retention policy linked to the Final Effective Date field
- A Word template for a contract document

It would be labor intensive to manually create this functionality in multiple sites and lists, so content types were introduced to SharePoint 2007.

To create a new content type in a site collection, the following steps should be applied:

1. Click on the **Site Settings** link on the Sites Action menu.
2. In the **Galleries** section of the Site Settings page, click on the **Site content types** link.

    This will display a list of currently defined content types for this site collection.

3. Click on the **Create** link.

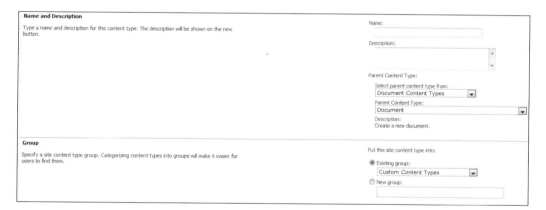

4. Enter a **Name** and **Description**.
5. Select a **Parent Content** from the drop-down list.

    If your contract document type is a Word document, the Parent Content type should be Document Content Types and the Parent Content Type should be Document.

6. Choose the group of the content type, or create a new group.
7. Click **OK**.

A new Content Type has been created. This Site Content Type will now be displayed:

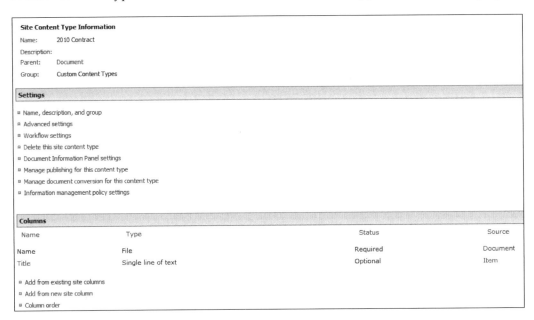

On this page you can edit and add to its functionality, such as workflows, policies, and columns.

It is possible to upload multiple document templates so that when you can create a new document from a template in the library it is saved into the library that it was created from. An advantage of this is that users are more likely to save the document in the correct location.

Managing content types

To add a content type to a list or library, the following steps should be taken:

1. In the list or library, click on **the List\Library Settings** on the ribbon.
2. In the **General Settings** section of the **Document Library Settings** page, click on **Advanced Settings**.
3. In the **Content Type** section click **Yes**.
4. Click **OK**.

You have just configured this library or list to have multiple content types in a list or library.

To add content types, follow these steps:

1. On the **List\Library** settings page, in the **Content Type** section, click on the **Add from existing site content type** link.
2. Select the Content Type you wish to add.
3. Click **OK**.

 You can have multiple content types in a list\library or even in a folder.

Content Types are discussed in detail in *Chapter 5*.

Information management policies

In this chapter, we have discussed record management and the process of marking a document as a record for legal and compliance reasons. **Information Management Policies** is the procedure of applying these processes as a set of rules that govern the record management policies to be correctly applied across a site.

These policies enable administrators to control retention, auditing, labels, and barcodes of content, and how effectively people are complying with the policy. The most common creators and enforcers of policy are compliance officers, records managers, IT staff, and others who are responsible for managing risk.

SharePoint Server 2010 has several out of the box policy features that you can customize for your needs across the SharePoint technology. The advantages of using polices is that you can set and manage *the rules* for a content type from a single location, including both client side policy features such as document deletion by a user and server side policy features such as expiration dates.

A policy is a collection of instruction sets for one or more policy features. Each policy feature provides a specific kind of content management functionality. You can assign a policy to:

- Site collection
- Content type
- Library or list
- Item level list document content type

Policies require little involvement from end users because corporate policies are automatically and transparently followed.

Policy features

There are four information management policy features to help you manage your content: **expiration**, **auditing**, **document labels**, and **document bar codes**.

Expiration

With an expiration in a policy there is the ability to retain information for fixed periods of time and manage the lifecycle of content. This is done at the end of the content's life. The expiration policy feature can dispose of content in a consistent way that can be tracked and managed. For example, you can set content that is assigned a specified content type to expire on a specific date, within a certain amount of time after the document was created or last modified, or based on a workflow activity or some other event.

After the document expires, you can determine the actions that the policy control takes. For example, the policy can delete the document, or define a workflow to have SharePoint Server 2010 route the document for permission to destroy it. In addition, the expiration policy feature provides the capability for you to build and use a custom plugin action to be performed on the item after it reaches its expiration date, such as a web service to move the document to another site collection.

It is not uncommon in an organization to have a separate site collection that only contains expired content of a live site. There are a number of benefits to this approach:

- The site collection can be branded so users know its content is expired
- There can be unique workflows to the site that are only associated with expired content
- The expired content can be moved or even removed from a site

To apply expiration to a content type in a Library or list, the following steps should be taken:

1. In the Library or list, click on the **List\Library Settings** on the Ribbon.
2. In the **General Settings** section of the **Document Library Settings** page, click **Advanced Settings**.
3. In the **Content Type** section click **Yes**.
4. Click **OK**.

To apply another content type to this list\library you will need to perform the following steps in the library to create another unique content type:

1. On the **Document Library Setting** page, click on **Information Management Policy Settings** link.

   You will now see the content types for this library.

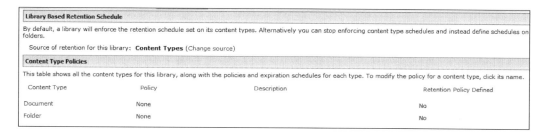

Please note that there are now two content types associated with this library.

2. Click on the **Document** link.

   The **Edit Policy** page is where the expiration, auditing, document labels, and document bar codes policy features can be applied.

3. Click on the **Enable Retention** checkbox.

4. Click on the **Add a retention stage** link.

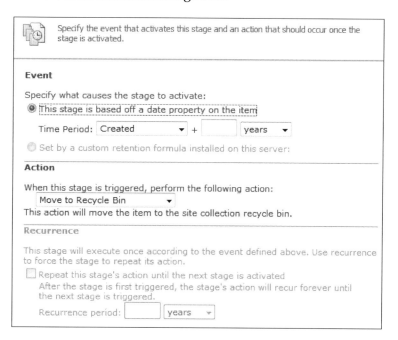

5. Set the time period of when you want this policy to be activated.

6. Set an action for this policy.

7. Click **OK**.

An expiration policy has been set up on this content type.

Why apply an expiration policy?

Content is not just about creation, but also management, deletion, and re-submission. Organizations always have initiatives to create information such as policies and procedures, but from a user's standpoint what really undermines these initiatives, is when this information becomes outdated and perhaps inaccurate. So, by applying expiration rules when moving updated content, or triggering workflows to content, owners' accountability to the content can be assigned and old content can be removed from a live site.

For corporate websites where the customers make decisions on published content, inaccurate or even wrong information can be expensive to the organization.

Typically, time sensitive information on a corporate website would include product information, executive bios, and vacant jobs, which would be associated with content owners' departments. By applying expiration policies, the content owners will be notified to renew or remove content.

In the scenario stated previously, the benefit to the business is that responsibility is now with the content owners, product managers, and HR who actually work in the departments that benefit the most from the published information, rather than the webmaster, who may not be involved with the intimate details of the published information.

This is a good example of SharePoint enterprise content approval and teamwork, where the webmaster can set up the policies for the content owners to act on.

By using expiration, content can now have lifecycle stages applied to it, such as pending expiration review, expired, and expired do not use. This is useful for users to know the credibility of content, if it is time sensitive.

Auditing

SharePoint 2010's auditing is all about the activities around both a document, or item, or Site during its lifecycle. It is the classic who, where, when, what, and how of activities.

SharePoint 2010's item-level auditing capabilities have the ability to report on who opened, edited, checked in, checked out, moved, copied, or downloaded the document or item.

 The Site-level activity is useful as it shows security changes and when metadata associated with content was changed. This is a powerful compliance feature.

Only administrators can see the details of the audited information. This information cannot be edited through the SharePoint interface.

Site Collection Auditing

To set up Site Collection Auditing, apply the following steps:

1. From the top level site in the site collection, click on the **Site Actions** menu and select **Site Settings**.

2. In the **Site Collection Administration** section of the **Site Settings** page, click **Site collection audit settings**.

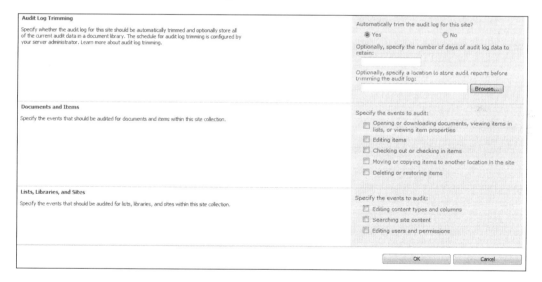

3. On the **Audit Settings** page, select the **auditing** functionality.

4. Click the **OK** button.

Now the auditing functionality is activated, you will need to run audit reports on the collected audited information. To do this, follow these steps:

1. Click the **Audit log reports** link in the **Site Collection Administration** section of the **Site Settings** page.

2. Select the type of report that you want to be running.

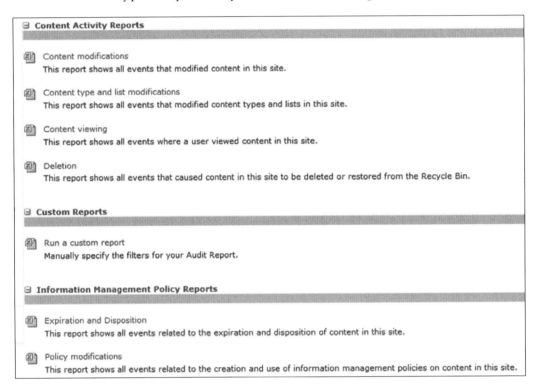

3. Choose the location where the report will reside.

4. Click **OK**.

We have two suggestions:

- Create a library in the Site collection called *Audit Reports* and save all the desired reports in this library. This makes it easier to find reports.

- On the Audit Log Reports page there is the ability to create up to nine reports. We suggest that you create all of the log reports because, over time, when there is more user activity on the sites, content owners begin to request audit activity information.

In the **View Auditing Reports** page there is a **Custom Report** option section. Click on the **Run a custom report** link.

You will be presented with the following screenshot:

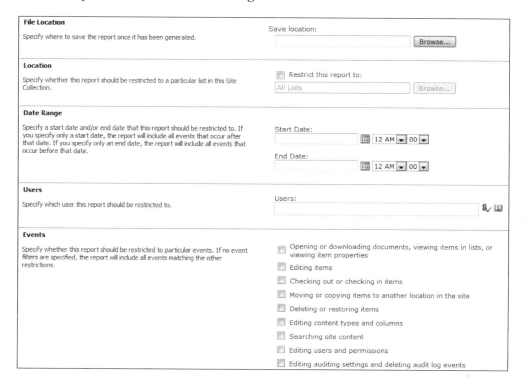

There is the ability to select date ranges of the auditing, security restrictions, and auditing events.

Document labels

The document label feature and the bar code feature are designed to assist you in organizing your documents for systematic storage and retrieval. You can use either feature to assign a unique label to a document, whether the document is a physical copy or electronic file, which enables you to track it.

Document labels are text labels that you can have SharePoint Server 2010 generate automatically based on a content type's metadata. For example, a law firm might want to attach a document label consisting of client name, subject matter, and date assigned to each document of a given content type.

You can print and affix document labels to a physical copy of the document, or insert them as images into a Microsoft Office 2010 document.

To apply document labels to a content type in a list\library, follow the steps outlined for an expiration policy and select the **Enable Labels** checkbox.

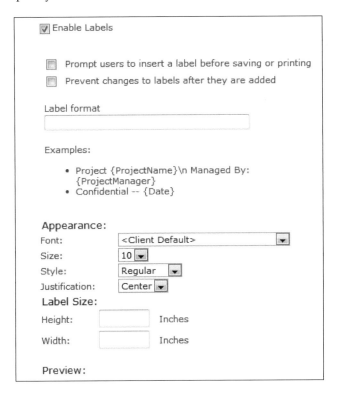

Apply the desired labeling requirements.

To further assist content organization, metadata should be used because this makes content easier to search and categorize. Labels are unique to content, while metadata will categorize content.

Document bar codes

Document bar codes are similar to document labels, but instead of text they are a **generated unique ID,** which is linked, but separate to, the document ID (this is a number generated at random so uniqueness cannot be guaranteed). You can print and affix the bar code to a physical copy of the document, or insert it as an image into an Office 2010 document. You can also extend and customize the format of the bar code.

This feature is useful if you are printing documents and have a bar code reader. If you are looking for a document unique identifier, the Document ID may be more appropriate as this is searchable, and if the document is moved, the ID stays with it.

> When content is stored in SharePoint Server 2010, instances of saving the content from the client to the server are captured by auditing events. If a user downloads content to their desktop, it is viewed as outside SharePoint's control and any policies are not enforced on the desktop copy.

Policy deployment

We recommend when you plan your policies, first determine your organization-wide policy needs. Then, design Site Collection policies to meet those needs and distribute those policies for inclusion in the Site Collection Policy galleries of all relevant site collections.

A single Site Collection policy is designed to be applied to all product specifications so that they are consistently audited and retained. After defining the Site Collection policy and testing it, it can be exported and then imported to Site Collection Policy galleries of other site collections in which product specifications are stored. It is then associated with all product specification content types in the various site collections to impose the policy on all products.

This should be coordinated with the SharePoint administrator.

Overview of enterprise content management planning

Planning content management is important if you wish to achieve your organization's records management goals. As part of this planning, we recommend the following steps:

1. Identify records management roles, such as compliance officers, to categorize the records and to run the records management process; IT personnel to implement the information management policies that efficiently support records management and content managers to find where content resides and manage their teams to follow records management practices.

2. Before creating a plan, you must determine which documents and other items are required to become records.

3. After you have analyzed your content and determined retention schedules, you must develop a plan to state what should be a record, indicate where this content should be stored, describe retention periods, and identify who is responsible for managing this content.

4. Develop retention schedules for each record type to determine when it is no longer being used, how long it should be retained after that, and how it should ultimately be disposed of.

5. Determine whether to create a records archive to manage records in place, or to use a combination of the two approaches.

6. Define content types, libraries, policies, and, when it is required, metadata that determines the location to route a document to.

7. Plan how content becomes records. If you are using SharePoint Server 2010 for both active document management and records management, you can create custom workflows to move documents to a records archive.

8. Create a training plan to teach users how to create and work with records.

Summary

This chapter's focus has been how to organize and promote true enterprise-wide content management. This can be a challenge because policies affect not only teams or groups, but in many cases an entire organization.

With this release of SharePoint, the product has the functionality to act "as a true ECM system" as there is the ability to:

- Directly link to content with document IDs, store once, yet use in different locations and scenarios such as search, tagging, and notes
- Act as a Record Management Center, with policies being able to be applied to content
- Use metadata
- Have reusable content types
- Implement granular security
- Audit content

When record management, content types, and defining policies are applied to the SharePoint technology, the compliance capabilities are cost effective to any organization.

The next chapter discusses pages and web parts where lists\libraries are discussed with users.

12
Blogs, Wikis, and Other Web 2.0 Features

Blogs and **wikis** are two characteristic elements of interactive information shared on the Internet that is commonly referred to as **Web 2.0**. Blogs and wikis allow you to create and share information collaboratively on the web.

A blog is a site where you can share your ideas and work information in an informal format. Blogs provide a space where your colleagues can comment on your entries and have a dialogue with you about the ideas you share. Like a diary, the contributions to a blog are also dated records that show the development of ideas over time.

With SharePoint 2010's blogs, you can add categories to blog entries to make it easier to find items on a common topic. Readers of a blog can add tags, alerts, and send links to inform others of items they find of interest on a blog. Tools to manage a blog are automatically provided when you create a blog.

Wikis are sites where information about a topic is collected from many sources and contributors. The most familiar example is the online encyclopedia, Wikipedia. The information can continually be updated and corrected with new information.

SharePoint wikis provide sites where the knowledge of an organization can be collected and organized. The tools in SharePoint for managing wikis allow you to create:

- Wiki pages
- Wiki libraries

In this chapter, will see how you can create and customize your blog and wiki sites. We will discuss how you can allow others to contribute to the sites, and we will also take a look at how to manage your sites.

Blogs

A blog is usually written by one author. The blog contains posts often made on a daily basis with the posts appearing in reverse chronological order.

Blogs can be used to share experiences, opinions, best practices, or lessons learned. The blog often takes on the character of its author, sometimes expressing a distinct point-of-view.

People who have permission to read and contribute to the blog can make comments on the author's posts. Posts and comments are themselves lists that can be managed on the blog.

We will take a look here at creating a blog, contributing posts and comments, and managing blog lists.

Creating a blog

To create a new blog, perform the following steps:

1. Click the **Site Actions** menu and choose **New Site**.

2. In the **Create** dialog box, choose **Blog** and enter a **Title** and **URL name** for your blog.

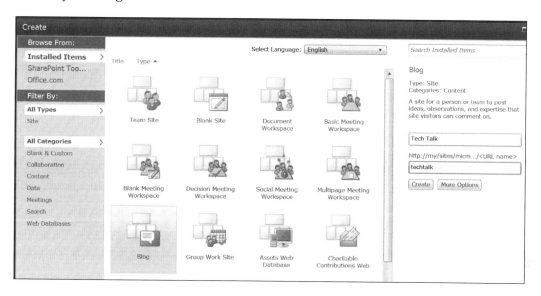

3. Click **Create** and the blog page appears.

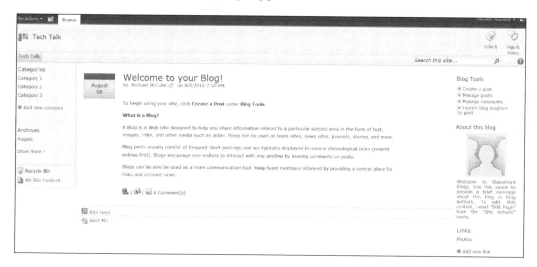

Contributing to a blog

You can contribute to your blog with posts. Others with permission can manage blog posts. Posts can be added by anyone with permission to read the blog, or permission can be given to post anonymously.

To create a post, first look for the **Blog Tools** list on your blog site, and then follow these steps:

1. Click **Create a post**.

2. In the form that appears, enter a **Title** for the post and the content of the post in the **Body** section.

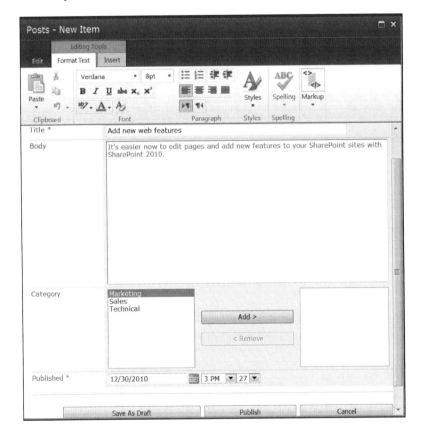

3. Click **Publish**.

The post will appear at the top of the blog as the most recent post.

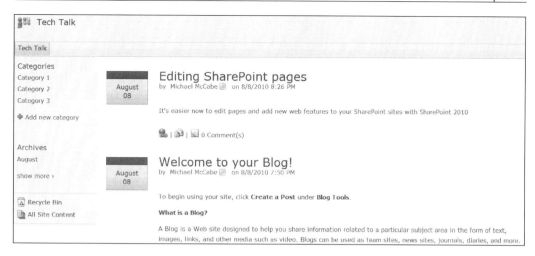

 Use Microsoft Word to create blog posts

By selecting **Launch blog program to post** from the **Blog Tools** menu, you can launch Microsoft Word. In Word, you will be able to use all of its formatting and style tools to enhance the look of your blog posts.

To make a comment on a post:

1. Click the word **Comment(s)** just below a blog post.

2. Type the **Title** and **Body** of your comment.

3. Click **Submit Comment**.

When someone adds a comment to a post, a comment count will appear below the original post. Comments can be read by clicking on **Comment(s)**.

Managing blog posts and comments

You can manage your blog posts and comments by choosing the appropriate links on the **Blog Tools** list.

For example, the **Manage posts** link opens the list of posts on your blog.

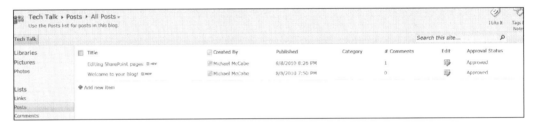

By clicking a link in the **Edit** column, you can open a form to edit your post.

This procedure is the same for managing comments. You would simply select **Manage comments** from the **Blog Tools** list, instead of **Manage posts**.

Categories are another easy way to manage your blog posts. Others can read posts grouped together in common categories, making it easier to see all contributions related to one topic.

Categories are kept in a list on a SharePoint blog. So, to edit categories you only need to click on the link under lists, and then edit or add categories as you need them.

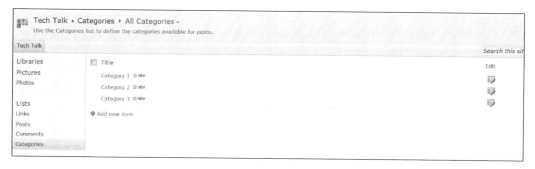

You can then apply categories when you create or edit a post. As shown in the following screenshot, you can add or remove categories from the blog's category list in the dialog box that appears.

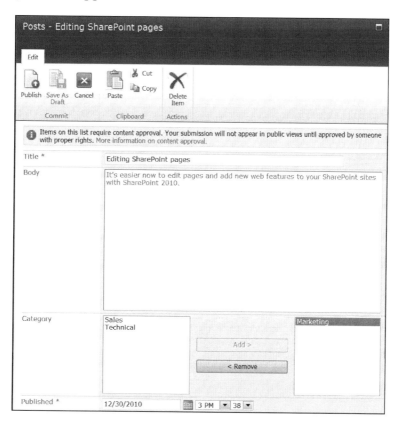

In the preceding screenshot, the information banner points out that the site owner has set up the site so that a site manager must approve posts to the site. Once a manager approves the post, it will be published to the site so others can read it.

Tagging is another tool for managing blog posts as well as other SharePoint sites. You can add a tag to a blog to help you remember links and organize sites. You can click the **I Like It** tag on a site, or click **Tags & Notes** to create your own tag. Your tags will be saved on your My Site for easy reference.

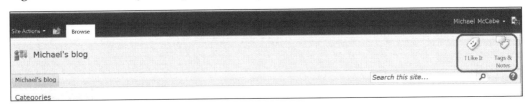

Wikis

In SharePoint 2010, wikis are designed to make it easy for you and other team members to contribute information. The format of a wiki page is open, and you can easily edit wiki pages using a browser without any other special editing tools. In SharePoint 2010, the default page format is a wiki page. When you create new pages on a SharePoint 2010 site, they are by default stored in the **Site Pages** library. The first time you create a page on a site, the Site Pages library will automatically be created for you.

If you want to manage a wiki separately from the pages in the Site Pages library, you can create your own **Wiki Library**. This allows you to manage the properties and permissions of your wiki library as a separate group.

 If you want to manage all your wiki pages in one place, we recommend you first create a **Wiki Page Library**. This makes managing your wikis easier because they are organized in one place.

We will first create a wiki page library, and then create a wiki that will be stored in the new library.

Creating a wiki page library

To create a wiki page library:

1. Click the **Site Actions** menu on the site where you want to create the library.

2. Click **More Options**.

3. Select **Wiki Page Library** in the **Create** dialog box as shown in the following screenshot.

4. Type a name for the library and click **Create**.

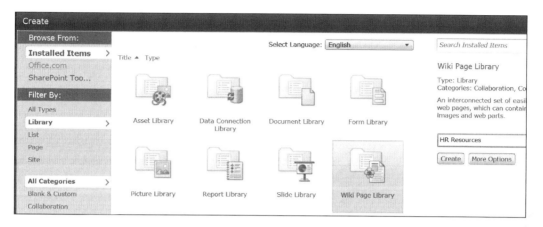

Creating a wiki page

The easiest way to create wiki pages, once you have created the wiki library, is to first create a link on the Wiki Library's Home page.

> It may seem odd at first to create the link *before* creating the page and its contents. But, as you will see, this is the easiest way to create wiki pages.
>
> This also makes it easier for you, as a first step, to outline the contents of your wiki before drilling down into the details.

To create the page link:

1. Edit the library page by clicking **Edit** on the Ribbon.

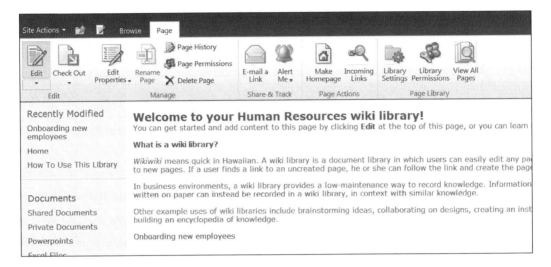

Note the additional capabilities on the wiki page ribbon.

These include:

- **Manage Properties**, **Page History**, and **Page Permissions**
- **Make Homepage** — to make the current wiki page the homepage for your site
- **Incoming Links** — to view pages that point to this one

---

2. Type the name of the page link in double-square brackets, as seen in the following screenshot with `[[Insurance Benefits]]`.

When you type the square brackets, you will automatically see a list of page links that already exist so you can select one. You will also have the option to create a new one.

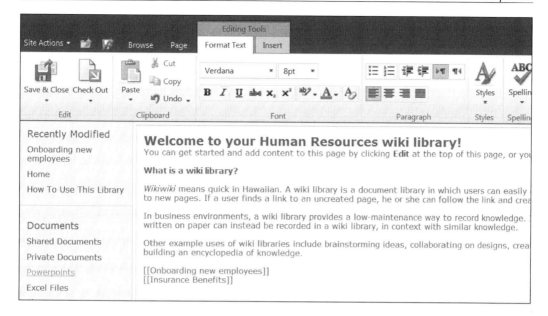

 When in **Edit** mode, existing links such as **[[Onboarding new employees]]** in the above example, as well as new ones, will appear within double-square brackets.

3. Save the library page.

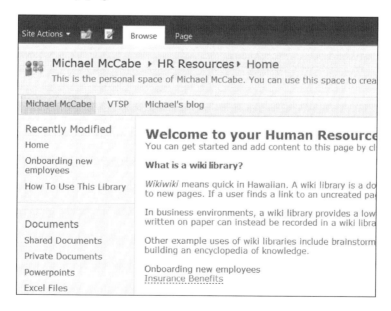

Once you save the page, the link will appear with a dashed underline if the linked page has not yet been created.

Now, to actually create the wiki page:

1. Click the link with dashed underline as shown previously.
2. Click **Create** in the dialog box that appears.

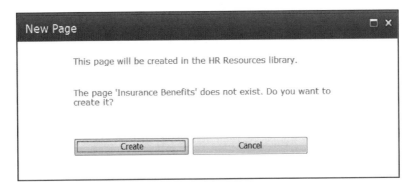

3. Enter content on the wiki page as in the following example:

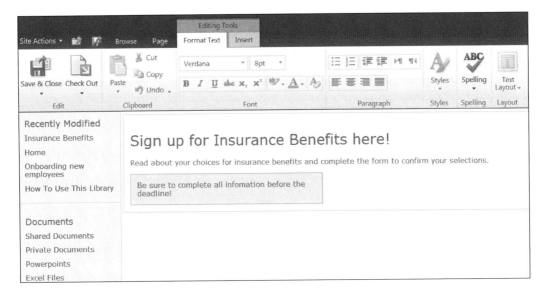

4. Click **Save**.

Editing a wiki page

To edit an existing wiki page:

1. Open the wiki page.
2. Click **Edit** on the Ribbon.

 Note the tools on the Ribbon available to edit the styles and effects on your wiki pages, or to insert pictures, video, audio, and web links. More information on these capabilities is covered in *Chapter 7, Office Integration with SharePoint* and *Chapter 13, Pages and Web Parts.*

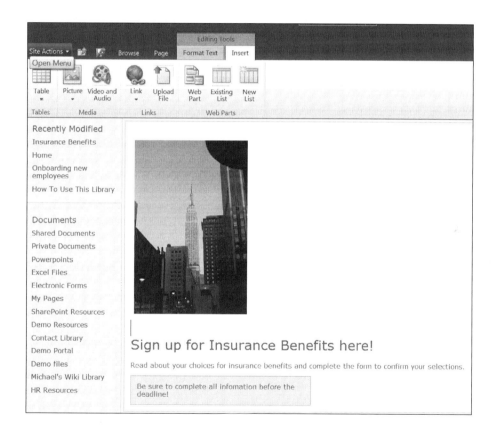

Summary

We have taken a look here at two important features of Web 2.0 that are now available for you to enhance your SharePoint sites.

Blogs give a single author the ability to share ideas and experiences and invite comments from others.

Wikis give teams of contributors the ability to collaborate and develop definitive documents on any subject. Contributors can continually update and enhance the documents with new information.

In the next chapter, we will look more closely at how SharePoint pages are composed and the tools new in SharePoint 2010 to make that process easier.

13
Pages and Web Parts

In this chapter, we will take a look at the basic building blocks for displaying content on SharePoint sites: **pages** and **web parts**. We will discuss what a page is, how you create one, and how you can modify it. We will show how you can add functionality to pages with web parts. We will discuss the types of web parts and how to work with them.

Pages

When you create a site in SharePoint, a **home page** is automatically generated from a template. SharePoint pages organize content for presentation to users, and SharePoint sites will contain multiple pages for presenting information.

You might ask why you would want to create a page instead of including the same information in a document that you could post to a document library. One answer is that a SharePoint page brings the information on a page to the immediate attention of a wide audience. Another reason is to present the latest information using web parts that connect to other data sources. A document is a snapshot of information an author knows at the time of creating the document. The author can always update information in a document, but that is often a process done only periodically. Because of the live connections to the latest data, SharePoint pages and web parts can present the most up-to-date view of information to users.

You can create individual pages from templates that come with SharePoint. The templates provide ready-made layouts for organizing your information on a page, and this information can be in the form of text, images, lists, or small applications called **web parts**. We will discuss web parts later in this chapter.

Types of pages

For our purposes we will cover three types of pages: **standard pages**, **web part pages**, and **publishing pages.** In general, standard pages make it easy for you to enter and edit the text, images, and date on the page, whereas web part pages offer a more structured layout for adding only web parts to the page. We will take a look at all three types of pages, but focus on standard pages and web part pages.

Standard pages

Standard pages give you a less structured format than web part pages do, making it easier to format text and move items around on the page. You *can* add web parts to a standard page, but with more flexibility as to where you place them than you have with a web part page.

 Standard pages have the same format as wiki pages, and for that reason they sometimes are referred to as wiki pages. You will also hear standard pages referred to simply as pages.

The following screenshot is an out of the box standard page with some content that has been added and formatted:

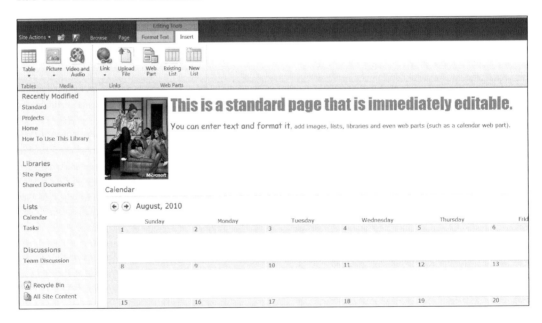

Web part pages

Web part pages have a structured layout. You can easily add web parts into this layout. The web part page is the best option if you are only going to include web parts on the page. The web part page gives more space to display web parts because there is no **quick launch** area on the left.

The following screenshot is a typical web part page, in edit mode, with some web parts inserted:

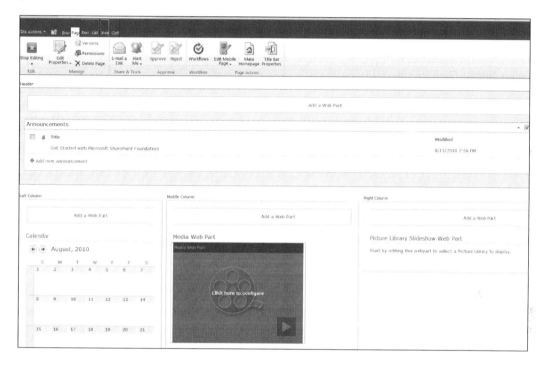

The preceding example shows the layout and the **zones** where you can **add a web part**.

While the structure of the web part pages is useful for presenting multiple web parts in a uniform layout, its tightly controlled layout does not make it the best option when you want to mix web parts with text, pictures, and other media.

As we will see, standard pages allow you much more flexibility in the layout of your information than you have with web part pages. You can include web parts on standard pages with more choice of how to integrate them with text and other media.

Publishing pages

The third page type is the publishing page. Publishing pages are less restrictive than web part pages in their structure. They give you the freedom to include text, images, links, and web parts. The layout of publishing pages, however, provides more control of the layout than standard pages. Publishing pages are most useful for managing content on extranet and internet sites, where a consistent layout is required.

Publishing pages also include tools for approval workflows, and the staging processes necessary as content moves from a draft to the final published version.

 To make publishing pages available, an administrator has to activate the SharePoint server publishing site feature. This is not activated by default.

Standard pages are the easiest for most users to work with and provide greater flexibility for layout. We will focus on them for the rest of our discussion here.

Creating pages

To create a new page, follow these steps:

1. Click **Site Actions**.
2. Choose **More Options...**.

Note that selecting **New Page** in the preceding menu would default to a standard page, whereas **More Options...** allows you to create either a standard page or a web part page.

3.   Under **Filter By** choose **Page**.

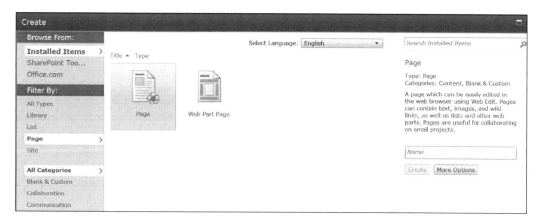

4.   Type in a **Name** for the page.
5.   Click **Create**.

The page you create will look like this before you enter content:

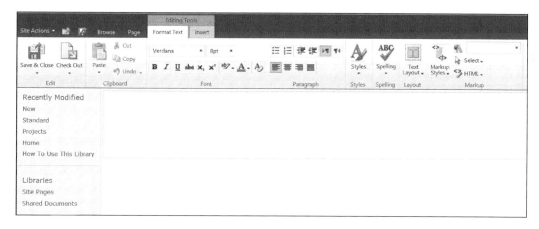

You can then begin entering text and format it with the **Editing Tools** available in the **Format Text** tab, or you can insert content with the tools on the **Insert** tab, as shown here:

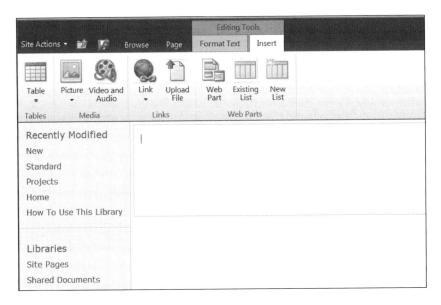

 Note that you can include **Tables**, **Media**, **Links**, and **Web Parts** on a standard page.

Viewing pages

You can view the pages you create by clicking the quick link to the **Site Pages** library:

Then, choose the page you want to view:

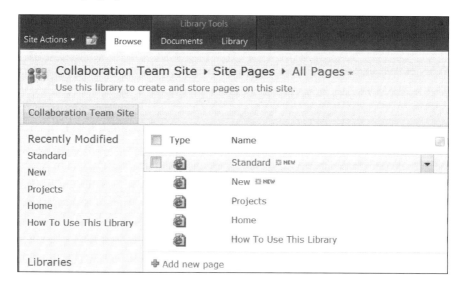

Your page will display with the content you have added already:

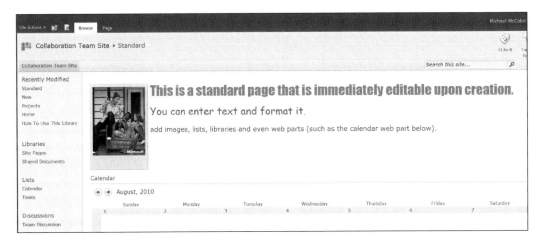

When you return to a page at this point, it will not be in edit mode.

 You can add a link on the left to allow users to go directly to a page by editing the **Site Settings** of the parent page. Look for **Navigation** under **Look and Feel**. There you will be able to add a link to the **Quick Launch** menu on the left.

Editing pages

To edit a page, click the **Edit** icon that will appear if you have permission to edit pages on the site. It is the icon that looks like a paper and pencil, to the left of the **Browse** tab.

This will open the page in edit mode and display the ribbon with the **Editing Tools**:

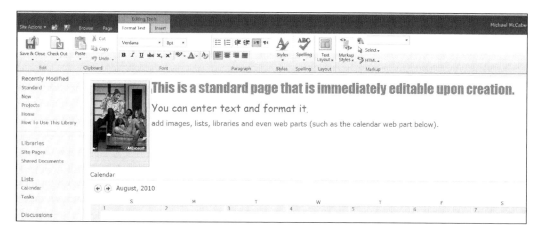

Select the text you want to format and then click the icon from the ribbon for the format you want to apply.

Formatting content on a page

On the ribbon under **Editing Tools**, click the **Format Text** tab.

Tools include the usual groups of choices under the **Format Text** tab:

- Edit
- Clipboard
- Font
- Paragraph
- Styles
- Layout
- Markup

Note the formatting choices here are consistent with those in the Microsoft Office 2010 products. This makes it easy to understand because users will be familiar with them whether working in SharePoint or Office.

Inserting content on a standard page

On the ribbon under **Editing Tools**, click the **Insert** tab.

Items that can be inserted in a wiki page are:

- Tables
- Media (pictures, video, and audio)
- Links
- Web parts (for example lists)

 Media can be added either from your local computer or from a URL. Refer to *Chapter 12, Blogs, Wikis, and Other Web 2.0 Features*, for a discussion on creating links on wiki pages.

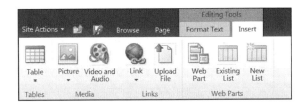

To insert media such as a picture, follow these steps:

1. Click the **Picture** on the **Insert** ribbon.
2. Browse for the picture file you want to insert.
3. Click **OK**.

The image will be uploaded to the **Site Assets** library on your SharePoint site and will appear on your page where you can move or resize it within your text.

Changing layout on standard pages

You can choose from a list of layouts for your page by selecting **Text Layout** in the **Format Text** tab, and choosing from the list.

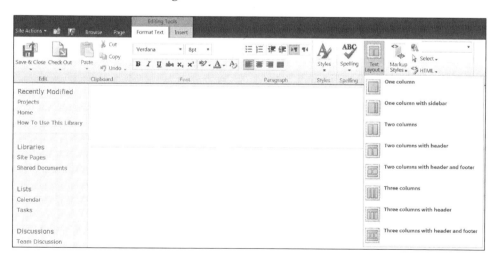

Deleting pages

In order to delete a page, follow these steps:

1. In edit mode, click the **Page** tab.

2. Click **Delete Page**.

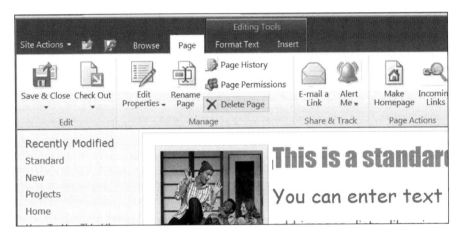

3. Confirm that you do want to delete the page by clicking **OK**.

Web parts

Web parts are small applications that add functionality to a SharePoint page. SharePoint comes with dozens of web parts you can simply select from libraries and add to your pages.

Typical web parts allow you to expose SharePoint lists and libraries on a page. There are list web parts to display calendars, links, or tasks for example. Business data web parts can display views of data from other sources, such as accounting or inventory systems, and media and content web parts will display the contents of picture or video libraries.

There are additional categories of web parts for exposing Office applications, search results, and social collaboration elements such as tags. In addition to the web parts that are included with SharePoint, by default developers can create customized web parts to deliver additional functionality.

The web part in the following image is a list web part:

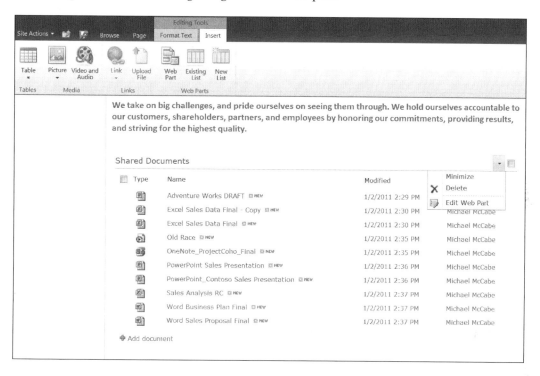

This web part shows a view from the **Shared Documents** list. The title of the web part appears towards the left. In the upper-right a drop-down menu allows you to **Minimize**, **Delete**, or **Edit Web Part**.

Clicking **Edit Web Part** opens a panel where you can modify the characteristics of the web part as illustrated as follows:

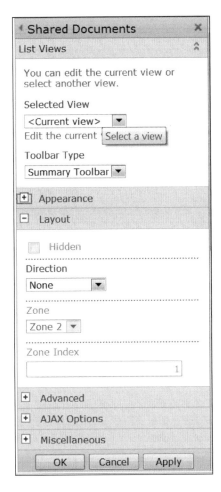

An example of another useful web part is the **Silverlight Web Part** that can be added from the **Media and Content** category to include video on your web page:

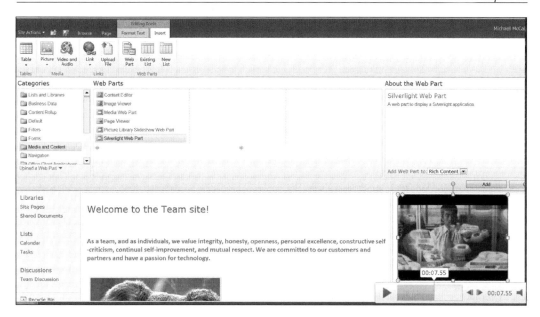

Next, we will show how to add a web part to a page, and how to edit or delete a web part.

Adding a web part to a page

Web parts are grouped into **categories**. Examples of categories include **Navigation**, **Lists & Libraries**, **Media & Content**, and **Business Data**.

When you add a web part they are listed by categories.

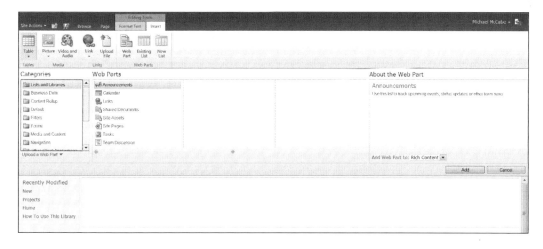

To add a web part to a SharePoint page, follow these steps:

1. Make sure the page is in edit mode and click the **Insert** tab under **Editing Tools**.

2. Click the **Web Part** icon.

3. Select one of the **Categories**.

4. Select the **Web Part**.

5. Click **Add**.

In the following example, we are selecting the **Team Discussion** web part from the **Lists and Libraries** category.

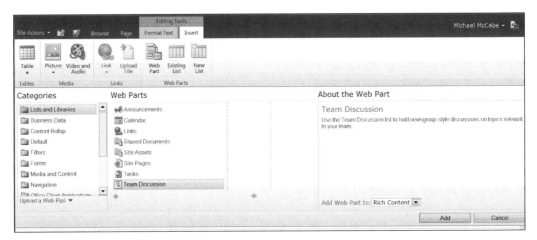

The web part is added to the page:

Editing a web part

To modify or configure a web part, follow these steps:

1. Make sure the page is in edit mode.

2. Click on the area of the web part on the page to activate the **Web Part Tools** tab on the ribbon.

3. Click on **Web Part Properties** to expose the properties panel.

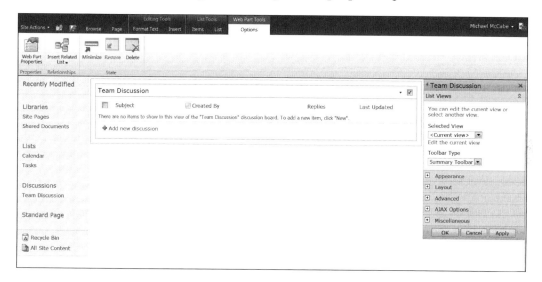

4. Under **Appearance**, for example, you can change the **Title** and **Borders** for the web part.

When you save, the web part appears like this:

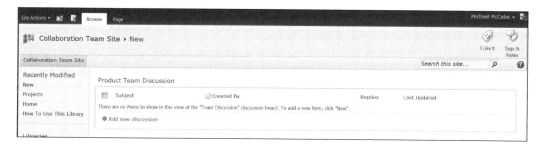

To delete a web part, follow these steps:

1. Point to the web part while the page is in edit mode.

2. Click on the **Delete** icon in the **Web Part Tools | Options.**

3. Confirm the deletion by clicking **OK**.

Summary

In this chapter, we have covered the types of pages you can create on SharePoint sites and how you can add functionality to pages with web parts. We took a look at standard, or wiki pages, and web part pages. We showed how you have more flexibility in laying out information on a standard page. You can even add web parts to a standard page along with text, pictures, or video.

We have seen the standard web parts that are included with SharePoint out of the box. We took a look at how to insert a web part on a page, and how to modify the appearance of a web part.

Pages and web parts are your tools for delivering content to users. You can easily build pages and add functionality with web parts using the templates, layouts, and libraries that come with SharePoint.

For advanced users, templates and web parts can be developed using tools such as Visual Studio and SharePoint Designer. Many web parts, though, can be downloaded for free or for a nominal fee. These web parts can supplement the functionality provided out of the box, often for specialized applications.

In the next chapter, we will take a look at My Sites, the personal web page for each individual SharePoint user to share information about themselves, their work, and area of expertise.

14
My Sites

Microsoft SharePoint Server 2010 significantly builds on the social networking features made available in the previous two releases of SharePoint technologies. **My Sites** in SharePoint 2010 have been redesigned with a completely new layout, navigation, and a rich new feature set. My Sites are a very important construct in the SharePoint environment that help users keep track of their personal content and information, along with discovering information about other users. This chapter's objective is to make you aware of the importance of My Sites and to ensure you learn how to effectively use them in your organization.

It is not uncommon in organizations that the My Site feature has been disabled as IT has viewed this feature as a gimmick or a time-wasting activity for users, but social networking has come of age in recent years and the Facebook generation has entered the workforce. My sites are growing in popularity in corporations as the management begins to understand the business value of social computing, which can be as simple as looking for a relevant skill set of an employee set for a project.

This chapter examines My Sites and how to manage them to build an effective personal landing page and storage area for individuals. You will learn about the structure of My Sites, all of the old and new features available to you as an end user, and how to use these features to help you network effectively with others in your organization. Topics covered include:

- Managing Your Newsfeeds
- Managing Your Content
- Managing Your Profile
- Tags and Notes
- Colleagues
- Memberships
- Common My Sites Operations

It's important to note that the My Sites functionality is not available with SharePoint Foundation, and otherwise it must be enabled by the administrator.

What are My Sites?

My Sites are unique to SharePoint server, and within a site collection of a SharePoint installation they offer individual users a place to store information that is only relevant to them. My Sites provide you, the end user, with a place to manage personal content, information about you, and communications with other users in your organization. The feature could be described as the **corporate Facebook**. There are many potential uses of My Sites in SharePoint Server 2010, and the following list outlines some of the most common ones.

Repository for personal content

My Sites allow you to consolidate and store your personal documents, files, and pictures in your own personal web space, effectively replacing the traditional network share or home directory.

In previous chapters, you have been introduced to SharePoint's functionality with team sites, within a site collection. My sites are associated with a site collection, and your My Site can be found at the top right-hand corner of the ribbon.

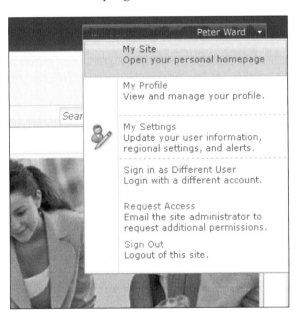

You should view your My Site as another SharePoint site, with the list, library, alert, and web part functionality that has been described in earlier chapters, and with the added social networking component that is similar to Facebook, such as profile updates, colleagues, and personal information.

Other users can view your My Site, and what they can view or edit will depend on how permissions have been set up.

Organizing sites, links, tags, and so on

You can efficiently organize all of the sites you are a member of, metadata tags and notes you have created and the associated content that they are linked to. This is discussed further in *Chapter 4, List Management* and *Chapter 8, Managing Metadata*.

Manage personal profile

My Sites provide you with a mechanism to update all of your current information so your organizational profile is up-to-date. You also have the option of creating and managing a personal blog site, which is by default visible to all other SharePoint users.

Normally, the My Site feature is configured for internal user access within an organization, rather than external access.

Mailbox and calendar integration

As long as SharePoint 2010 is integrated with Microsoft Exchange Server 2003 or higher, you can directly view your mailbox and calendar(s) through your My Site. This is discussed further in *Chapter 13, Pages and Web Parts*.

The feature is useful if you are often working in an environment where you are not working on your own computer, so your Outlook client is not configured.

Organizational information

My Sites easily grant visibility into colleagues' blogs, profiles, published content, and other relevant social information. SharePoint 2010 even includes a new interactive organizational chart.

Social aspects of My Sites

SharePoint's My Sites social networking component was originally introduced with **SharePoint Portal Server 2003** and was rebranded and included in SharePoint Server 2007, with minimal feature changes. With SharePoint 2010, you will notice a myriad of new features. Some notable new features are explained in the following sections.

Ask Me About

This feature allows you to list topics that you feel you are knowledgeable about so that other people know to come to you for assistance on the subject matter.

Colleagues

This page consolidates and displays all of your colleagues. You can configure how this information is presented to other SharePoint users.

Note Board

This feature displays notes and comments written by you that other users will see when you visit your My Site. It is similar to the wall displays used on Facebook.

Organizational chart

The **organizational chart** has been redesigned to be much more interactive and user friendly. You can easily locate your colleagues in the organization as well as navigate the organizational hierarchy.

The structure of the organizational chart is based on the organization's Active Directory. This is a good example of SharePoint leveraging corporate information in another system.

What's happening?

This *micro-blogging* feature allows you to enter a brief description of what you are currently up to. It is very similar to functionality provided by Twitter, with the exception that the audience consuming your updates is your organization's SharePoint community. This feature can be very useful to quickly post information and to engage in concise, directed conversation.

Office Communicator 2010 will display this information status from your My Site.

Creating your My Site

My Sites are comprised of two components: a **personal site** for each user, and one that is shared among all SharePoint users. When an administrator configures the **User Profile** service application in **SharePoint Central Administration**, only the shared component of your personal site becomes available to end users. The personal site is automatically created and integrated with the shared site when a user clicks on the **My Content** hyperlink. It only takes a few seconds, and the site is made ready for the end user.

1. Log on as yourself to your company's intranet (for example `http://intranet`).

2. Click on your name at the top right-hand corner of the page and select **My Site**.

3. Click on the **My Content** link and the personal portion of your My Site will be created momentarily.

 All SharePoint users have a profile, but the My Site feature must be explicitly enabled by the administrator.

My Site features

After your personal site is created, it is initially populated with a basic set of features. These features are divided up between, and accessible through, the following three pages:

- My Newsfeed
- My Content
- My Profile

My Newsfeed page

The **My Newsfeed** page displays updates relating to your colleagues, **newsfeeds** that you subscribe to, and other SharePoint content. By default the page is subdivided into three columns: **My Colleagues**, **My Interests**, and **Newsfeed Settings**.

My Colleagues

This section allows you to add people as colleagues and follow their activities in the SharePoint environment. This includes updates to colleagues' profiles, social tags, blogs, and so on.

My Interests

This section enables you to identify your interests using keywords that will act as metadata. When other users tag content using the keywords that you specified, you will start to see newsfeed activities populate the My Newsfeed page.

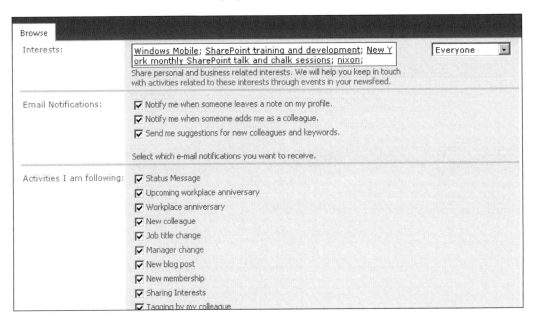

Newsfeed settings

This section allows you to glance at changes to content from colleagues such as changes to their profile details, or when content is tagged with keywords or commented on.

What's New

Stay Connected!

There are no activities in your newsfeed. Stay connected by adding colleagues and interests.

My Colleagues	My Interests	Newsfeed Settings
Add people as colleagues to follow their activities such as profile updates, blog entries, and tagging.	Enter keywords that describe your interests so that you will see newsfeed activities when people tag content using those keywords.	Select activities such as tagg updates, and comments that see in your newsfeed.

My Newsfeed can be viewed as virtual water cooler talk—where co-workers gather around a water cooler at work and talk about their or other co-workers' activity. This information that is exchanged is more than just gossip, but rather snippets of timely information that would not be normally announced via e-mail or other communication methods. The value of this form of information exchange should not be overlooked as it creates comradely teamwork and encourages an active understanding of what other people are doing during the day.

We have seen this feature work very well in organizations when users that share the same job function and have become colleagues with each other start tagging content or applying keywords to content. For example, if a developer writes a blog entry on their My Site about changes to the corporate firewall and tags this with a keyword that you are interested in such as **infrastructure**, you read this and tag it. This passive update can now be referenced in the future through a tag cloud, which is a visual depiction of user-generated tags.

Refine by type:

All | Tags | Notes | Private | Public

Refine by tag:

Sort: Alphabetically | By Size

Document Libraries I like it nixon Promotion Training

Tagging is a better way of communicating, storing, and referencing content than asking the person to e-mail the details, which may be lost in your inbox.

My Content page

The **My Content** page acts as a repository for your personal document images, and so on. As with SharePoint Server 2007, it includes lists and libraries that you can use to manage your personal resources, both shared and private.

Personal documents

This document library is private and can only be accessed by you. It is the same in principle as a user's home directory on a file server, and can be used to store documents that you do not want to share with anyone else.

It is not uncommon for users to be reluctant to save incomplete files on a SharePoint site and prefer to save the file to their desktop. This is understandable, but there is no version control or selective feedback from team members through a workflow. By using the personal documents library, the benefits of SharePoint are available where the content is restricted to you. Saving important documents to your desktop is not advised because content is not backed up on a daily basis.

Because you have designer permissions to your My Site, you have the ability to create lists and libraries, which may be restricted on other SharePoint sites.

To view another user's My Site, click on the **Modified By** column in a view of a list or library, or use SharePoint's search functionality.

Shared documents

This document library is intended to be shared with other SharePoint users that access your personal site. Everyone in the organization can read and copy content, but they cannot update content that is stored in this library.

My Sites should not be used as a permanent repository for team collaboration content because your My Site can grow into a mini website. It is designed for personal end user use rather than a fully functional team site. If end users beg to store a lot of content here, the content managers should consider moving it to an appropriate site.

Also, if an employee leaves the company, the user account may be deleted along with their My Site and its content.

Shared pictures

This library can be utilized as a photo album: a place to store and share pictures with other SharePoint users that access your personal site.

Other

Additional libraries available in your personal site include **Customized Reports**, **Form Templates**, and the **Style Library**. The Customized Reports library is meant to act as a repository for web analytics. The Form Templates library is meant to host form templates that would be made administratively available to you, based on organizational need. The purpose of the Style Library is to host style sheets and other files associated with branding and customization of My Sites. These libraries are used less frequently and an in-depth examination of each is outside the scope of this book.

My Profile page

The **My Profile** page is the default landing page for your personal site, for you and for others accessing your site. This page provides an abundance of information and gives you the ability to manage details about yourself, colleagues, and memberships.

In addition, the content and information that is displayed can be managed using views. A few out of the box views are as follows:

- **Everyone**: This view will enable every user that has access to your SharePoint site to see your content

- **Only Me**: This view will only enable you (the site owner) to see your content

- **My Colleagues:** This view will enable every user that you have listed in your My Colleagues list to see your content

- **My Manager:** This view will only enable your manager (pulled from Active Directory) to see your content

- **My Team:** This view will enable specific users that you have identified in your My Colleagues list to see your content

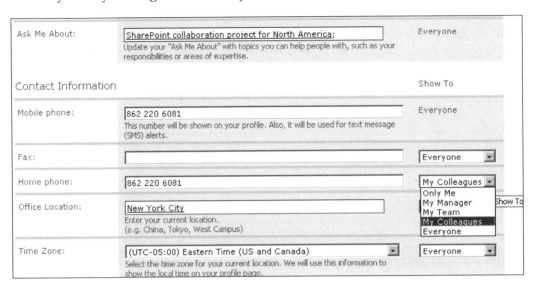

These settings provide useful personalization of information to certain groups of workers and team members who are more active than others in their day-to-day work.

We encourage you to apply settings that you think are most beneficial to you and your team. However, if you work in a large company and everyone can see your cell phone numbers, you run the risk of being inundated with requests from co-workers because the SharePoint site will probably be the tool of choice for workers to find someone with a specific skill set and their corresponding contact number within the company.

The My Profile page is divided into the following six tabs:

- Overview
- Organization
- Content
- Tags and Notes
- Colleagues
- Memberships

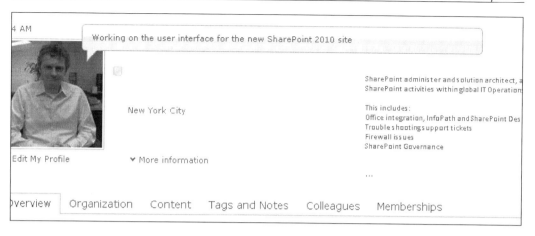

You navigate through the different portions of your personal site by clicking on these tabs:

- **Overview**: This tab displays general information about you via a few web parts on the page (refer to the following screenshot). The **Ask Me About** web part allows you to list topics that you feel you are knowledgeable about and where you should be involved so that other people know to come to you for assistance on the subject matter. The more detailed this is, the more status and credibility within an organization you will have as your team, colleagues, and co-workers will understand your role and what activities you are accountable for in this role.

- The **Recent Activities** web part lists relevant social actions that you have performed throughout the environment, such as the creation of tags and notes. The **Note Board** web part allows you and others to share notes and comments. The **My Organization Chart** shows where you are in relation to the organizational hierarchy. The **In Common with You** web part shows common traits that you share with users accessing your personal site. This information propagates other colleagues' My Site news feeds.

- **Organization:** This particular tab displays an interactive organizational chart using the Microsoft Silverlight plugin for your web browser. This chart is constructed using SharePoint profile manager relationships, and allows you to see a user's position in the organizational hierarchy. The actual data is pulled from your organization's **Active Directory** during the user profile import. You can use this chart to move up and down the hierarchy to find information about any user.

- **Content**: This tab displays all of the lists, libraries, and blog posts that you manage through your **My Content** page.

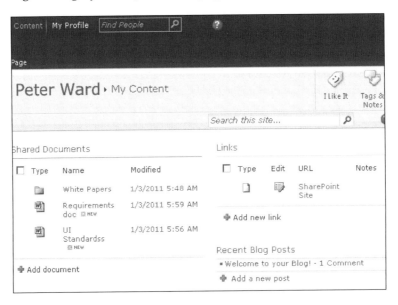

The My Site design does not have a link to return you to a team site within the site collection. We recommend that you add a **My Links** web part to your **My Content** page on your **My Site** and add in a link to the site collection (home page).

- **Tags and Notes**: This tab displays the tags and notes that you have created throughout the environment using SharePoint's social tagging mechanisms way. Social tagging of content in SharePoint 2010 consists of two links on all SharePoint pages: **I Like It** and **Tags and Notes**. These mechanisms enable you to identify content important to you and add personal descriptions of the identified content. In your personal site, these tags and notes are aggregated so that you can filter and sort through them in a structured, effective manner.

 One way to think of Tags and Notes is as an online equivalent of Post-It notes on a bulletin board or refrigerator. If you are the kind of person who is intuitive and likes to have information neatly categorized, this SharePoint functionality is ideal for cataloguing content.

- **Colleagues:** This tab lists all of your colleagues. It enables you to define your relationships with colleagues, to manage your team members, to delete colleagues, and so on. If you need to find out more information about a colleague, just click on their name. You will then open up the shared component of their personal site.

- **Memberships**: This tab lists all of the SharePoint groups that you are a member of. If you are viewing someone else's memberships on their My Site, the memberships in common will be displayed. From this page, you can manage your group information. This is a useful feature if you are taking over the role of another user; instead of asking them which groups they are a member of, you can look at this page.

The last two points, colleagues and memberships, are very useful during an on-boarding process of a new colleague to the team because they can very quickly see who the team members are and the groups to which co-workers belong.

Summary

The focus of this chapter was to introduce you to My Sites and the social networking features provided by SharePoint Server 2010.

We recommend that you take some time exploring the concepts and features examined in this chapter, particularly setting up colleagues, team members, and sharing content through your personal site. The more you practice, the easier it will get and you will quickly begin to reap the benefits of My Sites' functionality.

The described social element of My Sites only works if a team, group, or entire organization is managing the profile information, and tagging content. There is not much value if only a few people are using this functionality, not just in the updates, but also the information discovery process with SharePoint's search.

One of the best ways for this functionality to gain traction is for senior management to use this functionality to communicate to their team. This is to use the functionality, rather than tell their team how to use the social networking functionality. In short, we must all be social!

We have seen that once some traction begins in one department, the user uptake is viral and very quick, and a tipping point occurs where everyone is tagging content, adding colleagues, and micro blogging. Once this occurs, the value of SharePoint will go to a new level because a lot of knowledge in an organization is not stored in documents, but is sitting in cubicles and walking around corridors. The *people* element of information has become engrained into the technology.

We recommend that if possible you review the My Site functionality with the human resources department, and have the update profile process become part of the new employee initiation.

All of SharePoint's functionality has now been discussed in the previous chapters. This includes Sites, Lists, Libraries, Workflows, and web parts. The next three chapters explain how and where to apply these functionalities to your organization and to roles within your organization.

15
Applying Functionality for Business Initiatives

You should now have a good understanding of SharePoint's functionality and be wondering where and when to start applying functionality to the business collaboration activity. This chapter looks at where SharePoint's functionality can be applied with regards to the following business areas:

Department	Business Process
Sales Department	CRM tracking, RFP management and response process, contact management, workflow approval, and pipeline status.
IT Department	IT Support, knowledge base, and change/release management.
Project Management Office	Project management workbench-Document management, issue tracking, and change orders.
Human Resources	Resume approvals, onboarding, and yearly reviews.

SharePoint's functionality is most appropriately used when a department's or users' main collaborating activity is mostly dependent on unstructured communications such as e-mail or when third-party applications are not used with both this collaboration and communication processes.

If a business process of third-party application is being considered to be migrated to SharePoint, there are both technological and interpersonal considerations that need to be factored into the decision making process.

In this chapter, where to apply SharePoint's functionality is broken down by department. However, it will be beneficial for you to read the entire chapter and understand where to apply relevant SharePoint functionality to a department's related collaboration activities.

> The functionality discussed in this chapter has been explained in greater detail in *Chapter 3, SharePoint Team Sites, Chapter 4, List Management,* and *Chapter 5, Library Management,* but from the standpoint of technology functionality. This chapter will discuss this from a business standpoint.

Sales department

Typical scenario example: the sales team has seven members:

- Four field account executives whose responsibility is to generate and track leads, develop the proposal, and close the sale
- Two sales support members whose role is to keep subscription renewals of the product up-to-date with existing clients
- Sales Director whose role it is to manage the department so that it works as a team

Challenges

The main challenges of the sales department are:

- All internal communications and meeting notes are e-mailed among the department, so it is difficult to track information and respond to requests in a timely manner
- At times the team does not know which proposals have been submitted to clients, or the win-to-lose ratio of these proposals
- There is no campaign management with prospects or clients

SharePoint's functionality can be applied to the Sales department to remedy these challenges.

Customer Relationship Management (CRM) system

If the sales process is not too complicated, SharePoint can be customized to provide very basic CRM functionality by applying the following high level steps:

1. Create a **Contact List** to store leads from trade shows. The Contact List template has most of the columns required for contact management. Additional CRM-related fields could be added to identify the vertical and lead source. By adding these fields too, this list can be categorized with **Views**. The SharePoint contact list can also be connected to the user's Outlook so contact synchronization can occur. This is an excellent centralized repository, where if contact details change or notes need to be added, the information can be automatically shared among a user base. The integration with Outlook can resolve a major issue that corporations have with CRM systems, which is that contact information is entered once, but rarely updated. When the contact is edited by the sales person, it is only done in their Outlook. With the SharePoint approach, Enterprise information integration, and Outlook personalization is retained.

> It is possible to cut and paste an Outlook contact into a SharePoint contact list through the Outlook interface.

2. Create two custom lists, one called **Companies** to store the companies that have ongoing sales opportunities (suppose that your sales department has sent them a proposal for review), and one called **Contacts**. By using the column type **Lookup (information already on this site)**, the **Contact Name** and **Company** entry in the **Companies** list can reference the **Contact Name** and **Company** column values in the **Contact List**. Additional columns could be added to the **Companies List**: **Industry**, **Lead Source**, and **Annual Revenue**.

3. Create a **Document Library** called **Opportunities** to store the ongoing sales proposal documents. By using a column type **Lookup (information already on this site)**, columns such as **Company Name**, **Full Name**, and **E-mail Address** in both previously created lists such as the **Contact** and the **Companies** can be referenced from this list. Additional columns to the **Opportunities** list could be added:

Field Name	Field Type
Estimated close date	Date
Status: Won, Lost, Undecided	Choice
Dollar amount	Number

These would provide a CRM tracking functionality for management.

 Note that all fields in the Opportunities Library can be edited by the user in the Word document. This simplifies the user experience when making changes to information as the interface remains the same.

 You can see that structuring the information this way has a standard relational database structure of a one-to-many or a many-to-one relationship, which is the same table structure often found in an Access database.

Additional features to the described functionality

To provide additional user experience, the following bullet points should be reviewed and applied by the reader:

- In the **Opportunities Library**, create a **View** to show a sales pipeline or estimated sales to close in the next four to six months.

- In the **Opportunities Library**, create a View to filter the **Status by Won**.

- Set up an alert on the **Status by Won** view and subscribe the sales team to this alert. With this notification rule set up, every time a submitted proposal is won, the team is notified of the win and a workflow is triggered to copy the proposal to a work orders site or the **Record Center**. This is so that the project management office knows that this scope of work needs to be factored into resource schedules.

- When the sales team reviews the documents in the **Opportunities Library**, use the **Tags & Notes** feature to add comments to documents, such as side conversations about what the client is expecting from the **Statement Of Work (SOW)**, their timelines, and feedback from demonstrations.

- Create a standard document approval workflow to the submitted proposals and assign members of the sales team to approve these and provide feedback.

A Request for Proposal (RFP) response

The type of RFP received by an organization will determine how the sales teams will respond, particularly if industry vertical expertise is required. A useful feature within SharePoint to assist with this process is called the **Rule Based Submission**. This feature lets you define rules on a folder for the routing of documents on a timely basis. These are settings that the SharePoint administrator can configure. When a document is uploaded to the folder, depending on a defined rule, it can be moved to the correct library/folder because rules are dependent on the metadata that the user has associated with the document. This is an example of the vertical of the RFP document type.

This saves time for users because they no longer need to navigate to a specific location within a document library; it is done automatically for them!

To do this, set up the **Content Organizer** feature that must first be enabled on the **Site**:

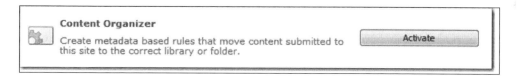

This is done via **Site Settings**, (**Manage Site Features | Site Actions**), and creates a document library named **Drop Off Library**.

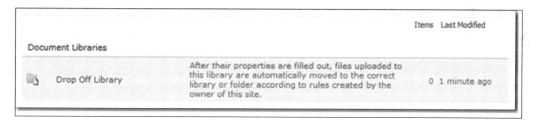

After enabling the feature, go to **Site Administration** and click on **Content Organizer Rules**:

This displays a form where you can add the routing criteria. In the following example there is a rule called **RFP** that will move all documents with the keyword Gov to the folder Gov in the **RFP** document library.

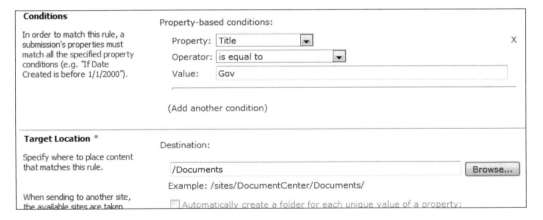

In the following screenshot, the **Managed Keywords** can be changed to **Gov** and the uploaded document will trigger the Content Organizer Rule **RFP Gov** so that the document will be copied to the Gov folder in the RFP's library. Regardless of where the document was uploaded to, the item will be redirected to the **Drop Off Library** before being routed elsewhere. Users *will* be able to see the final location of the document. Because this content indexing is automatically done by this rules engine, there is less user error and more confidence that the information in the target location is correct.

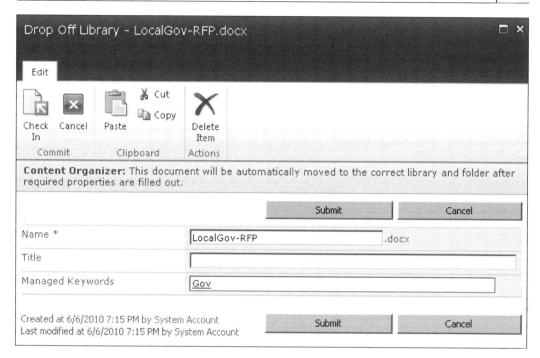

Campaign management

Because the sales contacts are now stored in the Contact centralized list that can be synchronized with Outlook, there is the ability to perform an e-mail mail merge (**e-mail blast**) using these contacts. This can be done by performing the following steps within Microsoft Word:

1. Select **Mailing** from the **Ribbon**.
2. Click on **Start Mail Merge**.
3. Click on **Select Recipients** from the Ribbon.
4. Choose **Outlook Contacts**.
5. Select the **SharePoint Contact** list that is connected to your Outlook that you wish to send e-mails to.

You can now send e-mails to contacts regarding upcoming events.

The preceding steps assume that the SharePoint contact list is connected to your Outlook. If this is not already done you can enable this setting by performing the following steps:

1. Select **Connect to Outlook** from the **Ribbon**.

2. Click **Allow** when you are prompted with the dialog box asking, **Do you want to allow this website to open a program on your computer?**

3. Click **Yes** when you are prompted with **Connect this SharePoint Contacts List to Outlook?**

This SharePoint list is now connected to your Outlook. The list in Outlook is available when you are offline, and if new items are added to the list in SharePoint or Outlook, the content will synchronize.

Simple SharePoint tips for a sales department user base

Generally, a sales department collaborates with e-mail more than other departments because so much information is received from outside of the organization by e-mail. Using SharePoint's e-mail-enabling feature of lists and libraries to store and reference this content is a huge win.

It is common that sales material such as price sheets and product literature from a third-party is e-mailed to a sales person and is of interest to other co-workers in the department. Instead of that person forwarding the e-mail to the sales department, this e-mail could be forwarded to a SharePoint library and categorized using the subject field of the e-mail.

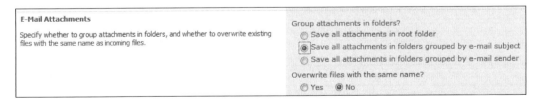

The library will store the attachments from the e-mail in a folder.

A daily alert subscription can be set up on the library to notify the sales department when content is added. This method of document categorization is very effective in storing content that can be quickly referenced, with minimal effort from users.

An e-mail-enabled team sales discussion list can also be created to capture sales-related activities, or industry-related news, with a daily alert to the sales group.

With both examples there are a few observations of the small yet valuable benefits that SharePoint is providing:

- The content is for reference, rather than content that requires an immediate response. This is why storing it in SharePoint (a searchable repository with a delayed notification) rather than sending an e-mail to the department is more appropriate.

- By setting up a daily notification rather than an immediate one, the constant drip feed of e-mails entering people's inbox is reduced. With the daily summary notification, users only need to glance at a single alert notification e-mail and decide whether it is of interest is or not.

 We have noticed that often co-workers are reluctant to e-mail FYI reference information to colleagues because people complain they receive too many e-mails. With the SharePoint approach of a daily notification from a SharePoint list, the e-mails are reduced and the content is searchable.

- The content rating field can be added to the list or library so the sales department can rate items or documents, so if users are periodically glancing at a list or library, their attention is drawn to what content their co-workers thought was good.

Type	Name	Rating (0-5)	
📁	Sales		⊃ 6:16 AM
📄	Final Memo	☆☆☆☆☆	⊃ 4:25 AM
📄	Sales Monthly Forecast	☆☆☆☆☆	⊃ 4:26 AM
📄	SOW	☆☆☆☆☆	⊃ 4:27 AM
📄	Top 10 Customers	☆☆☆☆☆	⊃ 4:28 AM

- A decision has been made in the department to store the content in two different locations: sales literature and sales activities. This has been agreed upon by the department. It is important that this is understood by the department.

IT department

Typical scenario example: The IT department has four members, one of which includes a manager. The department supports helpdesk requests submitted by various departments, as well as the company-wide e-mail and network infrastructure.

Challenges

The main challenges for this department include:

- Managing support issues for the user base
- Managing change control
- Centrally storing server names, IP addresses, IDs, and passwords for the team to use

SharePoint's functionality can be applied to the IT department with the following sections:

Supporting issue tracking

The challenges of support issue tracking can be addressed by applying the following high level steps:

1. Create an **Announcement List** to contain raised issues from users that IT support can track. The announcement list can be **e-mail enabled** so issues can be e-mailed into the list by the user base.

   You may ask yourself why we are proposing using an *Announcement List* template, rather than an *Issue Tracking* list template that is designed to track issues. The announcement list template can accept incoming e-mails, and we view this as the easiest and quickest way users can submit issues with screenshots embedded.

The Issue Tracking list template is more suited to track issues where the user base is already using SharePoint and knows which page to click and complete the web-based form. The e-mail approach of the announcement list is more suited for a non-technical user base that just wants the issue fixed.

If the user base does not have direct access to the SharePoint site, the e-mail approach may be the only way to submit support tickets to a SharePoint list.

 Custom lists and Issue Tracking lists cannot be e-mail enabled.

2. In this list, create the following additional fields:

   ° **Status** (Choice type) that has the following values: **Unassigned**, **In Progress**, **Complete**, **On Hold**, and **Unresolved**. This field will represent the status of the submitted issue. Its default value should be **Unassigned**, so when an issue is e-mailed into the list its value will be **Unassigned**.

   ° **Assigned To** (Person type): When an issue is e-mailed into the list, this value will be empty as this field requires manual input.

   ° **Technology** (Choice) that has the following values: **SharePoint**, **Email**, **Phone**, and **Blackberry**.

   These fields can be used to filter views that could be added to web parts on a page.

   The Announcement list template has the following pre-defined fields: **Title**, **Body**, **Created By**, and **Creation Date**.

3. Create the following views on this list:

   ° **Unassigned**: This will show all submitted issues that are unassigned to a support person. The filter on the view is **Status is equal to Unassigned**.

   ° **Assigned**: This view will show the submitted issues that are assigned to the support team, so it is possible to see who is working on which issue. The **View** should be **Grouped By**; the field value **Assigned**.

   ° **Assigned to Me**: This view will show the submitted issues that are assigned to a support member. The view should be filtered with the value **[Me]**.

4. Create an alert subscription to this list, with the **Change Type** set to **New Items Are Added**. So, when items are added you are notified that there is a new support issue and it needs to be assigned to a team member.

Support Tracking Process

The steps of the support tracking process are outlined as follows:

1. An end user submits an issue via an e-mail to the e-mail address that is defined in the list.

2. The e-mailed issue now resides in the list and has a status of **Unassigned**.

3. An alert notification is triggered and sent to the support team indicating that there is a new support issue that requires their action.

4. A member of the support team edits the submitted issue, changes the status to **In Progress**, and assigns it to a member who is then notified via an alert to begin work on the issue.

With the preceding example, you may be thinking, *Isn't the idea of SharePoint to reduce e-mail dependence....and this solution generates two e-mails?*

With the user raising the ticket through e-mail rather than completing a web form, there is an advantage. Not only is it quicker for the user to send an e-mail in Outlook, but it is also possible to paste screenshots in an e-mail, rather than uploading them to a web form.

Although a web form can capture additional fields for the user to complete, often a user will prefer to write a short descriptive e-mail of the problem with the screenshot of the error pasted into the e-mail body.

Once the e-mail has been received by a SharePoint list, someone in IT support can complete more specific information, such as ticket type and priority.

Regarding the alert notification, the e-mail notifies IT support that a support ticket requires action. The e-mail body contains details and has links to the SharePoint list. The content is now centrally stored in a list.

With this business scenario, SharePoint functionality is complementing e-mail with centrally managed information, rather than replacing it.

Obviously, this can be more complicated, but it is a good start to defining and deploying a support tracking process in SharePoint.

Managing change control

The best way to manage change control of software releases or a hardware upgrade is to create a list based from the Calendar list template as the calendar view functionality is already provided. This gives you visibility of upcoming change control activity.

Other changes that should be applied to this list can include:

1. Set **Content Approval** so all entries require approval.
2. Set up weekly subscriptions to this list with **Alerts** for the department so there is a weekly e-mail notification of activity.
3. Change the field title to **Brief Description**.

This is a very good example of a simple, yet effective approach to change management within a department.

Storing technical information

Usually, technical information is stored in Word documents and Excel files on a network drive. Using SharePoint's **Wiki** list template there is not only a centralized approach to storing technical information such as shared IDs, passwords, and IP addresses, but also a version history of entries stating what has been changed by who and when.

The functionality of a wiki is that it allows the easy creation and editing of any number of interlinked web pages via a web browser using a simplified markup language or a **What you see is what you get** (**WYSIWYG**) text. In this business scenario, confidential information should not be stored in a wiki because if pages need to become restricted, links to restricted pages may not work for certain users, and to manage the restricted pages and links to them could be a challenge.

Simple SharePoint tips for an IT department user base

An IT department has multiple requests from users to perform actions, such as new hardware, onboarding requirements, or software upgrades. These requests should use custom form lists rather than e-mail, where fields can capture essential information, such as username, location, and manager. The forms can trigger simple workflows to relevant users to perform and complete the work.

By structuring requests in forms, SharePoint views of lists can display requests in different stages on a single page so the IT department can understand the status of requests and also gauge workloads for resources.

Project Management Office

Typical scenario example: the **Project Management Office (PMO)** has a program manager and a number of project managers and consultants for their projects. A standardized methodology has been defined with phases, goals, and a document template. The projects are similar in resources and time length.

Challenges

The main challenges for the PMO include:

- Project issue tracking
- Storing documentation
- Restricting access to certain documents

SharePoint's functionality can be applied to the described PMO activity with the following sections:

Project site

The project collaborative platform can address all of the challenges of this department by following these high level steps:

1. Create a site with the Project Site Template. The Team Site name should be the project name.

2. In the **Shared Document Library** create folders after each of the phases in the PMO's methodology and upload project-related templates, such as Change Request forms. Metadata fields could also be added to this library, which could be applied to filter views or aid information discovery.

3. Create a custom list called **Project Goals** and create the following fields in this list: **Status: Incomplete** and **Finished**.

4. Adjust security levels on the folders so budgets can be restrictive.

5. Save this site as a Site Template called **Custom Project Site**.

With this saved team site now stored as a template, there is a repeatable layout for all projects, so each time that a new project requires a SharePoint Team Site, this Team Site template should be used with the project. It also specifies the path to the site gallery to view other site templates to confirm if a similar template already exists.

Simple SharePoint tips for a PMO office user base

One of the ways a PMO can undertake more projects with the same amount of resources is to define repeatable processes in the way projects are managed. This has been mentioned in this section of the chapter, with team site templates that contain documentation and custom lists.

The site template approach can be sophisticated enough to accommodate different types of projects with different templates, but this can only be done if the project methodology and project types are understood, or you are willing to create new site templates ad hoc.

We do not see anything wrong with an ad hoc approach, but it is important that project managers know the most appropriate site template to create a site.

Human Resources

Typical scenario example: the **Human Resources (HR)** department has three hiring managers and review thousands of resumes each year, and interview hundreds of potential candidates for roles within the organization.

Challenges

The main challenges for this department include:

- Too many e-mails of resumes to multiple people, with lost comments of feedback
- The whole resume review process is unstructured, at best
- Often, talented candidates are not hired because the hiring process is too long
- When a new employee accepts an offer they are often not able to start immediately because various departments are slow to complete onboarding tasks

SharePoint's functionality can be applied to the HR department processes with the following sections.

Resume approval

Resumes can be approved more quickly by applying the following high level steps:

1. Create a **Document Library** called **Resumes**. In this library, all resumes of potential candidates will be stored and reviewed by the HR members.

2. Set up **Content Approval** in this library so the status of resumes will be **Pending**, **Approved**, or **Rejected**.

3. Set up two alert subscriptions to this library for:

   ◦ **New Items Added**: so, when resumes are added, the team is notified that they need to review the newly created resumes.

   ◦ When the status is changed to **Approved**, the team members are notified that an interview is scheduled.

4. Create a **View** that is sorted by the rating of a document.

Resume approval process

Managing submitted resumes of a job opening within an organization can be challenging because this is usually managed via e-mail, by multiple people, so information can be lost or duplicated multiple times.

The steps of the resume approval process are outlined as follows:

1. Potential candidates' resumes are added to the Resume Approval's **Document Library**.

2. An alert notification is sent to the team members so they know that there are resumes that require their review.

3. The team members can write comments to the resume with SharePoint's Tag & Rate feature. By rating a resume, more suited candidates' resumes will be shown at the top of the rating view, which would indicate that they are more suited for the job.

4. The resume's status is changed to **Approved** and an interview is scheduled.

The defined resume approval process can be taken further with a workflow being triggered to the interviewer of the candidate with a link to the resume in the e-mail. The workflow will also store the interview comments, and at the end of the interview process the team can be notified that all the interviews for a candidate are complete with the interview comments in a single place for review.

HR onboarding process

Once a candidate has accepted the job there is a checklist of activity that needs to be done prior to their start. This process can be streamlined following high level steps:

1. Create a **Custom List** called **Onboarding** and create a series of checkbox fields that indicate a series of steps that are required. These could include **Bank Account Details provided**, **Photo ID**, and **Building pass**.

2. Set up a workflow to route a new item (new employee) to the relevant departments.

Simple SharePoint tips for a Human Resources user base

One of the roles of the Human Resources Department is the communication of company policies, standards, and processes. This information is ideal for a company SharePoint intranet site where documents, forms, announcements, and external links can reside.

Typically, HR content such as policies are time sensitive and if they are out-of-date, yet seem to be current, there can be repercussions not just to the department but the company as a whole.

There are a number of out of the box SharePoint intranet functions for this that are well-suited for HR information:

- **Record management and policies**: This allows documents to have expiration dates set to them.
- **Workflows**: Approval of documents and the auditing of the approval process.
- Permission restrictions for sensitive documents.
- **My Sites**: To display user personal information such as skills, colleagues, and manager and organization chart.

Your company may already have an intranet site, but if the content is static and requires a webmaster to add forms and documents, it may be a challenge to keep content up-to-date.

If there is not an area for HR activities on the current company intranet, request IT creates a SharePoint site purely for HR activities and link this site to the intranet site.

Summary

This chapter's focus has been *where to apply SharePoint's functionality to business activities*, with relevant business scenarios and functionality tips to help you decide which lists, libraries, and site to use for different purposes, and how and when to use them. The chapter covered only a few department scenarios and their challenges, but you can get a sense as to how to apply functionality to a department's business collaboration processes.

Further application of SharePoint functionality is discussed in the next chapter, where you will see how SharePoint's functionality can be applied to lists, libraries, notifications, search, pages, team sites, and My Sites.

16
Creating Exceptional End User Experience for You and Your Team

This chapter looks at where SharePoint's functionality can be applied to give exceptional user experience with the following SharePoint features:

- Lists
- Libraries
- Notifications
- Search
- Pages
- Team sites
- My Sites
- Frequently used web parts and web part connections
- Dashboard design

What creates exceptional end user experience in SharePoint?

Exceptional end user experience is about more than just deploying the SharePoint technology; it is about **simplicity**, **empathy**, **listening**, and **measuring success** so that improvements can be made.

In short, it is about users not only using the deployed SharePoint technology to assist with their work, but also with other unthought-of activities related their job. When this kind of enthusiasm occurs, SharePoint technology can be said to be making a difference, ultimately resulting in exceptional end user experience.

For this to happen, the following is needed:

- **Simplicity**: Just because you are familiar with SharePoint's interface does not mean other co-workers are. So, information must be presented in such a way that it is immediately obvious to the user what it is and how to navigate to it. This may require hand-holding and instruction manuals, but the key is simplicity. This idea should be applied to where to store content so there are fewer steps to perform simple operations such as uploading and editing content.

- **Empathy**: The user wants the comfort level of knowing that someone can address the concerns of SharePoint technology when they use it.

- **Listening**: This is much more than only asking for users' feedback. It is also observing the users and noticing how they use the interface, even if they can or do not verbalize their thoughts or response. Listening for unspoken cues in interaction or reaction is the key to understanding the impact of how SharePoint is working for them. In many ways, you actually need to be alert and in listening mode 24/7 to really hear the nitty gritty, the unspoken feedback; so, staying close to them during and after implementation is strongly recommended.

- **Measuring**: The value of SharePoint can be intangible, so defining key wins such as a percentage increase of completed daily orders, and so on will make it easier to build a business case for SharePoint.

 End users have a limited amount of time to spend visiting corporate intranet websites. So, if you don't make it easy for them, they're not going to come back.

Lists

As discussed in *Chapter 4*, lists have properties that determine their functionality:

- Data columns
- View definitions
- Entry form layout
- Validation

- Versioning
- Workflow
- Content types

Within this section are a few additions to lists functionality that enhances the end user experience.

Active default view

With a **project tasks** list there is normally a status field on an item, such as **Not Started**, **In Progress**, **Completed**, **Deferred**, and **Waiting on someone else**.

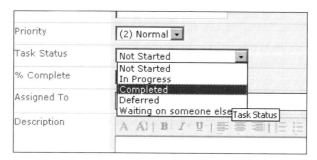

Project task items that are most important to a user are those that are **In Progress** as these are current and have most recently been created.

We recommend that you create a view with a filter with the Status set to Not Complete and make this the default view for the list, so every time this list is opened by the user, the active project tasks are displayed.

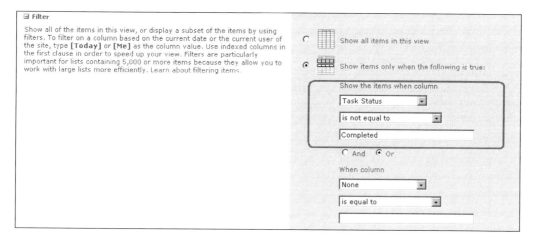

Make it personal

The Active View can be taken a step further by applying additional filters such as [**Me**], so that any tasks that are assigned and active to a user are immediately displayed.

Within libraries

In *Chapter 5*, you were introduced to the SharePoint's libraries functionality to store documents. Apart from storing documents and making these accessible to users, SharePoint has some easy and interesting functionality to enhance the user experience of document management in libraries. These are explained in the following sections.

Document sets

Document sets allow the user to bundle documents together. This is ideal for documents that are related that now can be associated and bundled together. The advantage of this is that certain actions can be done on a set of documents, rather than individually. These actions include:

- Sharing the same metadata
- Workflow management
- Permissions
- A single download and a single version control

Document Sets are a nice feature because a single document is rarely associated with a task or project, and now documents can be *bundled* together.

 Document sets are only available with SharePoint Server, not Foundation 2010.

Metadata

Documents can be tagged with metadata, which is now semi-automatic as the field has a **Suggestions** functionality, where keywords that can relate to the company's terminology have been defined in the site collection's **Term Store Management**.

Commit	Clipboard	Actions

Name *   Top 10 Customers   .docx

Title   Top 10 Customers

Rating (0-5)   ☆ ☆ ☆ ☆ ☆

Enterprise Keywords   sal

> **Suggestions**
> Sales [Keywords]
> Sales Manager, Regional [Keywords]
> Sales Rep [Keywords]
> Sales Representative [Keywords]
> Sales VP, Area [Keywords]
> Sales VP, Dedicated [Keywords]
> Sales VP, National Account [Keywords]
> Sales VP, Regional [Keywords]

Created at 12/28/2010 4:27 AM by USXEN
Last modified at 12/28/2010 4:28 AM by U

These keywords can be associated with entered content. SharePoint will intelligently make suggestions to which keywords you should choose.

By defining the keywords in the **Term Store Management**, there is one central place so keywords can be standardized.

File names

With documents stored on the network drive, one option is to choose relevant filenames that relate to a document. Filenames such as `Contract.docx` do not describe the information in the document, and the user would need to open it to understand its contents. A better description would be `ACMESalesContract2010.doc`.

With SharePoint, this approach is still useful, but a better approach is that metadata should be applied to the document or document set. One of the advantages of using metadata over the file-naming technique is that multiple keywords can be applied to a single item making the item more searchable.

SharePoint does not allow the following characters anywhere in a filename: Tilde, number sign, percent, ampersand, asterisk, braces, backslash, colon, angle brackets, question mark, slash, pipe, or quotation mark.

You cannot use the period character consecutively in the middle or at the start or end of a filename.

Notifications

With alert notifications, the alert title that is the subject of the e-mail message is based on the document library and the filename.

This is not helpful as a list and filename such as the one shown in the preceding screenshot, which is the **Alert Title**, could be in a number of libraries across a site.

A better approach is to make the alert tile more descriptive, such as **ACME Sales Contract Change** alert. This alert title indicates the filename that will be in the recipient's e-mail, and the type of alert that is being received.

Alert on a search

An alert can even be set up on a search page, so if there are any changes to the search results an alert can be sent out. This is a nice feature if, for example, you work in sales and want to know if there are any file additions to the SharePoint site that include any customer names. This is a good example of information being pushed to you when there is a change or addition to information that is of interest to you. The advantage of setting up an alert on a search is that it is relevant across an entire site collection, not just a list or a file.

An alert can be set up on a search page by performing the following steps:

1. Perform a search on a desired search criterion.

2. Click on the envelope icon at the top of the search page.

    You will be directed to an alert setup page. This alert page is slightly different to the alert page discussed previously in the book because this relates to subscribing an alert to a search results page, rather than a list or an individual item.

The difference that you will notice is the **Change Type** setting.

Change Type	Only send me alerts when:
Specify the type of changes that you want to be alerted to.	⦿ New items in search result
	◯ Existing items are changed
	◯ All changes
When to Send Alerts	
Specify how frequently you want to be alerted. (mobile alert is only available for immediately send)	⦿ Send a daily summary
	◯ Send a weekly summary

    3.   Complete the alert setup page and click **OK**.

You will now receive notifications related to content meeting the defined search results.

Outlook rules

If you have subscribed to multiple alerts it can be cumbersome to have your inbox full of alert notifications. So, you may want to set up a rule in Outlook to copy the alert e-mail to a folder.

Search

The SharePoint search feature is a quick way to find information fast. To make this process faster and more convenient for you, the following techniques could be applied when searching for information.

> Normally, when people wish to find information that is external to an organization, inputting a search into a search engine site is usually the first part of the process. SharePoint's search functionality should be viewed as a powerful tool to find internal company information.

Search refinement

On a search results page there are refinement options to assist you in narrowing your search results. They will show up on the left column of the search results page. It will consist of category headings and a list of links below these headings. Each link will have a number in parentheses. The number represents how many products match the refinement.

Result Type

- Any Result Type
- PowerPoint
- Webpage
- Word
- Adobe PDF

Site

- Any Site
- intranet.dev.usxp...
- usxhqvmsp10dev:82
- crmdocs.dev.usxpr...
- usxhqvmsp10dev:85

show more ⌄

Author

- Peter Ward
- Michael McCabe
- Paul Andrushkiw
- Scott Bobo
- Mark Westwood

show more ⌄

Modified Date

- Any Modified Date
- Past 24 Hours
- Past Week
- Past Month
- Past Six Months
- Past Year
- Earlier

Tags

- Any Tags
- NA sales

 Only the refinements relevant to your search results list will be displayed.

Recent content

Often, when you search for information that you know someone wrote recently, the quickest way to find that information is to perform a **People Search** on the person and then click on the **View Recent Content** link.

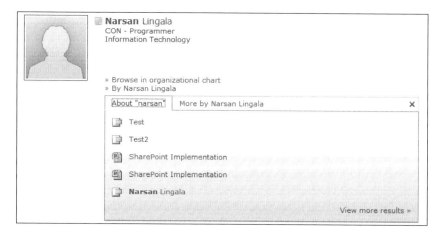

This will display the recently authored content by the user.

 This is also a good way to see what projects and activities that co-workers are working on as you can see the documents that they have edited.

Pages

The layout of a page in SharePoint is key to exceptional user experience as this makes information readable and quick to understand for the user. The attention to the layout of the information is often overlooked in a site design. This is unfortunate as the Page brings information from multiple sources in a site together.

Layout of the page

Given that most users read from left to right, put the most frequently read information in the top left-hand web zone of the page.

Limit views

If a view of a list or library is required to be displayed on a page, limit the number of items that can be displayed to five or ten. This will prevent the page scrolling down if there are too many items.

This feature can be set when the view is **modified**.

When a view has more than five items in it there is a tab button at the bottom of the web part:

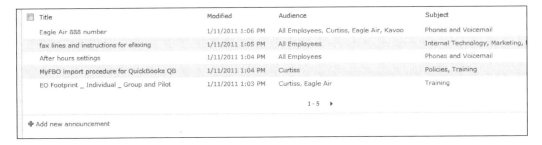

Avoid horizontal scroll bars

When adding a web part to zones on a page, avoid putting a list or a web part into a web zone that is very large as this makes it difficult to view the information without using the browser's navigation bars, which are additional steps for the user. This can be a challenge if users in the company have different screen resolutions.

Professional-looking websites normally have all the displayed content clearly displayed on the page, with the user only having to scroll down to view information.

Relevant documents

In *Chapter 13*, you were introduced to Pages and Web Parts. One of the most useful web parts to put on a page is the **Relevant Documents**.

This web part displays all of the reader's recently authored documents. This is useful because what most people want to focus on for the day are documents they have recently worked on, and this web part is only displaying files that the reader authored on this site, so the information is targeted to the logged-in user.

Team Sites

The purpose of Team Sites was discussed in *Chapter 3*. To design and deploy a team site with minimal overhead, the following tips and techniques are recommended.

Auto invite users

When adding users to a site, use the **Send E-Mail** feature. This makes the site setup process quicker as users are notified automatically via e-mail, with a link to the site team. Even with this, you can add a personal message in the e-mail stating what the site is and why you are inviting them to be a member.

While this might sound obvious, from our observations of the site creation process, most users create the site, add the users to it, and then send out a manual e-mail, even though this ultimately amounts to more work.

Inheritance

Team Sites inherit permissions from the parent site. To make security administration easier to manage, always try to keep the site inheritance on a Site, its libraries and lists, and documents and list items.

There is a tendency for the creator of a Team Site to feel that the site needs to be secure with access granted to a select few users, even when the information is not confidential. So, the site's security inheritance is broken, and they end up manually administrating the site for users rather than changing the setup of the parent site.

Site usage reports

Each SharePoint site has a usage report in the site settings. This site feature displays key features of information, such as the number of users using the site, which website they came from, and the page they are going to.

These reports are web pages within a site and can be found in the **Site Analytics Reports** of site settings.

This information is often asked about by users and can be displayed on the home page of a site. This can be done by using the **Web Analytics Web Part**, on the home page.

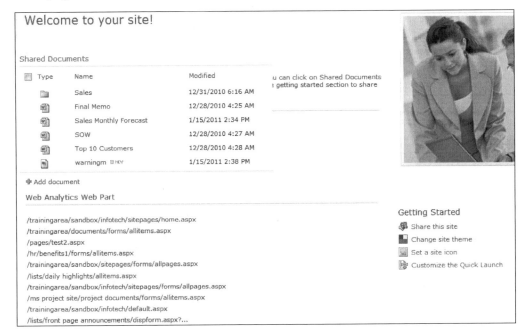

My Sites

In *Chapter 14, My Sites* you were introduced to My Sites, the personal portal for users to consume information from colleagues and those with the same interests. Take a moment and fill out your personal details and your job description:

- **Generic Details**
    - ○ **Name**: Diane Prescott
    - ○ **Job Title**: Director of sales
    - ○ **Job Description**: East Coast Sales
    - ○ **Hobbies**: Yoga, fitness
    - ○ **Skill Set**: Sales
- **Interesting details**
    - ○ **Name**: Diane Prescott
    - ○ **Job Title**: Director of sales
    - ○ **Job Description**: East Coast Sales from Florida to Montreal and east of Chicago.

- ○ **Hobbies**: Enjoy swimming and tennis and am always looking for an after-work tennis partner.
- ○ **Skill Set**: Technical sales for the company's entire in-house product set.

We recommend you create this information so that it really says something about you and your job role. Often, when someone searches for a document and they do not know the author and origin of it, they will most likely not open it. By having access to background information about the author, they can be sure of the value and legitimacy of the document.

 The main reason why people constantly update their personal details and connections on social websites such as LinkedIn is not because they are particularly friendly, but rather they want to raise the level of their profile in their peer group. Your personal details on your My Site aim at providing this functionality to your current co-workers.

Frequently used web parts and web part connections

In *Chapter 13, Pages and Web Parts*, web parts and pages were discussed. The main advantage of adding multiple web parts to a page is to display content such as lists, images, and PowerPoint files from multiple sources on a single page.

Obviously, the web parts of existing lists and libraries can be added to a page. Where user experience can really be enhanced is when the page filters data of different lists, or displays information from the same list, but with a different filter.

The web parts include:

- **Filters**: Choice Filter, Current User Filter, Date Filter, Filter Actions, Page Field Filter, Query String (URL) Filter, SharePoint List Filter, SQL Server Analysis Services Filter, and Text Filter
- **Media and Content**: Content Editor, Image Viewer, Media Web Part (embed video and audio media in web page), Page Viewer, and Silverlight Web Part (a Web Part to display a Silverlight application)
- **Content Rollup**: Content Query, HTML Form Web Part, Picture Library Slideshow Web Part, and RSS Viewer
- **Social Collaboration**: Note board, Tag Cloud, What's New, and Whereabouts

In this section of the chapter, we listed four web parts that we use often with SharePoint deployments. This is not a comprehensive list, but does give you a vision of what is capable with web parts and how **Web Parts Connections** work.

Content Editor Web Part

The **Content Editor Web Part** allows you to add formatted text, tables, hyperlinks, images, and even HTML to a web part page.

This web part gives the content worker a **WYSIWYG (What You See Is What You Get)** experience for editing text, similar to a word processer. There is also a source editor where HTML can be pasted into the web part to be displayed on a page.

Usually, a site's home page will have this web part on it with static introductory text about the site.

We found this web part useful for adding further instructions to custom forms. In the following screenshot, there is a custom form with a content editor web part at the top of the page providing further instructions to the users.

The additional information could include a company logo or a contact name.

Data filters

SharePoint's **Data Filter Web Parts** can filter a list based on the selection of another list. This is useful when working with large amounts of data in lists. The following screenshot lists the out of the box filters available:

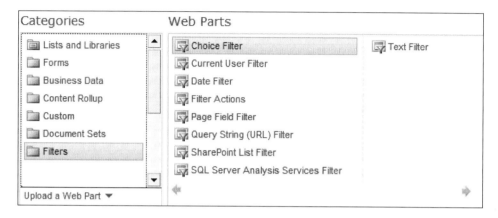

A data filter web part can be added to a page by performing the following steps:

1. Set the page in edit mode by clicking **Site Actions** and **Edit Page**.

2. Click the **Add a Web Part** text from the web zone.

3. Add an existing list web part to the page by clicking on **Lists and Libraries** and selecting the required list.

4. Add a filter web part to the page by clicking **Filters** and the filter web part. In this example, select the **SharePoint List Filter**.

5. Two web parts have now been added to the page. In this example, it is the **SharePoint List Filter** web part and the contacts list. The contacts list has a field that references another field in a list called **Companies** using the **Company** field.

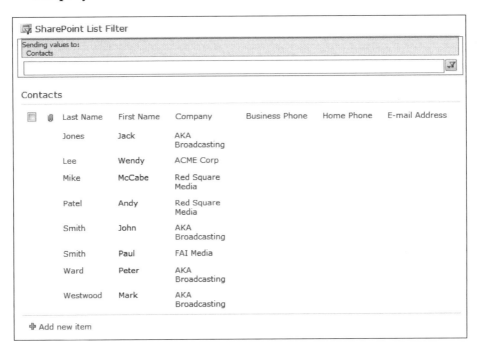

6. Edit SharePoint List Filter **Web Part**.

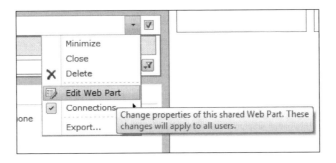

7. Select the companies list from the **list** field.

8. Select the company name as the value.

9. Click **OK**.

To filter the displayed items in the contacts list web part from this filtered web part, you have to apply web part connections to join the information together. This is done by performing the following steps:

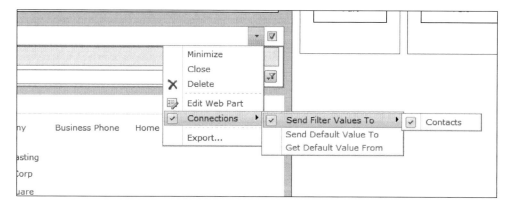

1. From the data filter web part, select **Connections** and choose the web part to connect to.

2. Select the field that both web parts have in common.

3. Click **Finish**.

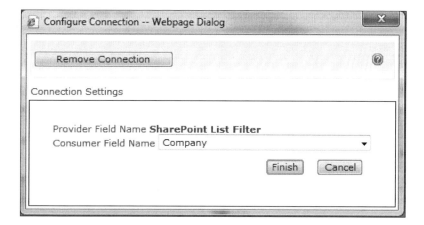

The contacts list is now being filtered by the end user selecting a company in the company list that is being displayed in the SharePoint list filter web part.

Outlook

Through the **Outlook Web App** web parts there is the ability to display your Inbox, Calendar, and Tasks. This is useful if you are often working on workstations that are not your own and you need to check e-mail and do not have Outlook configured to retrieve your e-mail.

These web parts should be added to pages on your My Site rather than a shared team site.

Content rollup

The **Content Query Web Part** can be best described as a *Site Collection rollup* view. This web part has the ability to display list items from different lists in different sites in a single web part.

This is very useful for reporting purposes of item information such as tasks or issue tracking items.

Dashboard design considerations

In SharePoint, there are a number of charting web parts in the **Business Data** web part category that can be added to a page.

These web parts can retrieve data from lists, external data sources, and Excel files, and make a page look very aesthetically pleasing. When adding web parts to a page, partially with dashboards or graphs, the following considerations should be taken into account:

- Because business data web parts are retrieving information from a data source, there can be a delay in the page loading. If there are multiple web business data web parts, the time delay could be unacceptable.
- The more items in a list, the longer it will take for the web part to display on the page. When the web part is added to the page, there may only be a few items in the list; over time this list may grow.
- Graphs and dashboards do provide an immediate **pop** effect to a page's look and feel, but does the information really provide valuable information beyond this?
- Use the web part title to name the graphical information.
- Keep it simple! At least to begin with; don't overload people with information. If one chart is a thousand words, then ten charts is a dissertation!
- Make sure the data sources of the dashboard are up-to-date and accurate.

Summary

The focus of this chapter has been *how to create an exceptional end user experience for you and your team*. The chapter covered just a few tips and techniques on how to apply SharePoint functionality, as explained in the previous chapters.

SharePoint's exceptional end user experience is not just limited to what has been explained in this chapter, so we recommend when you deploy SharePoint functionality that you ask yourself and your team the following questions:

- How can this be personalized?
- How can I make the information more relevant to me and my team?
- How can I get greater insight to who is working on what?

In the next and final chapter, we will discuss the golden rules for end user deployment, what's special about SharePoint, what SharePoint is not, and user requirement challenges.

17
Golden Rules for End User Deployment

If you have read all of the previous chapters and have attempted the recommended exercises, you will now be familiar with SharePoint's functionality and where it can be applied in day-to-day activities. This chapter outlines what SharePoint is *not*, what is special about SharePoint and why there is considerable value in using this technology, and the **User Requirement Challenges** that a deployment will cause.

What's special about SharePoint

Often, senior level management within an organization has already made a decision to make SharePoint the de facto corporate web platform, and users have to live with this decision and figure out a way for it to work for them. In many ways, this is what is special about SharePoint: the user base can define SharePoint's destiny within the company by embracing it or not.

SharePoint is a platform for the solution, and is not the solution itself, and this is often a challenge for management to understand. We recommend that some kind of SharePoint business architect should be employed to be the SharePoint owner, and a point of contact for its processes and upcoming collaboration initiatives from the business. This person should be accountable to ensure that the technology is working within the organization, and that it is meeting the business needs it was implemented for. This person does not need to be doing everything from the backups to the Site build-outs, but should have the following credentials:

- Some understanding of SharePoint's capabilities and limits

- Good knowledge of the business and its IT requirements

- Ability to speak to senior management about such requirements, and state if SharePoint is a good fit or not

If this person is the Exchange administrator or junior in the organization, there is a high likelihood that the SharePoint deployment process will not be successful because their role is focused not on the business needs of teams, but rather the technology side of the business. This is why business analysts should scope the requirements of a project.

In America, where job title inflation is rampant, the person's job title can be glorified to **Internal Collaboration Director**, **VP of Communications**, or **CCO – Corporate Collaboration Officer**.

What SharePoint is not

As we've already touched on earlier in the book, SharePoint is a product that can be a challenge to define, and the reality is that SharePoint has different meanings to different people. This is why we have described SharePoint as the "Ginsu knife" (an icon of "hard sell" marketing as *a knife that can do almost anything*) of web platforms because, depending on its application, individuals will perceive the product differently. While SharePoint can perform a lot of functions, the following descriptions of SharePoint are not a good fit for its true capabilities and prescriptive use, and thinking of it in any of the following ways should be avoided.

A generic "best of breed" technology

There is a lot of buzz within the IT world surrounding SharePoint, and it does not help to have a keen person always stating, '**SharePoint can solve this**' to understand if this is the appropriate technology. If SharePoint is customized enough, it can meet your required business needs. But, this is not the best use of people's time and effort, and in reality, without some customization SharePoint will not provide the benefits of an advanced **Customer Relationship Management** (**CRM**) system, or **Enterprise Resource Planning** (**ERP**) application. So, before you open up SharePoint in your browser, think about what your specific business problem is and how it can be solved.

If your company is looking for a very sophisticated document management system or a CRM application that is unique to an industry, SharePoint may not be the best tool without customization or a third-party add-on.

Yes, SharePoint does have very good document management functionality, but its functionality is geared towards the majority of users' needs in an organization, rather than one or two individual's specific requirements. This is so there is broader appeal to the technology within an organization.

The whole SharePoint architecture is based on customizable templates such as **Sites**, **Lists**, and **Libraries**. The moment that SharePoint Designer or Visual Studio is required for a project or task, the deployment should be viewed as an actual project, and a project manager will be required for help with development, staging servers, documentation, and perhaps a maintenance plan.

A defined end solution with an end point

Because functionality can be performed by an end user, there is often the notion among business users that *'this is the web so anything is possible'*. This creates the tendency to endlessly refine and make changes to the look and feel of field types and displayed information.

 A department does not request that IT change the UI colors for Outlook so it is branded with the corporate colors, or insist that the interface is redesigned so the tool bar is at the bottom of the page and menu links can go three levels deep. This is a common request for a SharePoint site, so managing these expectations is key to delivering projects within specific time frames.

With implementations such as a CRM or ERP system where there is a hard release date, and once the application has gone live, there is a freeze on requested functionality. Released SharePoint functionality in most organizations is constantly tweaked even after the go live phase.

This is not a good approach to an IT project. However, this is a common practice with SharePoint functionality releases and should aim to be minimized as far as possible.

An online transaction website

Information can be tagged and selected together, but this is not the right tool for shopping cart transaction user activity with credit card actions without a lot of development customization.

A standalone Business Intelligence tool

SharePoint provides the presentation layer for graphs and charts, and with its out of the box functionality, it can connect to a data source that could be an SQL cube or a list. SharePoint will not build or refresh the cube, or design the report.

People will often say, *'That's in SharePoint'*, referring to a graph displaying information from another database. In most cases though, SharePoint acts as a presentation layer to capture a graph from another application. An end user can easily capture web pages displaying cubes and graphs with the **Page Viewer** web part. For the more advanced user, **Business Intelligence Center** is more appropriate.

SharePoint will complement the BI functionality that is provided with other tools, rather than provide the functions of these tools itself.

 Excel files can be rendered in your browser on a SharePoint page using SharePoint's Excel Services, which is part of SharePoint Server. In this case, the Excel file is the data source, stored in a library that is being published to the SharePoint site.

An online Excel book in a list

The **Edit in Datasheet** functionality of a SharePoint list provides an Excel-like look and feel, which does work for basic information in a cell-like format. This is not a replacement for Excel's cell formulas and flexibility to manipulate data and forecasting models.

A public-facing company website

You may be surprised by this particular statement, but if your company is small and with mostly static content, and has not purchased the public connector licenses required, then SharePoint may not be a financially viable web technology.

When a public facing site is designed on the SharePoint platform, there are a lot more unknown variables such as browser formats, mobile devices, and search engine optimization, which can require a skilled team to maintain. However, with a company intranet environment, browser standards and devices can be enforced by the organization.

Significant customizations are required to make a SharePoint site look like a typical website.

Another challenge with public facing websites is that when pages do not load properly or functionally does not work, the website visitors generally do not notify the company that something is not working, unlike an intranet that has a content owner, or a help desk ticketing process to assist with feedback and troubleshooting.

Furthermore, if your company already has a company website set up with something else, why do a rip and replace of the technology?

Clearly for internal websites, SharePoint is the perfect tool.

A turnkey switch on solution

SharePoint is a web platform that will require manpower and effort to configure, but if there is a business process or something unique to a requirement, it will take some effort to have this functional in SharePoint. As you can see from reading this book, much can be done by the user without development, but this will require both learning SharePoint's functionality and understanding how to makes changes to it.

There is a perception by senior management in companies that SharePoint is a turnkey solution, and that once it is installed, benefits can be achieved in minutes. This may have something to do with the sales process, or that technology companies tend to focus on their solutions with SharePoint, rather than the process of implementing them.

An application that everyone will use on day one

While an accounting system upgrade will have a go live date where on a defined day all the invoices will be processed in the new system, SharePoint does not generally work like this, partly because people can use existing processes such as e-mail or the phone to perform their current tasks that SharePoint can also do.

So, during and after the go live release, users must still be constantly nurtured and educated to use the application, and will be questioned as to why they are not using it.

The biggest challenge for people in adopting a new system is for them to change their daily habits in going about their work.

The SharePoint platform

Because SharePoint is a platform for end user solutions and other third-party SharePoint applications to reside, the costs of ownership can dramatically decrease because installation costs and administration is spread across multiple business functions, and end user training is reduced because users are already using the application. This makes deployment of applications easier because the technology is already installed, and cultural acceptance within the company is in turn made easier because the users are already using the technology for other purposes.

This is why a lot of third-party applications have an interface deliberately designed to look like Microsoft's Office because it is easier to learn as people are more familiar with it, making the transition to using the technology go all the more smoothly.

Because there are multiple applications working off the same platform, integration of workflow, security, and file management is easier to manage as there is a single interface for administration, user authentication, and user management. This is a major win in breaking down the **information silos** of a company.

First impressions of SharePoint and what it can do for a department and the individual are very important. If these are not favorable then enterprise deployments can be difficult.

In the past, IT departments have deployed boutique applications for different business requirements that usually provide short term benefits and additional overhead for both users and the IT department. Because of an extended learning curve, more technologies are needed for support, as are additional licenses.

A hosted solution

SharePoint can be installed on premise or purchased as a hosted option from a third-party hosting company. Obviously, with the hosted approach, the IT department can be completely by-passed with a deployment. We recommend that if there is a business need that requires SharePoint, and the IT department is reluctant to deploy it in a desired timeframe, the hosted option should be considered with the IT department's involvement. This way, IT governance, security, and policy can be incorporated into the deployment.

User requirement challenges

There are a number of challenges that come with obtaining and implementing user requirements which have an equal impact upon the end users, the IT department and the SharePoint technology itself. These are outlined in the following sections.

The user

A department has requested that SharePoint assists with a business process and a requirements meeting is set up.

The department and users need to be aware that there is a process/methodology in achieving the end result. This is not a one shot deal, and they are involved in the success of the project.

Prior to the meeting, the department should have the following answers prepared.

Current environment

- What is the department trying to achieve?
- What are the **pain points** of the current environment?
- Is anything going to be approved (as an?) Excel DOC, submitted form PDF?
- How many steps are involved in the process?
- Who is involved in this process? (Submitters, approvers, or content viewers)
- If there is a business process, how should it flow?

SharePoint environment

- What are the critical success factors of using SharePoint?
- How does SharePoint help these critical success factors? (The more factors ticked off the better. If none are ticked then it goes to the back of the queue).
- How does the process start and end, and are there milestones involved?
- When the process goes live, who will be the owner of the process?
- Does SharePoint bring new business functionality to the process?
- What are the strategic objectives of this initiative to the business?

If the preceding points cannot be answered either prior to the meeting or during it, the business process has not been thought out, and the SharePoint solution is more likely to fail.

Often, the users will not be aware of SharePoint's capabilities, so there will be some educational aspects of such an engagement:

- SharePoint is a template technology. Must users work with this?
- The implemented approach will be out of the box with no coding—are there limitations?
- How can SharePoint be better than your existing process?
- What is required from you, the user?
- How much training is required by you?

At the beginning of an initiative, a simple process can become quite complicated, so it is important that complex requirements are identified at the beginning of the requirement gathering process.

IT department

Often, an IT department will implement the free version of SharePoint (Foundation) on a spare server, resulting in rumors within the company about a SharePoint deployment. This may have the effect that a tidal wave of requests for SharePoint applications from business units will come in, and this is all deployed on a **test deployment**.

Fast forward three months: the server has run out of disk space, the IT department is reading the manual to understand how to restore a deleted file, and users are complaining that SharePoint is not living up the hype. Unfortunately, it is all too often that the IT department will then adopt a *have-a-go* approach to the SharePoint technology.

A SharePoint installation and deployment needs to be carefully thought through with a one to three year plan of business usage and infrastructure considerations. This should be reviewed every year to assess the business requirements.

Just do it

SharePoint is a versatile platform, but all SharePoint business processes do not need to be deployed on the same server or within the site collection. Often, companies will install SharePoint on a server or server farm, and insist in driving all their initiatives off it, with the attitude that, *We have SharePoint deployed, let's do it on the existing SharePoint infrastructure.*

A good example of the **Just Do It** attitude is when a SharePoint application that was originally designed for employees is now being accessed by non-employees, and access levels are being set up as if they were internal users.

Good to talk

The IT department must engage with the business and users. This statement is not profound, but with SharePoint deployments, because users have the ability to customize and personalize so much functionality, the user experience, and ultimately the success of the deployment, is not a result of formal training sessions, but rather from users experimenting and making slight adjustments to features such as **alert** notification, meta tags, and their **My Site** so that it is personal to them.

We might estimate that 40 percent of the user experience is the personalization of notifications, pages, and the general look and feel, rather than what someone else did in building out the functionality. This is very different to other applications and is the reason why low touch, low value SharePoint deployments are as they are because the users are not aware of the functionalities that are all out of the box.

Recruiting evangelists throughout the organization is the only way to make a big project of any kind work. Usually, any new technology or process that is visibly promoted by only the IT department is difficult to be universally accepted across an organization.

People need to be nurtured, educated, and inspired to use the technology so they see the value.

Another challenge for the IT department is to understand the actual request from the business. Often, there is a request for a team site for a business function, when in reality a document library was all that was required.

SharePoint technology

One of the really nice things about the SharePoint technology is that the specifications do not all necessarily have to be required at the beginning of an initiative. Functionality can be added after the release, and even by the users themselves. This is different from traditional IT projects where requirement gathering is documented, but a true understanding by users of the process is incomplete.

With SharePoint deployments there is the ability to engage users with proof of concepts very early on in the process. This allows the users to become more confident with their own SharePoint skill-set and take ownership of projects.

By users taking ownership and personalizing content and design, the endless list of small requirements can be done by the users themselves.

We recommend performing follow-up coaching sessions, and having the more vocal people speak out about the small alterations they have made to a deployment to educate the other team members.

Summary

This brings us to the end of the chapter and the end of the book. In this chapter, you have been introduced to what is special about SharePoint, what SharePoint should *not* be regarded as, and the challenges of end user requirements. This book has introduced you to both the functionality of SharePoint and how and where to apply it to you and your team's collaboration activities.

As ever, we hope that you have been as impressed as we are with Microsoft's SharePoint 2010 release and how easy SharePoint makes it to create powerful applications. More than that though, we hope that you have enjoyed not just this chapter, but also the rest of the book, and that it has helped you to understand SharePoint's end user experience.

Glossary

This is a list of non tech speak definitions to many terms and acronyms related to SharePoint end user functionality, corporate intranets, and web user interface. We suggest that you glance at this appendix after you read each chapter, and you familiarize yourself with both SharePoint's functionality and relating technology.

Active directory

Commonly known as **AD**, this is a directory structure used on Microsoft Windows-based computers and servers to store information and data about networks and domains. Typically, SharePoint user accounts are managed in AD by the network administrator.

Audience

A named **Group** of users that is used for targeting content.

Audiences

Named groups that have information targeted at them.

Access Control List (ACL)

Contains a list of users or groups and their security permissions. Identifies who can update, modify, or delete an object on a computer or resource on the network.

Backstage

Office 2010 file menu system. In Office 2003 and earlier, you will recall the main menu with File, Edit, Insert, and so on.

Breadcrumb menu

A menu that shows the navigational hierarchy leading to a current location.

Business Connectivity Services

An external data integration feature of SharePoint to populate **lists**, **libraries**, and **web parts** with lines of business data.

Business Data Connectivity Service Application

A deployed instance of the **Business Data Connectivity Shared Service**.

Business Data Connectivity Shared Service

The **SharePoint Shared Service** that provides a means for storing and securing external content types, application models, and external data sources.

Business Data Catalog

The SharePoint 2007 equivalent of the **BCS** in the 2010 release. It displays information that exists outside the server farm. This service can be used to display business data in lists, web parts, search, user profiles, and custom applications.

Check in

Releases the lock for editing and enables other users to view the updated file or check out the file.

Check out

Enables users to lock a file while editing it to prevent others from overwriting or editing it inadvertently. Only the user who checks out a document can edit it.

Co-authoring

The ability for two or more people to edit a document simultaneously. Sections of the document are simply blocked off for each author to have exclusive control of a part of the document. This is a feature of SharePoint 2010 only.

Content types

This is reusable functionality such as columns, a workflow, lists, or libraries and allows you to manage the settings in a centralized and reusable way. By a list being selected to be multiple content types, there is the ability to have multiple forms in a single list.

Data connection

A link between an application and a data source. Data connections can be used to query and submit data.

Data connection library

A document library that contains a collection of **universal data connection** (.udcx) and Office data connection (.odc) files.

Data source

A database, web service, disk, file, or other collection of information from which data is queried or submitted. Supported data sources can vary based on application and the data provider that is specified.

Datasheet view

A view that provides the ability to edit items in a list as if it was an online spreadsheet. You can tab across fields, paste between them, and sort and filter columns.

Data validation

The process of testing the accuracy of data; a set of rules that specify the type and range of data that users can enter.

Data view web part

A web part that is used to display items in a list.

Discussion boards

In SharePoint this is the **Discussion list** functionality (refer to the following section).

Discussion thread

A series of messages or comments in a discussion board or web discussions in which replies to a message or a comment are nested directly under it.

Distribution list

A collection of users, computers, contacts, or other groups that is used only for e-mail distribution, and addressed as a single recipient.

Documents

Any form of document, both Microsoft Office or non- Office files, are stored in libraries. Events such as **workflows** and **alerts** can be initiated from an **item** in a library.

Document center

A **document site template** that is preconfigured to store a large quantity of documents.

Document library

A type of list that is a container for documents and folders.

Document sets

This is a new feature of SharePoint 2010 and is basically a container for multiple documents to which you can assign certain **metadata**, and treat as a single entity in many ways.

Document workspace

A document repository that enables users to collaborate on one or more documents.

Document workspace site

A SharePoint site that is based on a **Document Workspace site**. A document workspace site is used for planning, posting, and working together on a document, or a set of related documents, and information to a user.

Extranet

An external website for an organization; usually secured so that only authorized users can gain access to it.

Field

Also known as a **column**. Data items in a list or library.

Folksonomy

An informal flat list of terms. Folksonomies are collected by **social tagging** in SharePoint that a user can assign to documents, blogs, wikis, or in fact most of the information in SharePoint.

Gallery

A library that is used to store a collection of site resources, such as web parts, list templates, or site templates.

Global links bar

Located at the top of a page and displays links, regardless of the location of the user on the site.

Items

Items are records in a list. This is where metadata such as author, date, and keywords are stored.

Key Performance Indicator (KPI)

A pre-defined measure that is used to track performance against a strategic goal, objective, plan, initiative, or business process. A visual cue is frequently used to communicate performance against the measure.

Keyword

One or more words or phrases that site administrators have identified as important. A keyword provides a way to display best bets and definitions on a search results page.

Homepage

Main page of a website. It usually has hyperlinks to other pages, both inside and outside of the site.

Hyperlink

Colored and underlined text, or a graphic, that you click to go to a file, a location in a file, an HTML page on the World Wide Web, or an HTML page on an intranet.

Intranet

An internal website for an organization.

Lists

These are template-defined areas on a site that store web-based content such as team discussions, links, announcements, contacts, events, tasks, issues lists, or even custom-defined lists.

List column

A column defines what is stored in a field.

List content type

Policies that can be defined to an item or document.

List folder

A folder that is contained within a SharePoint list. A list folder can contain documents or list items, and it retains the characteristics of other items in the list, such as a customizable schema.

List form

A page that allows users to create, view, or edit an item in a list.

List form web part

A web part that is used to display, edit, or view an item in a list.

List item

An individual entry within a SharePoint list. Each list item has a schema that maps to fields in the list that contains the item, depending on the content type of the item.

List template

A based definition of list settings, including fields and views, and optionally list items. List templates are stored in `.stp` files in the **Content Database**.

List view

A named collection of settings for querying and displaying items in a SharePoint list. There are two types of views: **Personal**, which can be used only by the user who creates them, and **Public**, which can be used by all users who have access to the site.

List view page

A web part page that displays a view of a list.

List view web part

A reusable component that generates HTML-based views of items in a SharePoint list.

Libraries

These are collections of files that include documents and graphics that you can store/share.

Login name

A string that is used to identify a user or entity to an operating system, directory service, or distributed system. A login name uses the form `DOMAIN\username`.

Lookup field

A field of the Lookup type that allows a user to select an item from another data source.

Major version

An iteration of a software component, document, or list item that is ready for a larger group to see, or has changed significantly since the previous major version.

Managed keyword

A word or phrase that is added to a SharePoint item, either as a value in the **Managed Keyword** column, or as a social tag.

Managed metadata

A hierarchical collection of centrally managed terms that you can define and then use as attributes for SharePoint items.

Managed metadata connection

A connection to a managed metadata service that allows sites within a web application to access the service's term store and, optionally, content types.

Managed term

A word or a phrase that can be associated with a SharePoint item. Managed terms are usually predefined, can be created only by users with the appropriate permissions, and are often organized into a hierarchy. Also called **term** where **managed** is clear from the context.

Meeting workspace site

A website based on a **Meeting Workspace** site template that is used for planning, posting, and working together on meeting materials and following up after a meeting or series of meetings.

Metadata

Data about data.

Minor version

Used with version control with an item on a SharePoint site.

My profile page

Is the default landing page for your personal site, for you and for others accessing your site. This page provides an abundance of information and gives you the ability to manage details about **Yourself**, **Colleagues**, and **Memberships**.

My Site

A personal SharePoint site for a user that stores the user's personal content and information.

Office Data Connection (ODC) file

A file that stores information about a connection to a data source, such as an Access database, worksheet, or text file. This file facilitates data source administration.

Office Web Apps

Microsoft **Office Web Apps** give users the ability to view, create, and edit documents, presentations, and spreadsheets using a browser when the full Office application is not installed on the computer.

Page

A file consisting of HTML that can include references to graphics, scripts, or dynamic content such as web parts.

Page layout

A SharePoint page that contains content placeholders such as web part zones and web parts.

Paged view

A view that supports one or more visual pages. A paged view is used to break up large sets of data into smaller sets for increased performance and manageability.

Parent list

A list that contains a list item or list folder.

Parent site

The site that is above the current site in the hierarchy of the site collection.

PerformancePoint content list

A list that stores the elements that are used to construct a PerformancePoint dashboard. A PerformancePoint dashboard is a related group of interactive scorecards, filters, and report views that are organized together into a set of web pages.

Permission

A rule that is associated with an object to regulate which users can gain access to the object and in what manner.

Permission level

A set of permissions that can be granted to principals or SharePoint groups on an entity such as a site, list, folder, item, or document.

Personal site

A type of SharePoint site that is used by an individual user for personal productivity. The site appears to the user as My Site.

Personal view

A view of a list, SharePoint document library, or web part page that is available only to a particular user. The personal view of a web part page uses a combination of shared property values and personalized property values. Changes made to a personal view apply only to the list, library, or page in that view and are therefore visible to that user only.

Personalized web part

A shared web part that has been modified by a user in personal view. The changes made to a web part personalized in this way are visible only to the user who made those changes.

Private web part

A web part added to a web part page by a user who is working on the page in personal view. Private web parts are available only to the user who added or imported the web part.

Quick launch

Side navigation links of a site, normally displaying site content such as lists and libraries.

Portal site

A type of SharePoint site that can act as an umbrella to other sites and that can be used by a large organization.

Published version

The version of a list item that is approved and can be seen by all users. The **user interface (UI)** version number for a published version is incremented to the next positive major version number, and the minor version is zero.

Publishing level

An integer that is assigned to a document to indicate the publishing status of that version of the document.

Publishing page

A document that binds to a page layout to generate an HTML page for display to a reader. Publishing pages have specific fields that contain the content that is displayed in an HTML page.

Record

A group of related fields (sometimes referred to as columns) of information that are treated as a unit. Also referred to as a row.

Really Simple Syndication (RSS)

A web feed technology from blog entries, news headlines, audio, and video in a standardized format.

Record Management

The practice of maintaining and tracking records within an organization. This process is normally determined based on an organization's internal and external legal compliance requirements.

Recycle bin

A container for deleted items.

Ribbon

Toolbar menu style interface.

Sandboxed Solution

A custom solution that can be deployed to a site by a site collection administrator without approval from the farm administrator. Without that approval, the solution has full access to the immediate site and restricted access to system resources and other sites.

Security policy

In the form of a collection of security policy settings, the policy itself is an expression of administrative intent regarding how computers and resources on their network should be secured.

Shared documents library

A document library that is included by default in the team site template.

Shared view

A view of a list or web part page that every user who has the appropriate permissions can see.

Shared web part

A web part added to a web part page by a user who is working on the page in shared view. Shared web parts are available to all users of a web part page who have the appropriate permissions.

Shared workbook

A workbook that is configured to allow multiple users on a network to view and make changes at the same time. Each user who saves the workbook sees the changes that are made by other users.

SharePoint Foundation

Formerly known as **WSS**, and is ideal for smaller organizations or team-oriented web-based collaboration, as well as entry-level document management.

SharePoint Server 2010 Enterprise edition

This edition of SharePoint Server 2010 has further functionality than the Standard edition. This includes **Excel Services** and KPIs.

SharePoint Server 2010 Standard edition

Formally known as **Microsoft Office SharePoint server** (**MOSS**) in the 2007 release, this edition has further functionality than the SharePoint Foundation edition. This includes additional preconfigured workflow and search capabilities.

SharePoint site

A site usually represents a functional department or activity in an organization, such as sales or marketing in a project. It contains lists and libraries.

SharePoint workspace

Formerly known as Groove, this is part of the Microsoft Office Professional Plus 2010 edition and provides the ability to use content offline on your desktop, and then synchronize into the SharePoint lists when you are back online.

Site collection

A set of websites that are in the same content database, have the same owner, and share administration settings. Each site collection contains a top-level site and can contain one or more sub sites and can have a shared navigation structure.

Site collection administrator

A user who has administrative permissions for a site collection.

Site collection quota

An option for a site collection that allows administrators to set levels for maximum storage allowed, maximum number of users allowed, and warnings that are associated with the maximum levels.

Site column

A field that can be associated with a content type or list within a site or site collection.

Site content type

A named and uniquely identifiable collection of settings and fields that store metadata for lists within individual sites.

Site definition

A family of site definition configurations. Each site definition specifies a name and contains a list of the site definition configurations.

Site membership

The status of being a member of a site and having a defined set of user rights for accessing or managing content on that site.

Site property

A name/value pair of strings that serves as metadata for a site, such as the title or default language.

Site solution

A deployable, reusable package that contains a set of features, site definitions, and assemblies that apply to sites, and that can be enabled or disabled individually.

Sub site

A named subdirectory of the top-level website that is a complete website. Each sub site can have independent administration, authoring, and browsing permissions from the top-level websites and other sub site.

Taxonomies

Taxonomies are set up to provide consistency in the terms used across an organization. They define the terms that will most frequently be assigned to documents as metadata to provide identifiers that assist in searching for information.

Term Store Management tool

The **Term Store Management Tool** is used to create and manage terms and term sets.

Themes

Color formatting options for a site.

Top-level site

The first site in a site collection. All other sites within a site collection are children of the top-level site. The URL of the top-level site is also the URL of the site collection.

User profile

A collection of properties that pertain to a specific person or entity within a portal site.

Usage analysis

Data collected to evaluate how a website is being used, such as visitor usernames, number of visits to each page, and the types of web browsers used.

View

A table displaying items/documents in a SharePoint library or list.

Visio Web Services

In SharePoint 2007, Microsoft introduced Excel Web Services, allowing a SharePoint Server to publish content from an Excel spreadsheet file to a SharePoint page that could be viewed in a browser. Visio Web Services provides similar capability for Visio diagrams.

Visitors group

A default group of users on a SharePoint site. By default, the Visitors group is assigned the Read permission level.

Web part

A reusable component that contains or generates web-based content such as XML, HTML, and scripting code. It has a standard property schema and displays that content in a cohesive unit on a web page.

Web part connection

An element in a web parts page that defines a provider-consumer data relationship between two web parts. When a web parts page is rendered, data provided by one web part can affect how and what is rendered by the other web part.

Web part property

A configurable characteristic of a web part that determines the behavior of the web part.

Web part zone

A structured HTML section of a web part page that contains zero or more web parts and can be configured to control the organization and format of those web parts.

Web parts page

A SharePoint page that includes web part controls that enable users to customize the page, such as specifying the information that they want to display.

What's Happening?

A **micro-blogging** on a My Site that allows you to enter a brief description of what you are currently up to.

Workflow

The automation of business processes, where business documents and tasks are passed automatically from one user to another for action, according to a set sequence.

Workflow association

An association of a workflow template to a specific list or content type.

Workflow condition

A logical **if-then** statement that defines a specific situation in a workflow and any actions to be taken when that situation occurs.

Workflow history item

A list item that stores information about the current status of, and past actions for, a document or item that is associated with a workflow.

Workflow task list

A list that stores the sequence of actions or tasks for a business process.

Workflow template

A definition of operations, the sequence of operations, constraints, and timing for a particular process.

B
SharePoint Functionality Comparison

This appendix outlines a comparison of SharePoint's available functionality. This functionality comparison is particularly useful if you do not have the Enterprise edition of SharePoint and need to identify the functionality available in the Foundation version and Standard edition.

The following table details a comparison of the functionality available in SharePoint's **Foundation** and **Server** versions, along with the functionality differences between SharePoint **Standard** and **Enterprise** editions:

Foundation	Standard includes everything in Foundation plus	Enterprise includes everything in Standard plus
Accessibility	Ask Me About	Access Services
Blogs	Audience Targeting	Advanced Content Processing
Browser-based Customizations	Basic Sorting	Advanced Sorting
Business Connectivity Services	Best Bets	Business Data Integration with the Office Client
Business Data Connectivity Service	Business Connectivity Services Profile Page	Business Data Web Parts
Claims-based Authentication	Click Through Relevancy	Business Intelligence Center
Client Object Model (OM)	Colleague Suggestions	Business Intelligence Indexing Connector
Configuration Wizards	Colleagues Network	Calculated KPIs
Connections to Microsoft Office Clients	Compliance Everywhere	Chart Web Parts
Connections to Office Communication Server and Exchange	Content Organizer	Contextual Search
	Document Sets	Dashboards
Cross-Browser Support	Duplicate Detection	Data Connection Library
Developer Dashboard	Enterprise Scale Search	Decomposition Tree
Discussions	Enterprise Wikis	Deep Refinement
	Federated Search	

Foundation	Standard includes everything in Foundation plus	Enterprise includes everything in Standard plus
Event Receivers	Improved Governance	Excel Services
External Data Column	Keyword Suggestions	Excel Services and PowerPivot for SharePoint
External Lists	Managed Metadata Service	Extensible Search Platform
High-Availability Architecture	Memberships	Extreme Scale Search
Improved Backup and Restore	Metadata-driven Navigation	InfoPath Forms Services
Improved Setup and Configuration	Metadata-driven Refinement	PerformancePoint Services
Out of the Box Web Parts	Mobile Search Experience	Rich Web Indexing
Patch Management	Multistage Disposition	Similar Results
Permissions Management	My Content	Thumbnails and Previews
Photos and Presence	My Newsfeed	Tunable Relevance with Multiple Rank Profiles
Quota Templates	My Profile	Visio Services
Read-Only Database Support	Note Board	Visual Best Bets
Remote Blob Storage (SQL Feature)	Organization Browser	Includes Foundation and Standard features
REST and ATOM Data Feeds	People and Expertise Search	—
Ribbon and Dialog Framework	Phonetic and Nickname Search	—
Sandboxed Solutions	Query Suggestions, "Did You Mean?", and Related Queries	—
SharePoint Designer	Ratings	—
SharePoint Health Analyzer	Recent Activities	—
SharePoint Lists	Recently Authored Content	—
SharePoint Ribbon	Relevancy Tuning	—
SharePoint Service Architecture	Rich Media Management	—
SharePoint Timer Jobs	Search Scopes	—
SharePoint Workspace	Secure Store Service	—
Silverlight Web Part	Shared Content Types	—
Site Search	SharePoint 2010 Search Connector Framework	—
Solution Packages	Status Updates	—
Streamlined Central Administration	Tag Clouds	—
Support for Office Web Apps	Tag Profiles	—
Unattached Content Database Recovery	Tags	—
Usage Reporting and Logging	Tags and Notes Tool	—
Visual Studio 2010 SharePoint Developer Tools	Unique Document IDs	—
Visual Upgrade	Web Analytics	—
	Windows 7 Search	—
	Word Automation Services	—
	Workflow Templates	—

Foundation	Standard	Enterprise
Web Parts	Includes Foundation features	—
Wikis	—	—
Windows 7 Support	—	—
Windows PowerShell Support	—	—
Workflow	—	—
Workflow Models	—	—
	—	—
	—	—
	—	—
	—	—
	—	—
	—	—
	—	—
		—
		—
		—
		—
		—
		—
		—
		—

Summary

You have probably read most of the chapters in this book, so having this appendix at the back of the book is a nice conclusion to what functionality is available in which versions and editions.

C
List Templates

The following table presents the functionalities of SharePoint's out of the box lists and libraries, as well as accompanying business scenarios, illustrating when to use each type of list and library:

List Temple Name	Description
Announcements	Team Site, Blank Site, Document Workspace, Blog, Group Work Site, Visio Process Repository, All Meeting Workspace, Document/Record Center, My Site Host, Personalization Site, Enterprise Search Center, FAST Search Center, Enterprise Wiki, and Publishing Site.

 If your company communicates to its employees with company-wide e-mail, the announcements list is an ideal information repository to use because its content is searchable and the list is e-mail enabled, so the contributor can e-mail an announcement into the list and the contents of the e-mail will be copied into the list. So, there is no change in contributor activity.

List Temple Name	Description
Asset Library	Team Site, Document Workspace, Group Work Site, Visio Process Repository, All Meeting Workspace, Document/Record Center, Business Intelligence Center, Personalization Site, Enterprise Search Center, FAST Search Center, Enterprise Wiki, Publishing Portal, and Publishing Site with Workflow.

 This list is ideal as a corporate brand library of logos, graphics, and videos. SharePoint's workflows and policies can be used to manage the content. Creative teams can submit digital assets to the asset library where they are reviewed and published. The assets can be tagged and organized for end user consumption. Users will have access to official, authorized corporate logos or brand assets.

Calendar	Team Site, Blank Site, Document Workspace, Blog, Group Work Site, Visio Process Repository, All Meeting Workspace, Document/Record Center, My Site Host, Personalization Site, Enterprise Search Center, Basic Search Center, FAST Search Center, Enterprise Wiki, and Publishing Site.

 The calendar list is not associated with an individual, but rather a resource such as a conference room, or team-based activities. This list also integrates with your Outlook, with drag-and-drop functionality.

Circulations List	This list should be used to send information such as confirmation stamps or documents to team members. The list has inherent security trimming ability to recipients.

 This list is useful for managing confidential tasks or requests.

This template requires activation of the Group Work lists. This is done in the **Managed Site Features**, in **Site Settings**.

List Temple Name	Description
Contacts	Team Site, Document Workspace, Blog, Group Work Site, Visio Process Repository, All Meeting Workspace, Document/Record Center, My Site Host, Basic Search Center, FAST Search Center, Enterprise Wiki, and Publishing Site.

> This list integrates with Outlook, so a user can connect this list to their Outlook in order to send an e-mail to a contact in the list. Because the field names are the same as the contacts in Outlook, you can cut and paste contacts from Outlook directly into the list. This is a useful feature of SharePoint contacts that would normally reside in an individual's Outlook to be shared with other team members.

List Temple Name	Description
Custom List	Team Site, Blank Site, Document Workspace, Visio Process Repository, All Meeting Workspace, Business Intelligence Center, My Site Host, Personalization Site, Enterprise Search Center, Basic Search Center, FAST Search Center, Enterprise Wiki, Publishing Portal, Publishing Site, and Publishing Site with Workflow.

> If you have a requirement that requires custom fields, this is the template to use.
>
> Note: if you are going to use this template, views and fields all need to be added. With existing list templates, there are already predefined fields and views.

List Temple Name	Description
Custom List in Data view	Team Site, Document Workspace, Blog, Group Work Site, Visio Process Repository, All Meeting Workspace, Document/Record Center, My Site Host, Personalization Site, Enterprise Search Center, Basic Search Center, FAST Search Center, Enterprise Wiki, and Publishing Site.

List Temple Name	Description
Discussion Board	Team Site, Blank Site, Document Workspace, Blog, Group Work Site, Visio Process Repository, Document/Record Center, My Site Host, Personalization Site, Enterprise Search Center, Basic Search Center, Enterprise Wiki, and Publishing Site.
	This list is a message board, where groups of users can collaborate/have a two-way dialogue. We have seen this used very well in many environments. **Company communications forum**: Where there are announcements comments. **Technical knowledge base**: A user asks a question and there is dialogue among a team. This list can also integrate with Outlook, so you can synchronize content Office in Outlook. A nice touch is a discussion list to add the rating feature to the list as users' focus will be drawn to certain items.
Document Library	Central Administration, Blank Site, Document Workspace, Blog, Group Work Site, Visio Process Repository, All Meeting Workspace, Document/Record Center, Business Intelligence Center, My Site Host, Personalization Site, Enterprise Search Center, Basic Search Center, FAST Search Center, Enterprise Wiki, Publishing Portal, Publishing Site, and Publishing Site with Workflow.

List Temple Name	Description
Import Spreadsheet	Team Site, Document Workspace, Blog, All Meeting Workspace, Document/Record Center, My Site Host, Personalization Site, Enterprise Search Center, FAST Search Center, Enterprise Wiki, Publishing Portal, Publishing Site, and Publishing Site with Workflow.

Once a decision has been made to migrate the information from a spreadsheet into a list, the challenge is to actually migrate the information. If the spreadsheet contains multiple columns, a straight manual cut and paste of the information will be time consuming.

When this list is created, you are prompted to choose a spreadsheet file. Once this is selected, the contents of the spreadsheet will be copied to the newly created list.

Note: The spreadsheet should have column names to define the column names in the list.

Cell formulas are not copied into the list.

Issue Tracking	Team Site, Blank Site, Document Workspace, Blog, Visio Process Repository, All Meeting Workspace, Document/Record Center, My Site Host, Personalization Site, Enterprise Search Center, FAST Search Center, Enterprise Wiki, and Publishing Site.

Ideal for logging issues with, for example for a release of a product of activity or a general to-do list. The **Assign To** feature is an out of the box feature of the list, so when an item is created and the Assign To field is populated with a user, they receive a notification.

One drawback of this list is that it is not e-mail enabled, so a user cannot e-mail a support item into the list.

List Temple Name	Description
Links	Team Site, Blank Site, Document Workspace, Blog, Group Work Site, Visio Process Repository, All Meeting Workspace, Document/Record Center, My Site Host, Personalization Site, Enterprise Search Center, Basic Search Center, FAST Search Center, Enterprise Wiki, and Publishing Site.

A URL links repository

This is useful to have a single list containing links and displaying the list through a web part on a page, rather than the same links entered multiple times on different pages.

Picture Library	Central Administration, Team Site, Blank Site, Document Workspace, Blog, Group Work Site, Visio Process Repository, All Meeting Workspace, Document/Record Center, My Site Host, Personalization Site, Enterprise Search Center, Publishing Portal, Publishing Site, and Publishing Site with Workflow.

This list is ideal for storing graphics and photographs that can be tagged with metadata, size dimensions, and expiration date.

This library has a preview view for images, which is useful if you need to quickly search and review hundreds of items.

Project Tasks	Team Site, Blank Site, Document Workspace, Blog, Group Work Site, Visio Process Repository, All Meeting Workspace, Document/Record Center, My Site Host, Personalization Site, Enterprise Search Center, Basic Search Center, FAST Search Center, Enterprise Wiki, and Publishing Site.

This list has **project management light** functionality. The features unique to this list include a Gantt view to display project and dependent tasks.

List Temple Name	Description
Survey	Team Site, Blank Site, Document Workspace, Blog, Group Work Site, Visio Process Repository, All Meeting Workspace, Document/Record Center, My Site Host, Personalization Site, Enterprise Search Center, Basic Search Center, FAST Search Center, Enterprise Wiki, and Publishing Site.

> This list has the ability to survey users with questions that can dynamically change depending on the response. Because the responses are in a list, these can be exported into Excel for further reporting.

| Slide Library | Team Site, Blank Site, Document Workspace, Blog, Group Work Site, Visio Process Repository, All Meeting Workspace, Document/Record Center, Business Intelligence Center, My Site Host, Personalization Site, Enterprise Search Center, and Publishing Site. |

> This library stores slides from PowerPoint 2010 files, which can be distributed to users. PowerPoint files can become quite large and out of date, so with slides centrally stored in a single location, content can be managed, shared, and distributed easier to users. The slide library is discussed further in *Chapter 11, Enterprise Content Management*.

List Temple Name	Description
Tasks	Central Administration, Team Site, Blank Site, Blog, Group Work Site, Visio Process Repository, All Meeting Workspace, Document/Record Center, Business Intelligence Center, My Site Host, Personalization Site, Enterprise Search Center, Basic Search Center, FAST Search Center, Enterprise Wiki, Publishing Portal, Publishing Site, and Publishing Site with Workflow.

The tasks list is ideal for teams to collaborate **To Do List Items**. This list integrates with Outlook, so tasks can be created in Outlook and synchronized into the task list in SharePoint. This is useful if a request is e-mailed to you, so you can **drag-and-drop** the e-mail into the task list and assign it.

Note: There can be multiple task lists connected to your Outlook client. However, the more SharePoint lists that are connected to your Outlook, the slower it is to open and use.

The following sites do not have Lists defined in them and cannot have Lists created in them: **Asset Web Database**, **Charitable Contributions**, **Contacts Web Database**, **Issues Web Database**, and **Project Web Database**.

Index

B

C

W

Web 2.0
  blog 257
  wikis 257
Web part 367
Web part connection 368
web part property 368
web parts
  about 282
  adding, to page 285, 286
  configuring 287, 288
  Content Editor 334
  content rollup 333
  data filter 335-338
  example 284
  filters 333
  list web part 283
  media and content 333
  modifying 287, 288
  Outlook Web App 338
  social collaboration 334
Web parts page 368
Web part zone 368
What you see is what you get.
        See **WYSIWYG**
whitespace 70
Wiki libraries
  about 104, 118
  advantage 119
  pages, adding 119
wiki page
  additional capabilities 266
  creating 265-268
  editing 269
  page link, creating 266
wiki page library
  creating 264, 265
wikis
  about 257, 264
  in SharePoint 257
wildcard 213
workflow
  about 368
  activities 154
  authoring tools 149
  basics 138
  complexity, determining 153
  creating 141
  managing 145
  types 146
  virtualizing 153-155
workflow, creating
  approval workflow, creating 141-144
  architecture 145
  steps 141
workflow association 368
workflow condition 369
Workflow Foundation (WF) 150
workflow history item 369
workflow task list 369
workflow template 369
WSS. *See* **SharePoint Foundation**
WYSIWYG 315

Z

zone
  about 273
  Web port zone 368

Thank you for buying
Microsoft SharePoint 2010 End User Guide:
Business Performance Enhancement

About Packt Publishing

Packt, pronounced 'packed', published its first book "Mastering phpMyAdmin for Effective MySQL Management" in April 2004 and subsequently continued to specialize in publishing highly focused books on specific technologies and solutions.

Our books and publications share the experiences of your fellow IT professionals in adapting and customizing today's systems, applications, and frameworks. Our solution based books give you the knowledge and power to customize the software and technologies you're using to get the job done. Packt books are more specific and less general than the IT books you have seen in the past. Our unique business model allows us to bring you more focused information, giving you more of what you need to know, and less of what you don't.

Packt is a modern, yet unique publishing company, which focuses on producing quality, cutting-edge books for communities of developers, administrators, and newbies alike. For more information, please visit our website: www.packtpub.com.

About Packt Enterprise

In 2010, Packt launched two new brands, Packt Enterprise and Packt Open Source, in order to continue its focus on specialization. This book is part of the Packt Enterprise brand, home to books published on enterprise software – software created by major vendors, including (but not limited to) IBM, Microsoft and Oracle, often for use in other corporations. Its titles will offer information relevant to a range of users of this software, including administrators, developers, architects, and end users.

Writing for Packt

We welcome all inquiries from people who are interested in authoring. Book proposals should be sent to author@packtpub.com. If your book idea is still at an early stage and you would like to discuss it first before writing a formal book proposal, contact us; one of our commissioning editors will get in touch with you.

We're not just looking for published authors; if you have strong technical skills but no writing experience, our experienced editors can help you develop a writing career, or simply get some additional reward for your expertise.

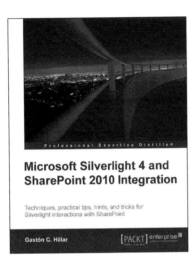

Microsoft Silverlight 4 and SharePoint 2010 Integration

ISBN: 978-1-849680-06-6   Paperback: 336 pages

Techniques, practical tips, hints, and tricks for Silverlight interactions with SharePoint

1. Develop Silverlight RIAs that interact with SharePoint 2010 data and services

2. Explore the diverse alternatives for hosting a Silverlight RIA in a SharePoint 2010 Page

3. Work with the new SharePoint Silverlight Client Object Model to interact with elements in a SharePoint Site

4. Use Visual Studio 2010's new features to debug Silverlight RIAs that interact with SharePoint 2010

SharePoint Designer Tutorial: Working with SharePoint Websites

ISBN: 978-1-847194-42-8   Paperback: 188 pages

Get started with SharePoint Designer and learn to put together a business website with SharePoint

1. Become comfortable in the SharePoint Designer environment

2. Learn about SharePoint Designer features as you create a SharePoint website

3. Step-by-step instructions and careful explanations

Please check **www.PacktPub.com** for information on our titles

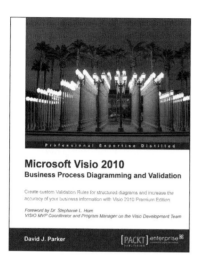

Microsoft Visio 2010 Business Process Diagramming and Validation

ISBN: 978-1-849680-14-1   Paperback: 344 pages

Create custom Validation Rules for structured diagrams and increase the accuracy of your business information with Visio 2010 Premium Edition

1. Optimize your business information visualization by mastering out-of-the-box, structured diagram functionality with features like the Basic and Cross-Functional Flowcharts

2. Create and analyze custom Validation Rules for structured diagrams using Visio Premium

3. Get to grips with validation logic for Business Process Diagramming with Visio 2010, by using the provided Rules Tools add-in

Microsoft Silverlight 4 Business Application Development: Beginner's Guide

ISBN: 978-1-847199-76-8   Paperback: 412 pages

Build enterprise-ready business applications with Silverlight 4

1. An introduction to building enterprise-ready business applications with Silverlight quickly

2. Get hold of the basic tools and skills needed to get started in Silverlight application development

3. Integrate different media types, taking the RIA experience further with Silverlight, and much more!

Please check **www.PacktPub.com** for information on our titles

Microsoft SharePoint 2010 Administration Cookbook

ISBN: 978-1-849681-08-7   Paperback: 288 pages

Over 90 simple but incredibly effective recipes to administer your SharePoint applications

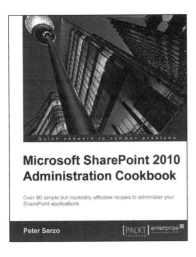

1. Solutions to the most common problems encountered while administering SharePoint in book and eBook formats

2. Upgrade, configure, secure, and back up your SharePoint applications with ease

3. Packed with many recipes for improving collaboration and content management with SharePoint

4. Part of Packt's Cookbook series: Each recipe is a carefully organized sequence of instructions to complete the task as efficiently as possible

Microsoft Windows Workflow Foundation 4.0 Cookbook

ISBN: 978-1-849680-78-3   Paperback: 255 pages

Over 70 recipes with hands-on, ready to implement solutions for authoring workflows

1. Customize Windows Workflow 4.0 applications to suit your needs

2. A hands-on guide with real-world illustrations, screenshots, and step-by-step instructions

3. Explore various functions that you can perform using WF 4.0 with running code examples

Please check **www.PacktPub.com** for information on our titles

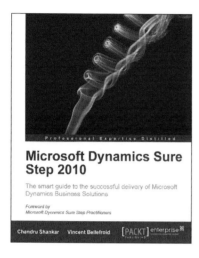

Microsoft Dynamics Sure Step 2010

ISBN: 978-1-849681-10-0   Paperback: 360 pages

The smart guide to the successful delivery of Microsoft Dynamics Business Solutions

1. Learn how to effectively use Microsoft Dynamics Sure Step to implement the right Dynamics business solution with quality, on-time and on-budget results

2. Leverage the Decision Accelerator offerings in Microsoft Dynamics Sure Step to create consistent selling motions while helping your customer ascertain the best solution to fit their requirements

3. Understand the review and optimization offerings available from Microsoft Dynamics Sure Step to further enhance your business solution delivery during and after go-live

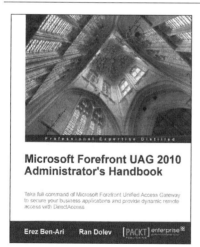

Microsoft Forefront UAG 2010 Administrator's Handbook

ISBN: 978-1-849681-62-9   Paperback: 484 pages

Take full command of Microsoft Forefront Unified Access Gateway to secure your business applications and provide dynamic remote access with DirectAccess

1. Maximize your business results by fully understanding how to plan your UAG integration

2. Consistently be ahead of the game by taking control of your server with backup and advanced monitoring

3. An essential tutorial for new users and a great resource for veterans

Please check **www.PacktPub.com** for information on our titles

Made in the USA
San Bernardino, CA
07 September 2014